'Hodkinson has a light touch and a modest, self-effacing style. He is a fine writer.' – *The Daily Telegraph*

'His writing is free of cliché and acutely on the money.' – *Q*

'His prose is never less than first-rate.' – *The Independent on Sunday*

'He writes with economy and elegance, self-deprecating but never self-pitying.' – *The Times*

'Hodkinson can weave poetry out of the mundane.' – *Daily Mail*

'If, like me, you have a habit of lending your new favourite book on the pretext of getting it back, you may think twice about letting Hodkinson's beauty out of your sight.' – *The Quietus*

'A deft writer, poignant and funny at different times.' – *The Guardian*

'He has an evocative turn of phrase with an impressive economy of language and the writing flows effortlessly.' – *The Observer*

'Hodkinson writes quite beautifully, which means that those of us with lesser gifts are given a glimpse into his soul. It is a richly rewarding place to be.' – *The Times*

# THE
# OVERCOAT
# MEN

MARK HODKINSON

# THE OVERCOAT MEN

## How Two Unsung Heroes
## Staved off the Bulldozers and Saved
## their Football Club from Oblivion

First published by Pitch Publishing, 2019

Pitch Publishing
A2 Yeoman Gate
Yeoman Way
Worthing
Sussex
BN13 3QZ
www.pitchpublishing.co.uk
info@pitchpublishing.co.uk

A CIP catalogue record is available for this book
from the British Library.

ISBN 978 1 78531 525 1

Typesetting and origination by Pitch Publishing

Printed and bound by TJ International, Cornwall

# Contents

Also by the author


*The Last Mad Surge of Youth* (Pomona)

*That Summer Feeling* (Pomona)

*Blue Moon: Down Among the Dead Men
with Manchester City* (Penguin/Random House)

*Life at the Top* (Queen Anne Press)

For George and Alec

'I've reached the stage where I don't like footballers. They're on £20–£30,000 a week [in 2007] and they're not earning it; it makes you resentful.'
**David Sullivan, Birmingham City owner.**

'If someone is a shit or a bastard, they deserve everything that comes their way. And they probably wouldn't care less. But if you are genuinely doing your best, making decisions for the right reasons and putting money in that you know you will never get back, then the unfair criticism does become hard to take.'
**Jason McGill, chairman, York City.**

'Football attracts a certain percentage of nobodies who want to be somebodies at a football club.'
**Brian Clough.**

'At a football club, there's a holy trinity – the players, the manager and the supporters. Directors don't come into it. They are only there to sign the cheques.'
**Bill Shankly.**

'First and foremost, the owners are the most important part of a club [Lewes is a community-owned club]. Then, the fans. The players are last because there is no loyalty in football, even at this level.'
**Stuart Fuller, chairman, Lewes.**

'The only way to make a small fortune from owning a football club is to start with a large one.'
**John Madejski, chairman, Reading.**

'We are reliant on owners, and football needs to look at how it treats the owners at some of its clubs. Fans not happy about the investment that is going into their club? Trust me, without them [the owners], they wouldn't have a club.'
**Shaun Harvey, ex-Football League chief executive.**

'We are enjoying it greatly. It's a wonderful franchise and we just love it.'
**Malcolm Glazer, owner, Manchester United.**

'Owning a football club is like drinking prune juice while eating figs. However much extra money came in, it would sift away, to players, transfers and agents.'
**Alan Sugar, ex-chairman, Tottenham Hotspur.**

'Chairmen seem to get themselves into a hole at times. They keep digging and all of a sudden the only way out is to sack the manager. There is a massive weakness in a lot of boardrooms.'
**Jim McInally, manager, Peterhead.**

'For too long, football clubs have not followed the basic principles of running any successful business.'
**Mark Rubin, ex-chairman, Southend United.**

'I've been a football fan and a gambler since the age of about seven or eight. My interest in both developed at the same time.'
**Tony Bloom, chairman, Brighton and Hove Albion.**

'Directors should really stick to what they do best, whatever that is, and keep their noses out of the playing side of the game.'
**Bob Stokoe, manager.**

'Even if I built a 50,000-seat stadium and bought Ronaldinho there'd still be complaints about crap hot dogs.'
**Simon Jordan, former owner of Crystal Palace.**

'Mr Chairman, when I want your advice I'll give it to you.'
**Tommy Docherty, manager.**

# Acknowledgements

The author wishes to thank the following for their help and support in writing this book: John Abraham, Les Barlow, Sue Berry, Mark Binner, Allen Brett, Christian Brett, Mark Brierley, Rod Brierley, Trevor Butterworth, Jane Camillin, Paul Camillin, Gary Canning, Austin Collings, Tim Davies, John Dennis, George Dodds, Chris Dunphy, Lisa Edgar, Terry Eves, Fred Eyre, John Faulks, Graham Hales, Dean Rockett, David Hammond, Derek Hammond, Andrew Hindle, Charlie Hindle, Steve Harrison, James Heward, Dale Hibbert, Mark Hilditch, Judith Hilton, Jean Hodkinson, Roy Hodkinson, Trevor Hoyle, Garfield Hunter, Chris Jones, Karen Kerr, David Kilpatrick, Michael Kilpatrick, George Lee, David Luxton, Richard Lysons, Jim McCalliog, Jane McCarthy, John McDonough, Ian McMahon, David Madden, Peter Madden, Julie Matthews, Rob Meaden, Beryl Morris, Christian Morris, Graham Morris, Bill Norris, Duncan Olner, Richard Partington, Guy Patrick, Dave Picken, Godfrey Pickles, Kevin Pocklington, Dan Plumley, Geoff Read, Eric Snookes, Jim Stringer, Nige Tassell, Julie Thomas, Helen Thompson, Joe Thompson, Alex Wade, James Wallace, Chris While, Mark Wilbraham, Graham Williams, Richard Whitehead, Rob Wilson, Emily Wood, David Wrigley, Dan Youngs. And, most especially, Kellie While.

# Prologue

Among its many qualities, football allows players and spectators to be resolutely *in the moment*. As a fan, once you're ensnared by the game in front of you, lost to it, there is no today, yesterday or tomorrow, especially when you are partisan and willing on your team, heart and soul. The noise of the crowd is all around you and you'll hear snippets of conversation, but you are elsewhere, a place where self-awareness, memory and protocol have been chased away.

All fans criticise or commend certain players or managers but they have an implicit trust in their team and everyone connected to the club; it seems part of the deal. In fact, there is a perverse pleasure in accepting that a football match and, indeed, a football club is an arbitrary concept and out of our control, much the same as the weather. A football ground, after all, is where we can stop the habitual thinking and fretting of 'normal' life. It is leisure time. We let go of our scepticism.

Sadly, I'm not sure this is true anymore, if it ever really was. Such a view seems old-fashioned and naive in a world where we scrutinise the motives and deeds of everyone in positions of authority or influence – doctors, teachers, politicians. When football clubs regularly fall foul of incompetent, negligent, profligate or downright corrupt owners, it is an absolution we can no longer confer. We need to be on our guard. We have to keep a look-out on who is passing through the reception area of our clubs and making themselves at home. Who are they? Why are they there? Where do they come from? What do they want?

My club, Rochdale, has had a long period of boardroom stability. It is an heirloom that has been handled with care and consideration for nearly 40 years, tended on a near-familial basis. It wasn't always this way. Back in the late-1970s and early-1980s the club teetered on the brink of folding and there was volatility in the boardroom, even suspicions of wrongdoing. I was a boy at the time, new to my club, but heady in love with it. I remember the carousel of faces in the local press, men in ties and jackets – directors, chairmen, vice-chairmen, life-presidents – and while I didn't understand what they did, I knew my club was in grave trouble. Many of us who are lengthy, one-club, do-or-die fans will most likely face this dreadful situation at some point in the lifespan of our support. Our clubs will be disrespected, mistreated or, at worst, pillaged from within; this is happening right now at several English clubs. Afterwards, we will still hold high the badge, the *idea* of the club, but the infrastructure may be devastated; several clubs have been forced to start all over again.

Rochdale AFC is a small kingdom but around it and within is the same type of person found at most clubs outside the higher echelons of football. Across more than 50 interviews, I have looked in forensic detail at Rochdale's period of great instability. I wanted to trace its origins, to understand the historical and social basis of what happened, and how it mirrored the turmoil of the town and its people. I also wanted to profile in detail the men who gravitate to the inner sanctum of football clubs, their backgrounds, their motivation, how they think, what they want to achieve. On a broader level, I have tried to capture the atmosphere of football back then, how it was administered and what it meant to be a player of small-town glory earning £70 per week to get whacked good and hard on muddy pitches in front of a few thousand fans in ramshackle grounds.

Hopefully this book will act as a guide and a warning. It is also, perhaps by chance, a rollicking good story. The rain falls hard on a humdrum town as our characters – despots, heroes, hard-nuts, the fallen, social climbers, optimists, chancers, baddies, cowards, dreamers and bit-players – move through a plot that veers from comical to profound. It may all seem a long time ago, barely relevant, but little changes under the sun (or clouds) and a similar cast of characters may soon be on its way to your club with a design that threatens the future of your match-day bliss.

* * *

The disparity between top-level football in England, the Premier League and Championship, and those at the thicker end of the so-called pyramid is colossal. They wear the same strips, run on the same grass and obey the same rules but otherwise everything is different. Only in cup competitions do they meet, and then the media gorges on the contrast: the glamour and the grit, the prawn sandwich and the meat pie, the gods and the journeymen. From the formation of the Football League in 1888, football remained largely unchanged for almost a century. A hierarchy still existed, based on wealth, extent of support and ensuing success but, ultimately, one club was very much like the next. Players and managers were British. There were no agents. Football matches were not routinely televised. Grounds were different sizes but very similar – functional, shabby. The wage differential of players was much narrower. In fact, until 1961, all footballers were, theoretically at least, paid the same maximum weekly wage of £20 during the season and £17 in the summer. Clubs circumvented this ruling, as they did others, by offering lucrative signing-on fees or bonuses. A common ruse was for club directors to confer 'jobs' at their companies to players or set them up in business so they could receive money via a different route than the club.

Within every community, in any town, a few men (for they were almost all men) were wealthier than others. The process of accumulating this wealth or, if inherited, expanding it, invariably made them adept at administration. They were born to organise and, catching the prevailing headwind of philanthropy and benevolent Christianity, many founded football clubs. They didn't do this to make money particularly; they had enough already. It was a charitable gesture, a gift to the weekend of the working man. This was the wellspring of most sporting organisations forged in the Victorian era – mutuality and egalitarianism, playing rather than working, the liberty of the weekend to the bondage of the weekday. Typically, the standpoint was codified, set down in the Football Association Rule Book drawn up by the wonderfully-named Ebenezer Cobb Morley. The subject of ownership was addressed in the 1899 edition and formed Rule 34: 'Directors cannot draw a salary from a football club; no one should take an income from owning a share in a football club and any money remaining from the winding up of a football club must be shared among local sports institutions.'

Football had a recognised 'golden age' after the Second World War, in the late-1940s specifically. The population was anxious to embrace peace once more and, with it, recreation. Spending power had also increased. The average attendance for matches played in the First Division in the 1948/49 season was almost 50,000. At the time, players were on a maximum wage of £12 per week and few clubs refurbished their grounds, which brings into question the final berth of all that money. Admittedly, a portion went on transfer fees.

The record transfer of 1948 was £20,050 which Sunderland paid to Newcastle United for Len Shackleton. The consensus was that clubs were flouting Rule 34, much the same as the ruling over the maximum wage. Shackleton himself seemed to be on to them: 'Professional players are no better than professional puppets, dancing on the end of elastic contracts held securely in the grip of their lords and masters. Sometimes the elastic is severed, always from above, never from below,' he wrote in his autobiography, *Clown Prince of Soccer.* Other players, meanwhile, doffed the flat cap to their patrons. Nat Lofthouse, in his autobiography, *Goals Galore*, was infuriated by those who 'look upon professional footballers as downtrodden individuals leading a hand-to-mouth existence'. He pointed out, bless, that 'many professional footballers have first-class accommodation provided for them by their clubs. A number of clubs also provide a mid-day luncheon.'

The modern age of football, the big change, can be traced to three momentous Thursdays over a 14-year period. The contagion of Thatcherism (generally defined as 'a belief in the primacy of competition and a free market') reached football on Thursday, 6 October 1983, when Tottenham Hotspur became the first sports club in the world to be floated on the stock market. At a stroke, the complexion, the focus, the philosophy of a football club was changed forever. The club had become a company, a commercial entity above all else.

The flotation meant there was no longer a need for directors to act furtively – if indeed they were – and they could, should they choose, accrue wealth from their football club, the same as any of their other business interests. At first, the club's lawyers were concerned about such an overt breach of Rule 34 but their solution was ingenious in its simplicity. They advised that Tottenham Hotspur FC be made a wholly owned subsidiary of Tottenham Hotspur plc and side-step the statute completely. The Football Association viewed the change as largely cosmetic, without any appreciation of its ramifications. The matter was considered so trifling that the FA failed to respond to Tottenham's request for permission, so it went ahead anyway. The share issue was over-subscribed four-fold and enabled the club to wipe out £4m of debt. The impact and change of ethos perturbed traditionalists within the club, even its own manager of eight years, Keith Burkinshaw. He left Spurs in 1984 after one of many fall-outs with the board and reportedly said, as he made his way to his car after leaving White Hart Lane for the last time, 'There used to be a football club over there.'

Nine years later, on Thursday, 20 February 1992, the 22 clubs that had previously comprised the First Division resigned en masse from the Football League. They formed a limited company called the FA Premier League with the commercial independence to negotiate broadcast and sponsorship agreements. The first major deal saw television rights sold to BSkyB for £191.5m, rising to £670m five years later. The current deal, running until the 2021/22 season, is for Sky Sports and BT to pay a combined sum of £4.4 billion to televise 160 matches per season. The 'reach' – as the marketing maestros term it – is phenomenal. The Premier League is broadcast in 212 territories to 643 million homes which forms a potential audience of 4.7 billion people: the world is a football.

On another Thursday, 29 May 1997, Mohamed Al-Fayed bought Fulham for £6.25m. The Egyptian-born businessman had twice been declined British citizenship, and, much the same as his purchase of Harrods department store and the satirical magazine *Punch*, his entree into football was presumed to be an attempt to fortify a claim to 'Britishness'. Whatever the motive, he became the first high-profile billionaire owner of a football club. Six years later he was followed by Roman Abramovich, a Russian magnate in oil and gas, who bought Chelsea for £140m. Abramovich, in an interview with the BBC, said he had done so because he was 'bored and needed a new challenge'. The truth, most likely, is that he wanted to disperse his assets globally and also 'soften' his image – Russian oligarchs are routinely accused of accumulating wealth by foul means. By 2011, Fayed had loaned Fulham £187m in interest-free payments. So far, Abramovich, the world's 151st wealthiest man, has invested £900m in Chelsea.

The international profile of the Premier League and the platform it provides has since proved irresistible to billionaires around the world. At the forefront is Sheikh Mansour, the deputy prime minister of the United Arab Emirates and owner of Manchester City via his City Football group which also includes Melbourne City FC and New York City FC. He has invested £1.4 billion in transfer fees since taking over Manchester City but this is a small portion of his family wealth, estimated at £785 billion. While foreign investment in football can seem arbitrary, if not foolhardy, it often has an allied agenda designed to impact elsewhere, thousands of miles from the anointed club. The venture by Sheikh Mansour, for example, is considered by some to be a gargantuan marketing initiative, nothing short of a re-branding of the Middle East.

At the start of the 2019/20 season, the only wholly English-owned clubs in the Premier League were Burnley, Tottenham Hotspur, Newcastle United and Brighton and Hove Albion. Although 'ownership', especially outright, is difficult to establish and fluid, the consensus is that during most seasons 75 per cent of clubs in the Premier League are foreign-owned as well as 50 per cent of those in the Championship. A foreign owner does not, of course, necessarily signify a soul gifted to Mammon. Avarice or ambition (take your pick) can also be home-grown.

The precedent set by Tottenham finally and irrev-ocably opened up football to the forces of unfettered commercialism. Board meetings, which had once been a hubbub of conversations ranging from possible signings to whether it was time to re-paint the spaces on the club car park, switched to musing on holding companies, joint ventures, portfolios, hedge funds, consortiums and parent corporations. Rule 34, much as it now mattered, was rescinded except for the provision on the winding-up of clubs. It meant certain well-placed individuals such as David Dein, the former Arsenal vice-chairman, were able to cash in shares which, in 1983, cost him £292,000, for £75m in 2007.

The money has cascaded, then, into top level English football and changed the sport beyond recognition. The standard of player his risen markedly, principally because they have been sourced on a global basis and also because their back-up team, psychologist to surgeon, dietician to podiatrist, is in place to ensure mind and body are in optimum condition to perform. The infrastructure of the top clubs has been utterly transformed, too. They are branded and marketed and the vocabulary has become suitably corporate: holding companies, multi-platforms, cross-collateralisation, inter-connectivity, multi-faceted. Even the sociologists have moved in. Professor Richard Giulianotti bravely confronts the theme in the 752-page tome, *The Blackwell Companion to Globalization*: 'Sport's appropriatisation by the forces of late capitalism place the economic (profit maximisation) ahead of the sporting (utility maximisation) to the extent that many may lament, but few could argue against the fact that contemporary sport, is, fundamentally, a vehicle for capital accumulation.' In layman's terms, the corner shop has become a hypermarket, and a black and white portable telly (more than ideal for Tony Gubba talking us through *Sportsnight*), a 55-inch widescreen, Smart LED, dynamic crystal colour 4K ultra HD home-cinema with Wifi, mirror frame and wall bracket.

Away from this shiny, super-capitalist, free-for-all extravaganza is a realm which, while not untouched or unchanged, has remained within sight of its roots. Only 15 per cent of clubs in League One are foreign-owned and six per cent in League Two. They each have a chairman and a board of directors who, unless matters go awry (and they sometimes do), run their clubs in a benevolent fashion on a long-term basis. They buy shares to validate their inclusion on the board and provide funds for the club, usually without expecting a return. Non-league football hosts many professional or semi-professional clubs which are similarly homespun, administered under the model set down more than a century ago; they remain 'clubs' rather than companies or mini financial empires.

Interestingly, there are exceptions, especially in non-league, where several often-eccentric characters have set upon a nurturing dream of turning a small club into a much bigger entity. Glenn Tamplin, owner of AGP, 'the No 1 Steel Fabricator in the Region', bought Billericay Town (founded 1880) in 2017 and made himself manager. He signed former Premier League players Jermaine Pennant, Paul Konchesky and Jamie O'Hara. The ground was renamed the 'AGP Arena' and a mural was painted on its outer wall which featured Tamplin, a heavily-tattooed, born-again Christian lying in bed with his wife, Bliss. He put the club up for sale in September 2018. David Haythornthwaite, a businessman with interests in leisure and the veterinary sector, bought Kirkham and Wesham FC of the North West Counties League in 2007 and renamed it AFC Fylde with an aim of achieving Football League status by 2022. The 'Class of '92', five former members of Manchester United's youth team who went on to great success, have taken Salford City from the Northern Premier League Division One North to the Football League in five years.

More commonly, directors tend to keep a low profile outside the higher leagues and work to ensure their clubs are financially viable and stable. Aside from the prestige, what is in it for them? 'Not a lot,' says Dr Rob Wilson, an expert in football finance at Sheffield Hallam University. 'They get local pride, I suppose. Most clubs have a history of changing hands between different generations of local businessmen embedded within their community.' Chris Dunphy is typical. He was running a shop and a heating engineering company in his hometown of Rochdale when, in his early 30s, he joined the board of Rochdale AFC who he had supported from boyhood. 'It seemed to be a natural thing to do, a way of stepping up your support,' he says. Fred Eyre, the ex-Manchester City apprentice turned author, ran a successful stationery business and in the early

1980s was offered the chairmanship of Derby County. 'It came at a time when my company was doing well. I had a little chat with them but it was at a time when Derby had about three owners in five minutes!' Clearly, the prevailing condition of a football club and a potential director's stage of life are crucial factors. Dunphy became involved with Rochdale largely *because* of its parlous state. 'No one wants to see their football club go to the wall,' he says. He left the board after two years to raise a family but returned later to become chairman. 'It's difficult quantifying how much time you put in but you just have to be there when needed. It becomes a way of life eventually.' Does it have a negative impact on family life? 'I'm on my third marriage,' he laughs. Often, people fall into directorships on an ad hoc basis. They are persuaded by pals or fancy 'giving it a go' and a football club can become an extension of a social grouping. Many are not necessarily passionate fans of the club on whose board they serve; most supporters would consider this a prerequisite.

The trickle-down effect of the Premier League's remarkable success plays a considerable role in the funding of lower league clubs, even if there is regular debate over whether the money should be so concentrated at the cone of the pyramid or divided more equally. John W. Henry (net worth: $2.6 billion), the American owner of Liverpool, has argued, for example, that the system 'subsidises competitors'. The current share of 'television money' each season, termed a 'solidarity payment', is approximately £1m per League One club and £500,000, League Two. This is a small portion of the overall income – the Premier League keeps 92 per cent of the total – but, for some clubs, it can be the single biggest source of finance during an average season. This largesse from the top table when amassed with gate money, club shop sales, lottery income, sponsorship deals, transfer fees and profit from the tea bars, etc., means that traditional, small-town, long-standing football clubs can continue in the thrall of the clock striking 3pm every Saturday. And, in sweet accord, up in the best seats, sit local middle-aged men made good, directors and chairmen, invariably in thick overcoats. It's chilly out there, from Carlisle to Plymouth.

**Mark Hodkinson, July 2019**

# Dramatis personæ

(in order of appearance)

Cyril Smith...obese, later-disgraced paedophile MP. Baiter of Graham Morris ('They're coming to get you.') and ex-employee of Fred Ratcliffe.

Bob Stokoe...ex-FA Cup-winning manager. Flinty but hyper-sensitive. Dog lover. Issuer of on-the-spot fines. Trilby hat growing ever tighter.

Fred Ratcliffe...Spring King industrialist. Mr Rochdale. Tough nut. Nearly four decades a director, chairman and life-president of Rochdale AFC.

Mark Hilditch...young, earnest striker. Fancy a game, son? Toilet-cleaner. Victim of crude retribution from dim-witted first-teamers. Don't throw snowballs!

Trevor Butterworth...sports shop owner. First outsider to see the malaise that was Rochdale AFC. Catalyst for change. Owner of pilot licence.

David Wrigley...man-about-town solicitor. Charming, handsome, tall. Meetings at the bank beginning to follow a familiar pattern.

John Faulks...estate agent entrepreneur. Gadder about town, searching for Spotland allies. Ever smiling, ever hopeful.

Judith Hilton...daughter of the Spring King. Still a Spotland regular.

27

Andrew Hindle...importer of Lada cars. Frequent flyer in private planes. 'Fairy Godfather' denier. Probably should have stuck with rugby.

Les Barlow...gnarled, chain-smoking (back then), Spotland-embedded sports reporter. Unwilling to sugar-drop the truth: 'They were crap!'

Rod Brierley...last of the old-timers. Wallpaper and paint mogul. Taciturn. One of few Rochdalians waking up each morning to a view over a Cumbrian lake.

Eric Snookes...tempestuous, door-attacking, cortisone-dosed full-back. Happy enough in his Rochdale terraced house to shun the palm trees of the English Riviera and cash-waving overtures of Torquay United.

Peter Madden...Big Pete. Gentleman Pete. Re-builder of the club – free transfer by free transfer – until the thwarted singing of a York City striker sends him as loco as a Stokoe.

Chris Jones...veteran profanity-issuing striker. An accomplice (of Jimmy Seal) in a plot to dislodge a bobble hat.

Graham Morris...the Morris Man. Accountant. Safe hands. My-word-is-my-bond. Inveterate worrier. An Overcoat Man incarnate.

David Kilpatrick...ex-boarder at top public school. Importer of granite, exporter of straight talking and common sense. Handy with concrete. Another Overcoat Man incarnate.

*Chapter One*

# Welcome to Rochdale

The junction at the end of the A627(M), the spit of road leading from the M62 to Rochdale, is substantial enough to accommodate a small village. Set yourself down on a grass verge, press a tissue to your face (to keep out the fumes) and start counting. There are 13, 14, 15 lanes of converging traffic. Maybe more. Or less. Does the slip road by the BMW garage count as a lane? Or the sneaky one to the left leading from McDonald's, the Odeon cinema and Homebase? Either way, it's a lot of concrete. And cars and lorries and vans.

'The Rotary Clubs of Rochdale Welcome You' is the first sign that isn't directing you to the town centre, another destination (Blackburn or Bury, say) or advising that the two lanes, one of which you're in, are about to become one with traffic merging from the right. More of this later. Within a second or two there is another reminder of where you have arrived: 'Rochdale – Birthplace of Co-Operation'. This is written in huge letters across a railway bridge. For many years, 'Co-Operation' was written, 'Cooperation'. That missing hyphen bothered me greatly. I pondered a moonlit walk across the bridge, paint pot in hand. I decided that it would be out of reach, even with a good pal holding on to my ankles. The sign relates to the Rochdale Pioneers, a group of 28 men who, as we were taught at school, banded together in 1844 to open a shop selling food they could not have afforded if it had been bought individually. They inspired the birth of a movement which, 50 years later, saw 1,439 co-operatives covering virtually every area of the UK. The principles were later adopted throughout the world. Go Rochdale!

The Dunlop Mill Tower is gone now, demolished in 2014, but most locals still instinctively look out for it, maybe in the hope of seeing it return as a tall ghost standing guard at the entrance to the town. It was clad in corrugated metal, painted soft blue, so that even on dark, rainy days (of which there are many – 140 per year on average), a piece of the summer sky remained unfurled and fastened down. Each year, at the beginning of December, a Christmas tree, complete with fairy lights, would appear on top of the tower. It was a scratty artificial tree, the kind rescued from a skip, but was made beautiful and proud again by its sash of twinkling bulbs and position high above the streets and houses. The tower was much like the bow of a huge container ship because fastened behind it was a seven-storey mill made from 14 million Accrington bricks. Dunlop Mill was believed to be one of the largest mills in the world, employing 3,200 at its busiest, making the cord used in tyres. As a kid, I'd travel from Rochdale to Manchester on the railway line which ran parallel to the mill, and marvel; it seemed to go on forever, brick after brick – it was half a mile long.

At the junction, by the huge Tesco store, is a direction sign shared by 'Spotland Stadium' and 'Gracie Fields Theatre'. 'Rochdale AFC' would have been more apropos because stadium is rather grand. In fact, the place is now officially called the Crown Oil Arena. No one outside of the media has ever referred to it as such, favouring its original title of Spotland – where the 'a' is pronounced as a soft 'u' or 'e' – otherwise it has the ring of a very peculiar theme park. It is significant that Gracie Fields is referenced seconds after arriving in town. Anyone from Rochdale knows this phenomenon. Utter the word 'Rochdale' and the Post-it Note falls immediately from the wall of memory – 'That's where Gracie Fields is from'. As if we didn't know. She made her last film 75 years ago but, like it or lump it (which sounds like one of her catchphrases), she clearly remains the pride of our alley and, if you dig out a 78rpm record, she can still tell you all you need to know about a thing-ummy bob. The theatre named in her honour, which opened in 1978, a year before she died, is seldom used for public performances, most likely because of its out-of-town location. The most recent programme contained a mere couple of shows – two performances of *Beauty and the Beast* described as an 'Easter panto spectacular' starring Kerry Katona as the Atomic Fairy, and Basil Brush as the 'beast's sidekick'. At Christmas there is a ten-date run of *Aladdin* ('star casting to be announced').

At the start of Roch Valley Way is a turquoise Mini with a Union Jack painted on its roof, perched on a flowerbed. The doors are open and the bonnet missing. The car has been filled with soil from which flowers bloom. According to Martin Taylor, head of environmental management at Rochdale Council, it is part of a campaign to 'make the borough cleaner and brighter by clearing litter from streets and planting colourful floral displays in a number of prominent areas.' The cost of buying the Mini, preparing it for the site and installing it on a concrete base was precisely £7,140. Cars as vases is clearly a theme in Rochdale because there is another in St Mary's Gate, the busy roadway that skirts the town centre. Here, a vintage Morris Minor van branded in the blue and white livery of the Co-Op has been installed at the behest of former council leader, Richard Farnell. 'Everyone is rightly proud of our links to the worldwide co-operative movement and although it's a historical connection it's one that still resonates around Rochdale today,' he said, probably while banging a bass drum.

Hidden behind a line of strategically positioned trees is a place known to everyone as the sewage works, but its Sunday Best name is Rochdale Wastewater Treatment Works. The landmarks thereafter become rather bleak and deathly: the Cemetery Hotel, Rochdale Cemetery, Rochdale Crematorium, Denehurst Cemetery. On a theme, the streets on the nearby estate are named after battle sites of the First World War: Verdun Crescent, Mons Avenue, Jutland Avenue, Marne Crescent. People are smoking at bus stops. A discarded tyre has been left on the pavement. A wall has been partially knocked down and police tape fastened across the gap. On the right, finally, is the home – whatever its name – of Rochdale AFC. It is the close season, so very few people are about. As I pass, I notice one or two familiar faces, fellow fans, walking from their cars to the office, perhaps renewing their season tickets. Still hoping, still believing.

I turn left into Edenfield Road. Half a mile up the road, The Star has shut down, another pub gone. I enter the car park at Rochdale Golf Club. Bentleys, Porsches and BMWs everywhere and, on the far side, a gleaming Jaguar F-Pace which will cost, as I soon discover, about the same as a terraced house on the other side of town. Back on the main road, the Horse and Farrier and Turf Tavern are still open but the Blue Ball is now N Bar and Grill – the 'N' standing for Norden, the district I am in. The businesses and shops reflect an upmarket clientele – accountants, gift shops (Pookys

Emporium), Norden and Bamford Financial Services, a shoe shop especially for children (Tip Toes), a tutoring centre, a florist (Garden of Eden, no less) and a skin clinic (The Aesthetic Rooms).

At the Bridge Chippy, a suitably elegant cafe boasting 'premium quality food', I turn round. I take a right up Bagslate Moor Road to the tree-lined residential area of Bamford. Many of the houses are individually built. They are large and all manner of shapes and designs. Some have verandas, others are wood panelled. Drives are long and wide. Lawns are carefully tended. Laburnum, lilac and cherry trees have been planted to provide variety and colour. Intercom systems are set into walls next to electronic gates. There is no litter. Benches are positioned beneath wide picture windows. There are no mills or workshops, nor backstreet garages. This is a seldom seen snapshot of a northern English town. I don't recognise it and as I drive through it reminds me of the setting of a suburban sitcom from the 1970s. Any minute now, I might see Sid James and Diana Coupland shouting to Sally Geeson that she can't go out dressed in *that* mini-skirt. Or I could be in another country; affluent America, perhaps, where the leafy peace will soon be disturbed when a Dodge Ram drives by and a wholesome, shiny-toothed kid jumps out, back from baseball practice.

On my way towards the town centre I pass a wonky sign at the entrance to Mitchell Hey Mill reading, 'Bter Dreams' and wonder what is the nature of its business. I take a quick left into Holmes Street, park up and do a search on my phone. Google proffers, 'Better Dreams – bedding suppliers to the trade.' On my left is wasteland where a shopping trolley has been tossed on its side. It has been there a while; the grass and weeds are holding it tight and snaking into the wire mesh as if trying to claim it for nature. A huge sycamore has joined in, forming a canopy of leaves that reach down and provide more cover from above.

Further down the street, a burnt-out car is on the other side of a wire fence at the end of a row of terraced houses. It is hard to tell whether it has been dumped or rests on land that was once the site of a mechanic's workshop. The brick-built houses are a hotchpotch. Some have been pebble-dashed, one or two clad in dressed stone. Thin dark trails occur at regular intervals where leaks from gutters have been left unrepaired and water has trickled down. Weeds thrive, little dots of green and yellow where the outside wall meets the pavement. The contrast in neighbourhoods is startling, just a couple of miles from Bamford.

Much of Rochdale is poor and scruffy. It has always been this way, it seems. During the Industrial Revolution life expectancy was 21 while, by comparison, several miles further north, in the more rural Westmorland, it was 38. At 13 years old, Rochdale boys were a full year behind boys from elsewhere in growth terms. In 1915 it was listed as the most polluted town in England. I check the local house prices. One of the two-bedroomed terraces nearby has sold recently for £40,000.

A middle-aged Asian man walks by the car and through the rear-view mirror I see him stop to shake the hand of a neighbour, also Asian. Rochdale has many émigrés; they were invited over originally to staff the mills. They arrived from Eastern Europe after the Second World War, Poles and Ukrainians chiefly, followed by Asians through the 1960s and 1970s. In 1966 about 1,000 people attended a banquet in Rochdale Town Hall organised by Asians as a thank you to the local population for making them welcome. The local MP, Cyril Smith, was the first to grasp the importance of the Asian vote and canvassed solidly in areas where they had settled – Deeplish, Wardleworth, Heybrook and Hamer, places which are now almost wholly Asian. Relations became strained briefly during the close-down of the textile industry when immigrants were perceived as filling positions ahead of indigenous people. This probably accounted for the 4,000 votes received by Jim Merrick, who stood on behalf of the British Campaign to Stop Immigration party in a by-election of 1972. By 1980, Rochdale, with a population of about 93,000, was home to approximately 10,000 immigrants. Today, nearly 35 per cent of the town's population identifies as being 'non-white British'. There was further tension in 2012 when a paedophile ring, eight men of Pakistani heritage and an Afghan asylum seeker, all living in Rochdale, were convicted of the rape of underage teenage girls, conspiracy to engage in sexual activity with children and trafficking girls for sex.

The road snakes to the right, becomes Primrose Street and passes the former site of Dexine Rubber Company which, from opening in 1941, provided work for hundreds before winding down to full closure in 2008. The area has been fenced off, the buildings left to decay and endure routine bouts of vandalism. Signs are fixed to the surrounding fence – 'Fly tipping is a criminal offence' and 'Dangerous Buildings, Keep Out'. Spray artists have scaled the fence and left their mark: 'KH', 'Cheesedraw' and 'Ned', among others. Again, nature is trying to claim and prettify the mess. Dashes of purple arch from the side of buildings where buddleia has managed to take hold. Rosebay willowherb stand as defiant sentinels among the piles of brick. The site had been a hub of industry from 1863 when Spotland Bridge Mill and Spotland New Mill were built there, initially for wool production, later for cotton. The River Spodden runs close by, a tributary of the River Roch, from which Rochdale draws its name. Spodden, by the same process, has lent its name to Spotland; the river was known previously as either the Spod or Spot and provided water power for the two mills and many others along its course.

Rochdale once had more than 130 mills, a huge number for a relatively small town. At its height, half a million people worked in Britain's cotton industry. The output per year was equivalent to providing a shirt and a pair of trousers for every man, woman and child on earth. Eighty per cent of the world's cotton products were once exported from Britain and it was said that the industry made enough to meet the UK's requirements within the first hour of the working day. The remainder of the day was for the rest of the world.

Growing up in the 1970s, there seemed to be a mill on almost every street corner, completely out of scale with the rest of the landscape. They usually had peculiar short names, presumably to fit snugly on the side of the tall chimneys: Elk, Pye, Flat, Harp, Mars, etc. I recall waiting with my mum for the 461 bus to Rochdale (via Deeplish) from nearby Castleton and being afraid as it set out along Queensway. This road, almost two miles long, was completely hemmed in by mills and factories and reaching the other end felt as if you'd emerged from a brick tunnel; you could breathe again. Without any discernible landmarks, the only way to mark off the journey was by the names of the mills you passed: Arrow, Linden, Ensor, Blue Pit, Castle and Dicken Green. As a teenager I would see older lads who had gone to work in the mills. The physical change was noticeable. They quickly bulked up from lugging bales and the other heavy work. When you spoke to them they seemed tired and uninterested, blaming the long hours and hot conditions in which they had to work.

The beginning of the end came with a lack of investment and the availability of cheap labour abroad. The last mill to be built in Lancashire was Elk Mill in Royton, near Rochdale, in 1926. Seven years later production was overtaken by Japan and later by the United States, India and China. In 1959 Britain, for the first time, imported more cotton goods than it exported. Mills closed at a rate of one a week in the UK during the 1960s and 1970s. Many were flattened, although this was often done in stages. As kids, we played in spaces where walls were still standing but the roof was missing. We'd find cotton spindles and pretend they were mortar bombs or throw stones at the pigeons roosting in the gaps where windows had once stood. A few working mills remained. They were noisy places with their own distinctive sweet, starchy smell belched out from metal grilles set into the walls.

Rochdale fell into torpor during the 1970s and 1980s, from which it has still not recovered. After the mills closed, unemployment was extremely high. Alcoholism and addiction to tranquillisers soared in the early-1980s and the suicide rate increased. Although conditions in the mills were poor, they still formed communities, taking in all ages, from different ethnic backgrounds and with a high percentage of women; about two-thirds of all cotton workers were female. After the mills closed I remember people, lost souls, suddenly hanging around, stopping to talk to us kids by the canal or when we played football on the bottom field. They had also lost a large part of their social scene. Many mills and firms had their own social clubs and sports teams and these disbanded. Afterwards, those that could find work were taken on as casual workers at the trading estates or retail parks installed on sites where mills had once stood. A company called Fashion Logistics moved into a large section of Dunlop Mill, for example, and staff loaded and unloaded racks of clothes from and on to lorries. There was little government support for redundant textile workers and, since the breakdown was less swingeing and dramatic than, say, the mining industry – it spanned several decades – there was scant acknowledgement of their plight: no pop concerts or poetry in their name or interest from a media eager to frame its documentaries with poignant pithead imagery.

I continue, heading down Spotland Road towards the 'seven sisters', a group of high rise flats, four of which are earmarked for demolition in the next few years. 'Three sisters' doesn't have quite the same poetic ring to it, Chekhov notwithstanding. The nearby districts of Falinge and Freehold have 75 per cent unemployment; in 2013 it was deemed to be the most deprived area in the country. This area, comprising mostly three-storey flats and cheap terraced housing, is where the after-effects of a workaday slow-motion demise of a single-industry (textile) town have hit the hardest. There are no jobs; there is nothing to do. The proliferation of cheap housing, some of it standing empty, means the town meets the criteria for acceptance of refugees. Figures released in 2018 showed that Rochdale has housed more refugees than the whole of the south-east of England, excluding London. Maidenhead, the constituency of the former Prime Minister, Theresa May, has accommodated none; Rochdale has accepted approximately 1,000. While the town has a long tradition of welcoming people from across the globe, the principal reason was the promise of a job. This no longer stands.

I pass a corner shop (remember them?) with a sign outside reading 'Booze 'N' Basics'. A shop called Hench Supplements on Whitworth Road has posters in the window of near-naked young men lifting weights. More closed-down pubs, chipboard nailed across the windows. The same with former bingo halls, some of them still with rain-scrubbed posters on their walls advertising half-price Wednesdays. Signs, lots of them, for nurseries and day-care centres with twee names, usually citing bees or butterflies. Plenty of care homes too, several set back and swathed in rhododendron bushes, others pressed tight to the busy road and its booming traffic. Betting shops, pizza outlets, kebab houses and car washes that appear to have been set up overnight. Postmen and postwomen pass by, almost running – probably meeting a delivery target; that's why they wear shorts and trainers. Most gardens along the main roads are overgrown, unkempt. The pavements are full of plastic bins, all at different angles, some tipped over like a drunken line-dancing team. A kid (no helmet) revs his motorbike and does wheelies on wasteland across from Albert Royds Street. His dog chases after him, bark, bark.

Eyes back on the road, I have to be careful because two lanes often and randomly become one without forewarning. This impromptu funnelling calls upon the better nature of drivers, to show consideration to their fellow man (or woman) because only one car can pass from two lanes into one at any given time. After you, Sir (or Madam), please pass this way. No, after you. In Chalfont St Giles, Lower Slaughter or any other similarly genteel environ this road design would function perfectly well. Not in Rochdale. These two-into-one lanes are council-sponsored showdown sites for boy (and girl) racers; queue jumpers; anger management subscribers; stubborn, I'm-not-budging middle-aged lane hoggers and random hotheads looking for a reason to shout at, gesture to, or, worse, set upon fellow drivers. If you survive the particularly challenging bottleneck at the Kingsway–Milnrow Road junction and need a lie down, head to the Bulls Head pub where bed and breakfast is a mere £20 PPPN, according to its sign.

I avoid driving into town because it's almost impossible to reach without putting aside an afternoon to traverse the one-way system, bus lanes and a tramway which does the hokey cokey across various roads. Congestion and frustration, that's what it's all about. I've been there many times before, of course, and there are several magnificent buildings to recommend. Magnificent and Rochdale in the same sentence, at last. The town hall (due a £16m refit) built in 1866 in the Gothic Revival style; the Georgian post office (now a pub) and Touchstones (art gallery, museum and local studies library) are all splendid ways to spend an overcast Tuesday, even if, to get there, you have to pass a statue of Gracie Fields doing a weird kind of curtsey. Perhaps she's doing the hokey cokey, too. There is also a spanking new sports centre and a 'multi-use' public building (library, coffee shop, council offices) called Number One Riverside which has a wibbly wobbly wavy design, but is a bit too close to the River Roch, which is prone to burst its banks. Sadly, there is no independent book shop or town centre cinema (though one is pending with six screens, apparently, as part of a £250m regeneration scheme). As in many other northern towns, the centre is clogged with charity and pound shops, nail bars, food outlets, mobile phone shops and downmarket clothes stores. And, to reach them, you've got to slalom around a fair number of beggars, druggies and drunks.

Thankfully, Rochdale is skirted by wonderfully rough countryside. A few miles from the town centre and you are engulfed in a grassy sea of moorland. From up there, where the curlews make their throaty, insistent calls and the landscape is hewn from millstone grit and soft peat, Rochdale, down below, can look quite beautiful. At night the best vantage point is on the car park of the White House pub on the A58, the top road to Halifax. As darkness falls and streetlights come on across town it appears as if this golden spread has been specially ladled from the Pennines. When you're so far away, you don't see the litter, the graffiti, the mess and the mucked-upness. All you see is light.

## Chapter Two

# Under a blanket, driven into the dark

There is always *that* point, which is why the word is often prefixed with snapping, breaking, boiling and turning. It arrives arbitrarily – a pin jabbed randomly into a map, a few letters in red ink among pages of black, hailstones on a summer's day. Here lies the spot, the line, the rupture, the place where everything changed: the mood, a routine, a relationship or even the course of history. Thereafter, what follows is unlike what went before, whether visited upon a person, a people, a place, a situation or a lower-league northern English football club.

Everything changed for Rochdale AFC during the 1973/74 season. On this occasion the adjectives summoned to describe a poor sporting episode are hollow, inadequate. The facts suffice. They won twice in 42 league matches. They conceded 107 goals throughout the season. They finished bottom of Division Three. They lost 5-3 in the FA Cup at home to non-league Grantham Town. On a Tuesday in February 1974 they played before the lowest ever post-war attendance for a match between two professional football clubs – between 450 and 588 people (the figure was thought to be inflated to reduce the humiliation) attended the 2-0 home defeat to Cambridge United. Still, at least supporters were well fed. So many pies were left over that the club handed them out free from trays.

As so often happens in sport, the downfall had followed an upturn. The preceding four seasons had seen the club at its highest point. Rochdale, formed in 1907, had been promoted in 1968/69 to play outside the bottom tier for the first time in its history. The promotion was 'natural', a team well-assembled playing to their maximum potential and not one borne from the sudden input of money. In fact, the club had sold only 98 season tickets and was being run at its overdraft limit of £60,000 when Bob Stokoe, the manager, built a team comprising, in his words, 'experienced and young tenacious players'. This task had been set upon many times before, of course, but had failed, usually by a considerable distance.

The club's season-upon-season losing habit was broken when they suffered just one defeat in the first 13 league games of 1968/69, which included a 6-0 trouncing of the division's nobility, Bradford City. Such wins burnish players, lift them higher. The departure of Stokoe to Carlisle United – to return 11 years later in very different circumstances – did not affect the mindset or the momentum. Len Richley, the assistant manager, replaced Stokoe in October 1968. They carried on winning and lost only twice in the last 24 games of the season. Promotion was sealed with a 3-0 home win against Southend United on Saturday, 10 May 1969. A civic reception was held two weeks later at Rochdale Town Hall. The players, Reg Jenkins, Tony Buck, Steve Melledew, Joe Ashworth, Chris Harker, et al, who had finally severed the club from perpetual defeat and despondency, were patted on the back until they almost bruised.

Initially, Rochdale performed well in the higher division, as promoted teams often did. They finished ninth in the first season and then 16th, 18th and 13th.

During 1972/73 there was little to indicate the forthcoming long dark night of a season. In October 1972 they had been in second place, one point behind the leaders, Walsall. They faded as the season progressed but won three of their last five games, indicating ostensibly that all was well as they went into the summer break.

The club appointed Walter Joyce as manager, a former youth coach at Oldham Athletic. He was 35, young for a manager, and this policy of putting faith in the new and inexperienced stretched to the playing squad. Reg Jenkins, who had scored 119 goals in 305 league games across nine seasons, was released at the age of 35. Other established players were also moved on – Colin Blant, Gordon Morritt, Bill Atkins, Malcolm Darling, Len Kinsella and Dick Renwick. They were largely replaced by young cast-offs from the likes of Everton, Manchester City and Liverpool. Joyce's strategy might have reflected a steadfast belief in youth – many former youth coaches who become managers hold dear this belief – or, more likely, it was an edict from the board to reduce the wage bill.

Joyce was also asked to shed backroom staff. Amy Robinson had been the club laundress for eight years and voluntarily took on other jobs such as darning the kit, making toast for the players and cleaning the boardroom. She was paid £14 a week for a minimum of 21 hours. When Joyce made her redundant he told her the club was so short of funds it could no longer afford the rental on its television set. The redundancy was handled badly – this would become a common occurrence – and she took the club to a tribunal where she was awarded precisely £147. The tribunal heard that she washed three strips a week and up to 50 towels. She worked most Sundays and Christmas Day. She used her own washing machine plumbed in at the ground, where it was so cold she often had to wear 'slacks, a car coat, bonnet and football socks' to keep warm. She said she had been asked to work for less money and had agreed but the club laid her off anyway, without giving notice or covering holiday pay. She went to work in the laundry at Birch Hill Hospital in nearby Littleborough, where she was paid £44 a week.

Another staff member moved on to save money was Angus McLean. He had been a defender in a strong Wolverhampton Wanderers team which played in the top tier after the Second World War. He arrived at Rochdale as secretary after being manager at Hartlepools United; roles in football were not clearly delineated at the time so a manager becoming a secretary was not particularly unusual. He had spent five years at Rochdale when he was laid off without notice. He too threatened to take the club to an industrial tribunal. Fred Ratcliffe, the chairman, asked him not to be so hasty and presented him with a cheque for £750. McLean had clearly not been asked to sign a gagging order because he spoke readily to the press about his former job. He revealed that it was his duty to phone Lloyds Bank each Thursday and check whether there was enough funds in the club account to cover players' wages. If not, he had to hunt down a director and ask him to make a payment from his personal account. 'Sometimes this was up to £2,000,' said McLean. The club was constantly looking to save money, he said, and one time he was asked to call round as many off-licences and supermarkets as possible in Rochdale to see if he could undercut the amount paid to Standring's, its wholesale supplier of bottled drinks. After a full day on the mission he reported back that it *was* possible to save money by calling at individual shops – the total bill was £1.50p cheaper.

Much the same as a good start to the promotion season had broken the ingrained culture of losing (seven league games undefeated), a bad start to 1973/74 (seven games without a win) saw its return. The defeats quickly piled up and the young team soon had fear in its boots. Fans could easily read the players' body language. They were reluctant, afraid, staring hard at the ground; beaten before they started. They fell to the bottom of the division in November 1973 after a 3-1 home defeat to Watford and remained there for the rest of the season. They finished 21 points adrift of the team directly above the relegation zone, Port Vale. Attendances had fallen at an alarming rate, suggesting that the wider Rochdale public had regarded promotion as a blip, a one-off, a tilt of circumstance rather than a sporting transfiguration. During the promotion season the average home crowd had risen from 2,292 to 5,399. The first (and only) home league victory of the 1973/74 season, a 3-2 win against Shrewsbury Town, was witnessed by 957 supporters. In addition to the Cambridge United game in February, the attendance fell below 1,000 on three more occasions – an ignominy in professional circles.

Football clubs were in perpetual flux, especially at lower league level where players and backroom staff rarely settled for more than a handful of seasons. All this assimilation – young players and seasoned pros, the skilful and the scrappers, the brawny and the nimble, ball players and hoofers – was funnelled into the team which either succeeded, or didn't. Every decision had a cumulative effect on the overall fortunes of a football club, whether made by the board or manager or players on the pitch. The choices made at Rochdale during 1973/74 were almost universally amiss, for its season was one of the worst recorded by a Football League club. Many fans believed this nine-month spell, August to April, caused a rupture at the club, stole its soul, and led them to the point of extinction several years later.

Rochdale's malaise coincided with a tumultuous and wretched period in the country's history. At such times, sport can put a smile on the dirty face of life, provide cheer, but at Rochdale club and country were under a blanket, driven into the dark. The IRA was running bombing campaigns across England. Eight off-duty soldiers, two children and a civilian were killed when a bomb was detonated on a coach travelling along the M62 in Birstall, West Yorkshire, a few miles from Rochdale. In the autumn of 1974 five people were killed and 65 injured when bombs exploded in two Guildford pubs. Twenty-one were killed and 182 injured in the bombing of two pubs in Birmingham. There felt to be no sanctuary from danger; even post boxes were used to conceal bombs. An unusually high number of industrial accidents occurred, especially in the mining industry. Eighteen miners died at Markham Colliery, Staveley in Derbyshire, when the brake on a cage failed; ten died in a methane explosion at Golborne Colliery, near Wigan, and seven died at Lofthouse Colliery, Wakefield, after an inrush of water. An explosion at a chemical plant in Flixborough, north Lincolnshire, killed 28 people and seriously injured 72 others. A train travelling from London to Oxford derailed at Ealing, causing ten fatalities and injuries to 94 people. Disasters and death appeared to be constantly in the newspapers and on television.

There was also a severe economic crisis. The Yom Kippur War between Israel and the Arab nations in October 1973 led to Arab members of the Organisation of Petroleum Exporting Countries (OPEC) suspending deliveries of oil to

Western nations that had supported Israel in the conflict. This caused an energy shortage in Britain exacerbated by a protracted dispute between the miners and government. A three-day working week was introduced on New Year's Day 1974 to conserve electricity which was principally generated by coal. Firefighters and ambulance drivers took strike action as inflation exceeded 11 per cent, more than three times higher than average; by the end of 1974 it was almost 18 per cent. Edward Heath, the Prime Minister, called a General Election for February 1974 which resulted in a hung Parliament. Another General Election was held in October. Labour secured a narrow majority of three seats.

Although the textile industry was on a discernible wind-down, it was a few years from moving into recession. The *Rochdale Observer* still carried adverts for jobs, each presented in the knowledge that the local population was familiar with industry terms. They wanted winders, doublers, weavers, ring spinners, high-speed beamers, cotton feeders, doffers, cone winders, card attendants, creelers, loom oilers, cloth dressers and warp gaiters. It was much the same at the engineering firms – Farrel Bridge, E Brierley, Holcroft Castings, Rochdale Tool Company – as they sought fitters, capstan operators, horizontal borers, markers out, Plano millers and hand grinders. The companies did not request CVs or letters of introduction; prospective staff was asked merely to 'call round' or 'visit the site office'.

The lack of spending money and mood of despondency caused attendances to fall at football matches. In a bid to attract more fans, the Football League allowed a tranche of games to be played on Sundays. Rochdale's away match at Brighton and Hove Albion was one of 12 selected on Sunday, 20 January 1974. The Sunday Observance Act of 1780 prohibited 'the use of any building or room for public entertainment or debate on a Sunday if it invoked an admission charge'. So, clubs waived the conventional entrance fee but insisted fans bought a copy of the match programme instead, which sold at a much higher price than usual – the cost of a match ticket. Nine of the 12 clubs taking part in the Sunday football experiment reported their highest crowds of the season. Rochdale tried it two weeks later when they played York City at Spotland. The attendance was 2,205, much the same as it might have been on a Saturday. The increase in attendances at those first few games was widely felt to have been due to the novelty element. Fans didn't like having their weekend routine changed. The atmosphere was different, they said, walking to the grounds through empty streets – traders had to wait until 1994 before opening for limited periods was allowed on Sundays.

The shortage of power led to the use of floodlights being banned. Matches had to be played in natural daylight which meant kick-off times were brought forward on Saturdays and midweek matches were played in the afternoons – this had largely been responsible for Rochdale's low attendance against Cambridge United; the match was played on Tuesday afternoon when most fans were at work or school. A proposal was tabled to suspend the League and another to extend the season until June; neither was approved. Rochdale, incidentally, lost both of their Sunday games.

After being relegated to Division Four, Rochdale arrested the catastrophic form of the 1973/74 season. By mid-September 1974 they had already won more league games (three) than in the whole of the previous campaign. Towards the end of the season, they lost five out of six matches and this turned the final game against Swansea City at Spotland into a de facto play-off to see who could avoid the re-election zone. Bob Mountford, Rochdale's robust striker, scored the only goal of the game to lift the club one point above the zone and condemn Swansea to their first ever appeal for re-election.

The Football League's re-election system had been inaugurated at its formation in 1888. Although the League originally comprised only 12 clubs, those finishing in the bottom four places each season were technically suspended or, in the terms of statute, 'retired' from the league. At the AGM, the other clubs voted and, in effect, 're-elected' them back into the Football League. The plan was well-intentioned – the league wanted to maintain standards while still offering potential places to flourishing clubs outside the existing set-up. At this point, there was no real clamour to join. Several of the clubs that went on to garner huge support had not yet been formed or fully established. The Football League had grown in distinct stages, expanding the number of clubs in the first division and adding a second division. By 1921 and the formation of divisions three, north and south, it boasted 92 clubs; Rochdale was among this batch of new admissions. The re-election system remained but very few clubs entered the League via this route. Down the years, frustrated non-League clubs began to view the procedure as a restrictive practice. They argued that Football League directors, many of whom had forged long-standing friendships with one another, were unlikely to vote out each other's club. The regular indictment was that it was a 'closed shop' and 'an old pals act'. Rochdale, in particular, had benefitted and, by 1975, had been re-elected six times.

The voting system was peculiar and granted the greater say to clubs with seemingly the least interest in the outcome. The chairmen of the 44 clubs in the top two divisions had one voting 'right' each while the remaining 48 chairmen from the lower two divisions had six voting rights between them. The president of the Football League was also granted a single voting right. Each voting right entitled the holder to cast four votes – to select four clubs from however many candidates wanted to join the league and met the designated criteria, four of whom would be the 'suspended' pre-existing members.

Rochdale were stalked by the re-election system. Their lack of funds, low attendances, dilapidated ground and poor form undermined their status as a League club and made them a prime candidate for replacement. The inherent bias towards pre-existing League clubs could only deflect moneyed, ambitious non-League clubs for so long. Bradford Park Avenue had lost their place to Cambridge United in 1970 and Barrow to Hereford United, two years later. A pattern was emerging of greater admission to the League. The emphasis, therefore, for Rochdale was to avoid finishing in the bottom four at all costs.

In the 1975/76 season they finished 15th in Division Four, four points above the zone and, in 1976/77, 18th, two points above. The move towards greater fluidity of League members was further substantiated when Wimbledon replaced Workington in June 1977. Wimbledon, who had employed full-time professional players since 1964, had won the Southern League for the three previous seasons. In 1975 they had beaten Burnley of the First Division in the FA Cup and drawn with the champions, Leeds United, at Elland Road. Meanwhile, Workington, playing in front of barely 1,000 fans most weeks, had finished second from bottom twice in the preceding seasons and then bottom in 1976/77. The appeal of the new was becoming compelling.

## Chapter Three

# Catching the Rain

Rochdale's squad at the start of the 1977/78 season comprised 13 players, which included two goalkeepers. Apprentices Ian Bannon (18) and Ted Oliver (16) were hastily promoted to augment the numbers, along with Paul Cuddy (18), who signed on an amateur basis. The shortage of players was exacerbated by a raft of suspensions incurred when Paul Hallows, Bob Mountford, Dave Esser and Bob Scott were sent off early in the season. A run of eight consecutive defeats, from August to October, left them bottom of the league.

The former Rochdale midfielder, Mike Ferguson, replaced Brian Green as manager in October 1977. He was 34 years old; it was his first managerial position after nearly 500 games as a player. The defeats continued. The team was weakened significantly when Mike Poole, the goalkeeper, left for Portland Timbers in the United States, and Bob Mountford moved to Huddersfield Town. Mountford had scored 37 goals in 97 appearances – an impressive number for a striker in a struggling team. Poole was replaced temporarily by Andy Slack, aged 18, summoned from his job as a sorter in a tannery in nearby Heywood. He made 15 appearances before having to retire though injury. Local teenagers, Steve Shaw and Billy Boslem, were also added to the squad, to be pitted against match-hardened lower-league professionals. Another poor run after Christmas saw them lose seven out of eight games. Aside from centre back, Bob Scott, who stood 6ft 2in, the rest were nimble, slight men. Most weeks they were flattened as much as they were beaten.

Among the batch of young local players to join was Mark Hilditch. The easy way he fell into professional football was typical of the times. As a youth he played for Rushcroft Boys in Royton, a few miles from Rochdale. One evening, aged 15, he was walking home when he was passed by cars containing players from Heyside Juniors, another local boys' team. They recognised him and remembered him as a good player. He was invited to play with them that night in a match against the Rochdale 'town team' made up of boys considered the best players of their age in the area. Hilditch played well and was invited by Rochdale scouts, Brian Dodd and Jack Corless – two men whom Hilditch presumed worked for the club on a voluntary basis – to a training session with the first team, held the next day.

Rochdale trained at Sparth Bottoms, an area close to the town centre where the terraced houses ran into scrapyards and industrial units. Guard dogs barked on the other side of metal fences and the air was often scented with the sweet-sharp tang of burning metal from one of the foundries. Rochdale Gas Works was nearby with a huge gasometer jammed tight to the streets, looking like an abandoned UFO. Ratcliffe Springs (company motto: 'They never lose their temper'), owned by Fred Ratcliffe, Rochdale AFC's chairman, was based nearby at Crawford Spring Works in Norman Street. The company's site included a piece of grassland which was used for training by Rochdale. 'I didn't know what I was doing, really,' said Hilditch. 'I turned up with my boots and joined in. I was well out of my depth and knackered in no time.' Afterwards he was invited to play for the youth team at Bolton Wanderers and then for the reserves against Preston North End at their training ground. 'I was a big Manchester United fan and couldn't believe I was getting changed in the same dressing-room as David Sadler,' he said. Sadler, who had spent a decade at United, was in his early 30s and had signed to play under his former team-mate, Bobby Charlton, Preston's manager.

Over the course of a year or so Rochdale maintained a loose association with Hilditch. He wasn't asked to sign any papers and after each game was told, 'We'll be in touch.' He started an apprenticeship as a turner at Cobden Chadwick Engineering, a wallpaper printing company in Oldham. One evening, Jack Corless arrived unannounced at the family home and asked whether Hilditch would play some more games for the club. 'I then started playing regularly. One week, we'd be up against Manchester City or United's "A" team and the next we'd be at Marine, somewhere like that. I didn't feel out of place and was growing in confidence as a player,' he said.

Rochdale reserves trained on Thursday nights at Bishop Henshaw School, a mile or so from Hilditch's home. After one session, Mike Ferguson approached him and asked, 'Do you fancy playing for the first team?' He was invited to travel to the match at Southend United in April 1978. He skipped his usual Friday attendance at Oldham College which was part of his apprenticeship scheme. Unsure of what to pack, he jammed a suit along with his football gear into a bag. 'It seems incredibly naive now but I had literally no idea where Southend was. We'd been travelling a couple of hours and I realised it was a lot further than I'd imagined,' said Hilditch.

As far as he recalls, he had not signed for the club at this juncture and did not have insurance. He was effectively the '13th man' and would have been named sub if anyone had fallen ill en route – only one sub was allowed at the time. On a purely sporting level, he'd barely had a single word of counsel or coaching during his time at the club, let alone a briefing about Southend United.

The game would have been a considerable challenge for a 17-year-old newcomer. Rochdale were nine points adrift at the foot of the table while Southend had secured promotion a few days earlier and were all set to celebrate with a goal feast against the travel-weary northern toilers. Rochdale kept the score down to 3-1. Afterwards, Hilditch, still below the legal age to buy alcohol, witnessed the drinking culture prevalent in football during the 1970s. 'They all got bladdered,' he said. 'It was mind-boggling. No one had told me we were staying overnight so I'd not properly packed anything. They were running around with all these buckets of water, throwing them over each other and making a mess of the hotel rooms. Bobby Scaife and Bob Scott walked down the corridor carrying Mike Ferguson; he was completely out of it.'

Hilditch was asked to report to Spotland three days later, ready for an evening match against Reading. On the day of the game he worked as usual at the engineering plant, starting at 7am, and travelled to the ground by bus. Rochdale won 1-0, one of only two wins in the final 13 matches of the season. Hilditch scored the goal. Before he left to catch the two buses home, he was beckoned by Tom Nichol, club secretary and man of many roles, and presented with a £5 note 'for expenses'. 'I would have played for nothing,' said Hilditch. 'I wasn't bothered about getting the bus from Spotland. There was little chance of me bumping into any fans – we didn't have many back then.' Indeed, the attendance at the Reading game was recorded as 1,004 but was actually 734. When Hilditch arrived at work the next day he received a round of applause from colleagues in the milling section and the machine room. He set about his work but was soon tapped on the shoulder. The foreman gave him a dressing-down for clocking in 15 minutes late.

\* \* \*

A regular visitor to Spotland, invariably with a car full of playing strips, footballs and boots, was Trevor Butterworth, the owner of a sports shop in town. As a lifelong fan, he offered the best deals he could, sometimes augmenting his delivery with manufacturers' samples passed on to the club for free. The players each had four pairs of boots for the various surfaces on which they played, with Puma and Adidas the most popular. 'The place was a dreadful mess. The roof in the boardroom was leaking and there were buckets in the dressing-room catching the rain,' said Butterworth. 'It had become very rundown.' On one occasion, Mike Ferguson, sounding particularly downbeat, invited him to 'have a chat'. 'I got there and asked him what was wrong. He couldn't see any way the club could progress. He said he was depressed – the directors hadn't done anything to help and they were all getting on in years. He asked if I could help in any way. I'd been a fan since I was eight years old and it got to me, knowing the club was in such a state and the manager feeling as he did.'

In their 50th season as a Football League club Rochdale finished in the same position as their first: bottom. They were seven points adrift of the next club, Southport, whose goal difference was minus 21, compared to Rochdale's minus 42. The attendances for the last seven matches of the season at Spotland had each been a few more than 1,000. Clearly the club had not wanted to reveal that the real figures were a few hundred below 1,000; it would have attracted negative attention and weakened the case for re-election.

The club was understandably anxious. Four years earlier they had finished bottom of the Third Division by a large margin and had now done the same again in the bottom tier. By any definition, considering the shortage of investment and dilapidated state of the ground, they were the 'deadwood' which the non-League lobby was seeking to see replaced. All the same, it had been 11 years since Rochdale had last sought re-election and despite the shortage of funds the club had honoured its commitments, paid its players (even if occasionally late) and fulfilled fixtures.

Perhaps more importantly, Rochdale had friends in high places, where it most mattered on voting day. Fred Ratcliffe – also known as Little Freddie or Mr Rochdale – was a canny operator. In the parlance of politics, sporting or otherwise, he knew how best to crawl towards the light. He made sure representatives from clubs higher up the league were always welcomed warmly to Spotland. Cup of tea, Sir? Piece of cake? Before being relieved of his duties, Angus McLean had noted that no matter how impoverished, the club remained generous with its hospitality. 'At other clubs you had a cup of tea and a biscuit, and that was it. At Rochdale there was always plenty of drink,' he said. Ratcliffe was well aware of the goodwill garnered from a judiciously gifted bottle of sherry or brandy. A thank-you note or get-well-soon card, perhaps. And, for a visiting chairman's wife: a bouquet of flowers. They'd remember the visit, the warmth of the people, the delicious meat pies. So, everyone was left with a soft spot, a place in their hearts for Rochdale. Habitually, there was a parting shot as visitors were wished a safe journey home: 'Think of us in June [the time of the league's annual general meeting and re-election vote], we just might need you.'

Fred Simpson Ratcliffe was de facto King of Rochdale. If the title was unofficial and came without a castle, he'd bloody well build his own; he was that type of man. He was born in January 1914 to a working-class family living in a two-bedroom terraced house in Clapgate Road, Norden, near the Brown Cow pub. He had a sister, Hilda, five years older. His mother, Mary, died when he was 14 and his father, Herbert, when he was 19; their early deaths were thought to have contributed to his independent nature.

As much as it was a mill town, Rochdale was also home to scores of engineering works, often built from the same redbrick as houses, blending in on the same streets. Spring-making in particular had been carried out for more than 200 years and employed almost 1,000 people in the town. Ratcliffe started as an engineer at Milkstone Spring Works for Robert Riley, a spring-making company established for more than a century. At the age of 25, his brightness duly noted, Ratcliffe was invited on to the board at Riley. Four years later he formed his own company, FS Ratcliffe. He covered the staff's first week's wages by borrowing money from his aunt and uncle who owned a fish and chips shop. His timing was perfect. Huge quantities of springs were needed in the production of aircraft engines for the war effort and his company quickly grew to more than 300 staff.

He joined the board of Rochdale AFC, whom he had supported from a boy, on Thursday, 12 September 1946, aged 32. He was introduced to the wider public of the town in the *Rochdale Observer*. Readers were told that Ratcliffe was a member of Hopwood Golf Club and the Central and Balderstone Conservative clubs; he later stood unsuccessfully as a candidate for the Conservative party in the council elections of May 1949. He became, at 39, one of the youngest chairmen in the Football League and was widely accepted among football's hierarchy. He quickly became known for his authenticity, love of Rochdale AFC and small stature. He was the round-faced chap in the camel coat with pale blue eyes and a gap-toothed smile, far left on the press photo at the golf day at Everton, the sportsman's dinner at Manchester United or at a boxing night held by the Anglo-American Sporting Club in the Hotel Piccadilly, Manchester.

One of the people Ratcliffe met regularly at such events was Fred Eyre, the former Manchester City youth player, after-dinner speaker and author of the seminal football book, *Kicked Into Touch*. 'Fred was infectious and dynamic. He knew his football, especially when it related to Rochdale. He could have been by the pool in the south of France but he got up every morning and called at his works or made his way to Spotland,' he said. 'He ran the place as if it was his fiefdom and I mean that in a good way because, with Fred, it meant bonhomie and making everyone welcome. I honestly can't remember anyone ever saying anything bad about him. He was at all the games and made sure everyone got a pie – you can't say that about most chairmen.'

A club *was* jettisoned from the Football League in June 1978 but it wasn't Rochdale. In a break from the usual protocol which customarily saw, if any, the bottom club demoted, they chose the second from bottom instead. Southport received 26 votes, the same as League applicants, Wigan Athletic. In a two-way second ballot, Wigan were finally accepted on a 29-20 vote on their 35th attempt to join the Football League. Six years earlier, Wigan had been so frustrated with failed applications that they had petitioned to join the Scottish League. Hartlepool United, who had finished three places above Rochdale in the table and had 13 more points, received 33 votes, compared to Rochdale's 39. The man in the camel coat had done well, very well.

The failed re-election bid by Southport was not a surprise to those within the game. Again, it revealed that personality held eminence over a club's achievements or infrastructure. A year or so before the re-election appeal, John Church had resigned as Southport's chairman. Much the same as Fred Ratcliffe, he was a lifelong one-club man, a wealthy benefactor and, more to the point, a likeable, cheerful character. He had made his money supplying fruit and vegetables to market traders and shops. One of his frequent ruses had been to promise young players a five pound win bonus and present them with five pounds of potatoes. At other times, he bought expensive suits for the entire playing staff. He was a popular figure in boardrooms up and down the country, unlike his replacement, Walter Giller, who was described by Hughie Fisher, Southport's manager at the time, as 'bombastic and brash'. Another factor in Wigan superseding Southport was that Arthur Horrocks, their chairman, and Ian McNeill, the manager, had made personal visits to every first and second division club while Walter Giller and his directors had canvassed by letter only. Clearly, football people responded most favourably towards those that cared most about their clubs.

## Chapter Four

# The Secret Six

Mike Ferguson's plea for help had resonated with Trevor Butterworth. He was busy running the shop, but between placing orders and dealing with customers, it was on his mind. He was an itchy, chatty, amiable and straight-talking man, always happy to discuss football, especially Rochdale. His shop often became an impromptu meeting point for fans, leaning on the counter, passing the day, rueing how Saturday's game had gone. Another defeat, another disappointment. Why did it always have to be this way? These people, loyal to the bone, deserved better, he felt. 'It had got me thinking, how we could possibly turn it around and save the club if we got together half a dozen younger men with ideas and energy,' he said.

He contacted a local solicitor, David Wrigley. 'He was young enough and had the financial capability to help out,' said Butterworth. 'He was very charming socially, too.' Wrigley had done the conveyancing on a house Butterworth had bought and overseen a contract for the shop. They had also played amateur football together for several years in the mid-1960s. Butterworth had been a left winger for Whittle's Sports, and Wrigley, a centre-half. They were the works team of Whittle's Bakery in Littleborough, a small town three miles north-east of Rochdale. They had been extremely successful, boasting ex-professionals Kevin Walsh, who had played for Oldham Athletic, Southport and Bradford City, and Brian Sutton, a goalkeeper who had made several appearances for Rochdale. 'I told Wrigley what a mess the club was in and that it might go out of business if someone didn't get a grip. He was keen to find out more,' said Butterworth.

The pair met Mike Ferguson at The Deerplay, a remote pub high on the moors between Bacup and Burnley, close to where Ferguson lived. 'Trevor was a friend,' said Wrigley. 'I was flattered that he'd contacted me and that he thought I'd be able to help.' Wrigley, 40 at the time, was a staunch fan of Manchester United, but had been taken by his father as a boy to watch Rochdale and other local clubs, including the rugby league side, Rochdale Hornets. 'I used to like going to Spotland. Walter Birch was centre-half at the time [late 1940s/early 1950s] and it was a friendly little ground.' Butterworth and Wrigley set about finding cohorts. Within weeks they had assembled a team and met at Wrigley's office in Rochdale town centre. The others were John Faulks, a chartered surveyor and estate agent; Andrew Hindle, a motor vehicle distributor; Sidney Marks, personnel director at Turner Brothers Asbestos (TBA), Rochdale's biggest single industrial employer, and Jimmy Valentine, an accountant.

Although their union had not been particularly discreet and they were soon reduced in number, the group – effectively a shadow board of directors – became known in the local media as the 'secret six'. Their early get-togethers were easy affairs, a chat and a pint and a few ideas shared with friends and friends of friends. Butterworth, as the only one with first-hand experience of the club and the disarray it was in, was the catalyst. While the others held a largely passive interest in Rochdale AFC or felt duty-bound to heed the calling of their hometown club, Butterworth could count out his life in Saturdays spent behind the Sandy Lane End goal, lost to the roar or the groans.

Butterworth, born in April 1938, had been adopted as a child by Thomas Devaney, a chauffeur, and his wife, Annie, a millworker. They lived in a terraced house in Parish Street, close to Rochdale town centre. He was introduced to football and Rochdale in particular when some older children who had been evacuated from London during the war and were living next door to him, took him to Spotland. They were fans of Queens Park Rangers but they each cheered on Rochdale as they ran out winners against Chester, 6-0. 'I got engrossed in it immediately,' he said. 'I started going to nearly every game, walking down Spotland Road, over Spotland Bridge and up to the ground to stand behind the goal about two hours before the match kicked off.'

At the age of 27 he opened a sports shop in Rochdale with his team-mate from Whittle's Sports, Kevin Walsh. As well as Rochdale AFC, it also supplied kits and equipment to Bury and Oldham Athletic. The pair opened another shop, Lakeland Sports, in the Manchester overspill estate of Langley in Middleton; the council estate had a Lake District theme with streets and avenues named after its towns and villages. 'That led to us going our separate ways,' said Butterworth. 'Kevin was offering people credit and we were spending our evenings knocking on doors all over Langley trying to get them to pay up. I thought, "This is no bloody good".'

On the surface David Wrigley might have seemed an unlikely ally for Butterworth. They had been brought together through business and playing football, but mostly moved in different circles. Butterworth was a little uneasy in white-collar company but saw in Wrigley an assuredness, a level of articulacy without superciliousness that he thought would serve the club well and form a counterpoint to his own street-level nous. Wrigley had quickly built a reputation as a grafter and a go-getter. Many of the existing solicitors in Rochdale were viewed as fuddy-duddy and old-school, whereas Wrigley was keen and personable. He had established himself with the professional set residing chiefly in the districts of Bamford and Norden, and also among the flourishing tradesmen dotted around Rochdale who needed advice on company law. By 1976 he held directorships at 16 different companies, though some were notional to fulfil legal requirements. He held a financial stake in several pubs around town, among them the Ladybarn in Milnrow, and The Cemetery, close to the football ground. The Ladybarn was set up as a forerunner of the gastropub, offering generous lunches of rump steak and mushrooms (£1.25), duckling a l'orange (£1.30) or gammon steak and pineapple (95p); all with 'French fries and vegetables'.

Wrigley was a difficult man to miss, standing, by his own measurement, at 'one-eighth of an inch below 6ft 7in'. He had thick black hair, pale blue eyes and an engaging smile. Even in the defiantly manly environs of Rochdale he was referred to as a 'good-looking bloke'. He had been outstanding at cricket and football. As well as playing for Whittle's Sports, where he had worked over the course of a summer, he had also turned out for the university team and, on finishing his studies, Old Mancunians, a team made up of former Manchester Grammar School pupils. Back in Rochdale, he helped form Castleton Casuals, a team comprising players drawn from professional circles. During one game a team-mate, a lawyer, was fouled and reportedly asked the referee: 'Are you going to admonish him or shall I just hit him?' Wrigley was an all-rounder at cricket, playing at a high amateur level with Norden, Castleton and Cheetham Hill, where he captained the side. He played golf off a handicap of 10.

Among pals, Wrigley was noted as a prodigious drinker. He could knock back pint after pint with little apparent impact on his demeanour. He was known as 'Biggles' and thought to embrace similar heroic and gentlemanly qualities as the fictional pilot and adventurer. He denies that he is widely known by this nickname. 'It was and still is a friend in London who calls me Biggles. I have no idea why he does. It's most probably because he couldn't find anything to rhyme with my surname,' he said.

Wrigley grew up in a semi-detached house on Queensway, now a busy dual carriageway near the Rochdale junction of the M62. He lived with his father, Hubert, mother, Marian, and younger brothers, Keith and Julian. Both his parents were members of Castlemere Methodist Church and Wrigley said they created a 'loving environment' in which to bring up children. Hubert Wrigley, an engineer, had been in a reserved occupation during the Second World War. He volunteered as a special constable and later became a superintendent. David Wrigley attended Lowerplace Junior School and passed the entrance examination for the prestigious Manchester Grammar School. He wanted to study Classics at university but his father advised him to undertake a more vocational course. He read law at Manchester University, starting his degree in 1956.

David Wrigley began his career as a solicitor in December 1961 at the Manchester firm, Aubrey, Snowise & Co. He quickly specialised in civil matters – probate, conveyancing and company law. 'I hate public speaking,' he said. 'Criminal law wasn't for me, standing in a court and speaking out. I've never been a pushy person. I much prefer to be part of a team.' He practised under his own name until 1971 when he entered a partnership with Peter Toomey, as Wrigley & Co. They were later joined by Ian Ferris and William Goodwin. The firm was based in The Butts, in one of the finest buildings in Rochdale, a grand house which had once belonged to the Royds family, woollen merchants and grandees of the town. Wrigley & Co was upstairs while the ground floor housed the William and Glyn's bank.

The second person contacted by Butterworth was John Faulks. The same as many others in Rochdale, Butterworth had noted the impressive growth of Faulks' estate agency; its boards were all over town. Norford Estates (an amalgamation of Norden and Bamford), had grown to six branches and 22 staff. Faulks had forged links with local farmers and developers, making him ideally placed to specialise in newly-built properties when they came on the market. Norford's motto, carried on its television advert was, 'We've got Rochdale covered.'

Butterworth, Wrigley and Faulks had all played at various times for Norden Cricket Club, and while none of the three were close friends they had often found themselves in conversation at the cricket club, golf club or one of the pubs along Edenfield Road in Norden, perhaps the Horse and Farrier, Turf Tavern or Blue Ball. While very different to Wrigley, Butterworth imagined Faulks would be a boon to the football club with his enthusiasm, amiability and business acumen. 'Trevor rang me,' said Faulks. 'He said Rochdale FC was going down the pan and would I be interested in being involved. I shared similar views as Trevor, especially about sport, and I respected his view of the football club.'

Faulks had been a Manchester United season ticket holder but fostered an affinity for Rochdale AFC when his family moved to the town from Davyhulme in Manchester when he was 11. 'I went to boarding school [Lancaster Royal Grammar, founded 1235] where I was desperately unhappy. I was forging my own identity and mixing with boys from other towns and realised I was quite proud of what had become my home town – the blue and cream buses, Gracie Fields and the like,' he said. He had visited Spotland in the school holidays with his father, Frank, who worked in the district valuer's office at Rochdale Council. 'We'd stand on the slag heap that used to be at the corner of the pitch where crush barriers had been forced into the cinder,' he said.

Jimmy Valentine, an accountant, was a close friend of David Wrigley and had been best man at his wedding. He worked at a private practice but, soon after being invited to join the secret six, became a partner in the Manchester branch of Arthur Andersen, one of the largest accountancy firms in the world. On seeing the indigent state of Rochdale's finances, he said it might damage his professional reputation to be associated with the club (and its debts). He opted out of the group just weeks after first expressing an interest.

A rumour circulated the town that one of the six men 'taking over' at Spotland was heir to the Marks & Spencer family fortune. They were mistaken. Sidney Marks was no relation. He was originally from Liverpool and after leaving Cambridge University had joined TBA as a trainee manager, rising to earn a place on the board. He was a good friend of Faulks; the two played golf together. He was considered a 'people person' with a youthful outlook and an infectious personality. He, too, was destined to spend a relatively short period of time associated with Rochdale AFC.

Mark Hilditch had returned to his engineering job but decided to ask the club its intentions. 'I was getting fed up at work. They were long days. One dinner time I rang up Mike Ferguson and said if they didn't sign me, I'd try elsewhere. My dad had a few friends at Oldham Athletic. Ferguson said, "Leave it with me."' Hilditch played in a Lancashire Youth Cup match for Rochdale against Manchester City whose defence included the captain of England Schoolboys, Tommy Caton, and a future first-team regular, Nicky Reid. Rochdale lost 6-2 but Hilditch scored two goals. 'There had been talk about City being impressed with me. The next day I signed as a pro for Rochdale. Maybe it prompted them to offer me a deal,' he said. He was given a £250 signing-on fee – standard for any player joining the club – and put on a basic wage of £30 per week with an extra £10 for each appearance and another £10 win bonus. During the six years he would spend at the club, Hilditch was barely coached, at least on a one-to-one basis, and older professionals were reluctant to proffer advice – it wasn't in their interest to make a rival for their position an improved player. Hilditch was not spoken to about diet or told to hydrate before training or matches. He remembers doing a great deal of running, though. If they won, they ran. If they lost, they ran some more.

The last of the secret six was Andrew Hindle (full name: Brian Andrew Hindle), born in January 1944. Though he was from Rochdale, he was unknown to all but one of the group. 'I can't remember how he got involved,' said Wrigley. 'He said early on that he'd like to be chairman and nobody minded. It became a team effort and everyone played their part.' Hindle was considered to be the wealthiest of the group by some distance. He had property in the Isle of Man, presumably to take advantage of its reduced tax liabilities, and travelled occasionally in private planes. 'He seemed a bit of a white knight at the time,' said John Faulks. 'Unlike the rest of us, he was an out-and-out businessman and was used to dealing with finance.' Trevor Butterworth viewed him as a 'forward-looking young entrepreneur'. 'When he first came in, he said he'd put £500,000 into the club. He had plans to buy the shares from all the other directors,' said Butterworth. 'He had a lot of drive but wasn't the type to shout out about it. Looking back, I did wonder what was behind the facade and I wasn't totally convinced of his wealth.' Hindle denied ever making such a promise. 'This has come from Trevor's imagination. I definitely didn't say that. It would have been a ludicrous amount in those days,' he said.

Hindle was brought up in Newhey, originally a village but now considered a district of Rochdale on the border with Oldham. He attended the private, high-achieving Hulme Grammar School in Oldham. He was steeped in business. The family firm had been John Fielden & Son, coal merchants. Rochdale had more than 80 pits during the Industrial Revolution and coal was used to feed the boilers in cotton mills. Most homes had coal fires, too. At one point the company had 20 lorries delivering coal across the north-west. Hindle had an older brother by three years, David. Their parents separated when Andrew was nine. His mother later married Walter Hargreaves, a car dealer who owned two garages in Wakefield. Hindle went into business with his stepfather and became managing director of the company which, along with the routine dealership provision of servicing and repairing, sold about 100 new vehicles and 200 used, each year. 'I was quite close to Walter,' he said. 'He was pretty much a non-executive director when I came in, though. This meant he came in once a week to get his car cleaned and filled up with petrol!'

Unlike the other five, who each had jobs that brought them into regular contact with others in the town, Hindle's business interests were elsewhere. He had married Virginia [Gini] Lumb in 1967 when he was 22 and they had settled in Mirfield, near Huddersfield. They had two children – a son, Charlie and daughter, Sarah. 'Hindle wasn't known to anyone, really,' said Les Barlow, sportswriter at the *Rochdale Observer.* 'Put it this way, he'd not been seen on the terraces at Spotland before he joined the board.' Hindle had, in fact, visited the ground on several occasions as a boy. 'I'd stand at the Pearl Street End. I remember players like Reg Jenkins and one of the Milburns [Stan, a member of the famous family of footballers],' he said. 'We always seemed to be struggling but it was good fun and on the odd season we'd have a decent side.' His main love was rugby union. He played as a prop forward for Huddersfield until the age of 32. Hindle was connected by marriage to David Wrigley. Susan Wrigley, Wrigley's second wife, was the sister of Jennifer, Andrew Hindle's second wife. Their maiden name had been Cropper. Hindle had married Jennifer and became stepfather to her three children. 'I suppose it must have been me, then, who tapped up Hindle,' said Wrigley.

The secret six, though actually now five because of Valentine's departure, met several times and agreed on a strategy to 'save' Rochdale AFC. They had no experience of football administration but were giddy with enthusiasm and heart. There was only one snag, a roadblock standing resolutely in their path – Rochdale already had a board of directors. There were, appropriately, six of them, and their figurehead, Fred Ratcliffe, was cut from the millstone grit which formed large parts of the town. Fred and his pals, equally flinty, were set firm, happy in situ – going nowhere without a bloody big push. So, to fulfil their dream of building a winning football team playing in a modern stadium, the secret six had to first secure a victory against the solid six, a team of craggy, experienced opponents.

## Chapter Five

# The Spring King

The directors serving on the existing board of Rochdale were canny; they didn't miss much. Word had already reached them about what was going on, what the plan was and the names of the plotters. Fred Ratcliffe, initially at least, came out fighting: 'It is an insult to my fellow directors to think they can be replaced overnight. Losing experienced directors would be a big mistake.' For all his bluster, Ratcliffe was a pragmatic man. He'd already thought this through; all roads up, as they said in Rochdale. He was 65 and had been suffering chest infections, each one taking longer than the last to clear up. He was a heavy smoker. Family and friends were always on at him, nag nag, to give up fags, knock it on the head, take a rest. He'd also had back trouble and had spent time at Highfield Nursing Home in 1974. He loved his football club dearly, but it had been hard work down the years, a bellyful of trouble. This meeting, that meeting, the new signing moaning and wanting a few more quid, one of the apprentices caught nicking again, the groundsman's mower breaking down – there was always something going on, kicking off. It was getting too much bother for a man of his age, in his condition. If those daft buggers, Butterworth and the lot of them, wanted to take it from him, they were welcome, on a plate. Later, first drink of the day in his belly warming him up all lovely, he'd imagine life without the club, how he'd miss the banter and the brethren and those away trips, oh what fun. No, he was staying put. Bugger the lot of them.

Fred Ratcliffe was said to have two main loves in life – business and Rochdale AFC. 'I was brought up on Rochdale AFC from the cot,' said Judith Hilton, his daughter. 'I don't remember a time when it wasn't part of our family's life. It was my dad's first love and something he talked about every day. When I told him I was getting married, he said it would have to be a morning wedding so he could get up to Spotland afterwards,' she said.

Fred and his wife, Florence (nee Byron, and thought to descend from Lord Byron whose family resided in Rochdale during the 1600s), had lived in various houses in Rochdale with their children, Judith and Stuart, before moving in 1960 to Standrings in Norden, a listed house with six bedrooms built in 1791. Many years before package holidays became within reach of most families, the Ratcliffes spent a few weeks each summer in Spain, usually Majorca, Torremolinos, Barcelona or Lloret de Mar. Ratcliffe Springs also had a 25 per cent stake in a spring-making company in Madrid, to where Fred was a regular visitor. Fred had struck the deal in March 1961 with one of Spain's most famous entrepreneurs and reformers, Eduardo Barreiros, who wanted the springs to use in the mass-manufacture of car seats. 'To me, my dad was just my dad. I didn't know we were any different to anyone else, doing what we did,' said Judith. Stuart Ratcliffe had little interest in football, but his father encouraged his love of animals and he built up a menagerie at the house which included bush babies, monkeys, chipmunks, reptiles and snakes. Once, they were about to return from holiday in Spain, when Stuart saw a couple in a bar with a spider monkey. He was told they had bought it from a pet shop in Madrid. The flight back to England included a changeover in Madrid during which time they visited the pet shop and later had the monkey flown to England in a box placed on a seat in the cabin. 'Stuart had that monkey for years, long after all the other animals had died,' said Judith. 'They would have a cup of tea together when Stuart came home from school.'

Fred Ratcliffe drove a Rolls-Royce with the registration number 'FSR 880'. Wiseacres at the spring works joked that he was so small that he could barely see over the dashboard. His office at the factory was described as being 'like a posh living-room'. It contained leather settees, plants, a colour television and a cocktail cabinet. In 1974, FS Ratcliffe had declared a profit of £290,941 and Fred was listed as taking a 'wage' of £559 per week from the business. He had invited friends, mainly from the Masonic and Rotary community of which he was a keen member, to buy shares in the company and there were more than 100 local shareholders, including fellow Rochdale AFC director Edward Lord, who had more than £15,000 worth. Ratcliffe's family was aware that he had financed the football club for many years. 'But we never knew to what degree,' said Judith. 'He was very secretive about two things – his wealth and his age. I dread to think how much money he ploughed into it, though. If he had to pay the players' wages, so be it.'

He sat on various football committees, including the Lancashire Football Association. 'At one time he was asked to be a director of Manchester City but told them he had only one love and that was Rochdale,' said Judith. A profile of Ratcliffe ran in the March 1977 issue of *RAP* (Rochdale Alternative Press), a radical monthly magazine fashioning itself as a small-town *Private Eye*. He was featured on the front page beneath the headline, 'RAP Spies on Ratcliffe'. As a major employer in Rochdale and one of its wealthiest men, he was considered justified quarry. The magazine's co-editor David Bartlett trailed him over the course of a week to various pubs in Norden and Bamford. Ratcliffe's alcohol intake was listed assiduously – usually halves of bitter and whisky chasers. The time he spent at work was also clocked: 15 hours. His daily routine and general prosperity was contrasted with that of his staff who, of course, worked longer hours and had much less money. The article was a transparent attempt to ridicule and reduce Ratcliffe but his lifestyle was little different from any prodigiously rich, self-made man approaching retirement.

The timing of the revelations about Fred Ratcliffe's prosperity could not have been worse, even if it was completely out of his control. In the spring of 1977 it was disclosed that Rochdale had the highest death rate in the country of babies at birth or less than one week old. The main factors contributing to the statistic were social deprivation and low income. In simple terms, young women in the town had poor diets and lived in conditions (overcrowded, damp, cold) that significantly reduced their chances of giving birth to healthy babies. The government report highlighted high unemployment in the town and the traditionally low wages of the textile and allied industries which employed one-third of all working men in Rochdale and half of all women in work.

\* \* \*

The other five men on the board of Rochdale AFC alongside Fred Ratcliffe were Geoffrey Roderick Brierley (known as Rod), owner of Lancashire Wallpaper and Paint, born

November 1935; Leonard Hilton, bakery owner, born January 1924; Joe Stoney, solicitor; Harry Carter, owner of ladies' dress shops and with interests in property; and Edward 'Teddy' Lord, proprietor of an industrial decorating business, in which Ratcliffe held shares. They were a close unit, all pals together, as Judith Hilton confirmed. The Ratcliffe family often went on holiday with Joe Stoney's family and all six of them mixed at each other's houses or at Rochdale Golf Club. Stoney, perhaps the closest to Ratcliffe, had joined the board in 1954 and was vice-chairman for many years. When he qualified at the age of 21 he was thought to be the youngest practising solicitor in the country. 'Rochdale had such a lot of small businesses, especially in manufacturing, and they tried to help each other out. My dad treated everyone the same and never looked down on anybody,' said Judith.

They had each heard the rumblings emanating from Bamford. Any day now, they were told, these swaggering young (ish) men were due to appear with all kinds of fancy plans and ideas. They sat tight and waited. They held a view similar to Fred's – it was bloody hard work running (propping up, more like) an ailing football club. And it cost money, drip-dripping every week. If these fellows had cash, how could they turn them away? It would save them from dipping into their own pockets anymore – someone else could take a turn. But they did enjoy their jaunts and Saturday routines. This meant they were largely ambivalent to the idea of being usurped or amalgamated or appended – no one was quite sure of the definite plan.

Friends or not, the long-standing directors still had internecine disagreements typical of most boardroom associations. Teddy Lord, in particular, grumbled that the focus was too often on Ratcliffe to the exclusion of the rest of them. At other times, people inside and outside the club questioned exactly how much money had been introduced by the board and in what manner. Under perfectly legal arrangements, there were ways to transfer money which, while still supplying funds to the recipient, might, to varying degrees, also benefit the donator in tax relief. In other words, sceptics claimed that the board were merely redirecting money otherwise owed to the Inland Revenue to the loss-making (therefore non-tax accruing) Rochdale AFC.

The six had each shown sturdy, long-term commitment to the club. Leonard Hilton, the 'Pie Man', had first visited Spotland in the 1930s when he sold cigarettes from a tray to supporters as an 11-year-old. Later, his bakery supplied pies on match days. He had joined the board in 1964, despite also being a fan of Manchester City. 'We would meet up on a Tuesday and we'd have an agenda,' he told the *Manchester Evening News* in April 2010. 'First up would be last week's minutes. Second was the finance – money needed for the week. But we could never finalise the financial side. We knew we'd have to find something from somewhere but every week Fred would say "Gentlemen, I think we'll leave that until the end of the meeting." Under those circumstances, how can you possibly think about buying players when, at the end of the meeting, you know you're going to have to find some way to keep the club going and pay the players' wages?' The belief that the financial obligation was beyond him had been a longstanding issue for Hilton. He had left the board for eight months in 1973 and did so again in 1974, telling the press: 'It's a shame, but it got to the stage where I was dreading going to board meetings. The financial strain has become too great. Your pocket is only a certain depth.' He was later persuaded to re-join.

Rod Brierley was the youngest of the board and is the only one of the six still alive. He lives with his wife Gillian in a detached house with a wide veranda overlooking a lake. At the bottom of their long garden is a private jetty leading to a boathouse. A bit posh compared to Rochdale. 'Aye,' he says. How long had he lived here? 'A while now.' Did he miss Rochdale? 'Sometimes.' He doesn't elaborate or elucidate. His answers are cul-de-sacs. Occasionally he can't quite grasp the point or kids on that he can't; probably the latter. How did you feel when the new blokes came in at the football club? 'Let them have a try.' Were you offended that they considered you out of touch? 'Not really.' Eventually, after the question has been seasoned many different ways, he concedes of the incomers, 'I didn't think much to them.'

On the kitchen table Brierley has a pile of cuttings and letters that distil his playing days; he was a promising schoolboy footballer. The apex was playing for the Rochdale Youth League against Bolton Boys Federation in 1952. Afterwards his parents received letters from Eric Houghton, manager of Notts County, and Walter Rowley, the manager of Middlesbrough, inviting him to trials. Brierley had already decided he wanted to enter the family wallpaper and paint business. Rod, along with his brother Cedric, seven years the elder, built up the business until it had 75 staff and 25 vans delivering paint and paper to decorators throughout north-west England.

As a boy, Brierley had been taken by his father to Rochdale and his first heroes were Jackie Arthur and Jack Connor. He was one of the 24,231 – Rochdale's record home attendance – packed into Spotland in December 1949 for an FA Cup tie against Notts County. The main attraction was the appearance of Tommy Lawton, an ex-England captain and, at the time, the country's most expensive player when signed from Chelsea for £20,000. Brierley joined the board in 1966. One of his first acts was to persuade fellow directors that the club shirts should be changed back to blue after being white for several seasons. 'Rochdale's got to be blue, hasn't it?' he said. He was part of a new influx, including Edward Lord and Len Hilton. 'We had six on the board, which was a good number,' he said. He became close to Ratcliffe; their families went to Spain on holidays together. What was he like? 'He was all right, Fred. Straightforward.' How would you sum him up? 'He was quite hard.' How do you mean? 'You know, like a lot of people who make money, business people.'

Brierley's decision to focus on business made him a wealthy man. He worked extremely long hours. He and his brother collected classic, high-end cars. Among them were various types of Ferrari including a Monza and Testarossa; an Aston Martin; Jaguar; Rolls-Royce, Bentley and BRM (British Racing Motors) – some of which were shipped over from the United States. Cedric, with whom Rod was extremely close, raced cars at famous tracks such as Brands Hatch and Silverstone, and was featured regularly in the magazine *Motor Sport*. In the column for his placing in the Silverstone International race in May 1960 it reads DNF – did not finish. He crashed his Elva car and spent nine months in hospital. He was left without the use of his legs below the knees but still built and collected cars, working out of Victoria Garage in Littleborough.

The Brierley family sold Lancashire Wallpaper and Paint in 2000 and Rod retired to the Lake District. Cedric Brierley died in June 2007, aged 78. Rod remembers his time on the board at Rochdale as 'good fun'. 'The trouble was that if the team lost, you lost,' he said. He regularly divvied up with other directors to cover wages and sometimes contributed to transfer fees. The arrival of the 'secret six' coincided with a busy period at work for Brierley and it suited him to resign (though he would later return as director and remains a life vice-president). A fire had torn through the company's headquarters in 1975 and forced it to relocate from Sparth Mill to Sudden Mill which had to be completely refurbished. Brierley oversaw much of the work and was often unable to attend matches, though he was still close enough to form an opinion of the politicking. 'They thought it was time to step into Fred's shoes and try to get rid of him. He was a tough nut, Fred, though. A bit of a lad,' he smiles. Brierley's son, Mark, believes the club has had a positive impact on his father's life. 'It was a distraction from work, where he could think about other things,' he said. 'He was always one of the key people when it came to steering it in the right direction and protecting it from board members whose interest may have been more about themselves than the club.'

A meeting between the board and the secret six (now five) was set for Saturday, 7 October 1978. That afternoon, Rochdale drew at home against Halifax Town which meant they had still not recorded a win in the first 13 games of the 1978/79 season. The meeting was at the Crimble, a country hall standing in nearly three acres of countryside between Bamford and Heywood. The house had been built in 1810 by mill owner John Fenton, who became Rochdale's first MP. *RAP* dubbed it, 'that Mecca of middle-class aspirers' and 'home of the Bamford in-crowd'. It now belonged to Fred Ratcliffe, who had bought it in 1960 with Norman Ledson, a prominent Mason, Conservative party member and Mayor of Rochdale from 1961–62 – such alliances of dignitary were typical in the town.

The 11 men gathered amid the grand furnishings in the dining room, beneath two enormous crystal chandeliers, commandeered from a cruise ship. 'I got the impression that these men [the existing board] were very much on a gravy train with Fred at the helm. They were drinking shorts and I imagined them as a mobile drinks party, visiting all these football club boardrooms up and down the country,' said John Faulks. 'You couldn't dislike Fred, though. He was such a character and his heart was so much with the club.' The meeting went surprisingly well, it appeared. 'There was no friction at all. They were very polite with us and seemed happy that younger people wanted to be involved,' said Faulks.

The old-timers were crafty, each seasoned in the assessment of others and the politics of power. They had purposefully kept their counsel, offered handshakes and smiles. They'd do their talking, proper talking, when the new-boys had left the room, heading off home, pleased with themselves. The younger men had found it hard to tell what Fred Ratcliffe was thinking, especially when he slipped on his partially-tinted glasses and hid his eyes. He'd sometimes fiddle with the rims and then clean the lenses with a handkerchief. Or he'd make a movement, rolling his shoulders, as if checking on the fit of his jacket. These tics served as distractions, throwing you off the scent of working him out, reading his mind. He liked it this way. Keep them guessing.

For part of the evening Mike Ferguson called at the Crimble to deliver his 'manager's report'. Faulks, obviously new to such a forum, dared to proffer a question. He inquired if anyone had 'scouted' Droylsden, the non-league club Rochdale were due to play in the FA Cup. 'No,' he was told. 'We'll find out what they're like when we play 'em, won't we?' Faulks was left perplexed by the response. 'The talk, much as there was any, seemed to be along the lines of them being like a pub team,' he said.

The media – in this instance the *Rochdale Observer*, *Manchester Evening News*, *Radio Manchester* and the independent station *Piccadilly Radio* – dutifully covered the developing off-pitch shenanigans at Spotland. The concept of PR was a relatively new phenomenon, especially in sporting circles and little heed had been paid by the secret five as to how they, and their intentions, were portrayed. All the same, they did a sterling job. As much as anyone outside the fan base cared, their pincer movement on the club was related as the introduction of new blood, a happy union of new and experienced, a gentle and benign revolution that had long been overdue.

Letters passing between Andrew Hindle and David Wrigley revealed a much more clear-eyed and unambiguous scheme to acquire Rochdale AFC. In a letter dated 22 November 1978, still in the club's files, Wrigley wrote to Hindle: 'Although we have had no cause to worry about acquiring voting power during the past few weeks, I believe it now becomes a matter of immediate concern if your proposals are to succeed fully.' Wrigley had clearly studied the formal ownership of the club. He reported back that the 'old' directors held approximately 31% of the issued capital, almost 25% of this belonging to Fred Ratcliffe with the rest divided between the other directors, none of whom had more than 2%. There were 7,500 unissued shares at 50p each which, if bought by the 'old' board, would give them 53% of the share capital and a controlling interest in the club. 'I think we are faced with taking up the shares at par value [face value] even though they would be worthless [on the open market],' wrote Wrigley. If the five had bought these shares, presuming Wrigley was including the other potential directors, it would have been purely a defensive strategy, ensuring the old board could not hold a majority.

David Wrigley closed his letter by warning of the 'burden of responsibility' carried by directors under the Companies

Act. He was referring to the section which stated: 'Directors must act honestly and promote the success of the business and benefit its shareholders. They also have responsibilities to the company's employees, its trading partners, and the state.' Wrigley wrote: 'I have little doubt that the club is trading fraudulently at the present time [by running up debts while having no certain means to repay them]. I imagine that prosecution can be avoided, in the event of liquidation, by the directors providing sufficient funds to meet all claims. We all probably imagine Fred [Ratcliffe], at least, would ensure that all liabilities were met in the event of anything going wrong at Rochdale. In reality, it is nothing more than assumption on our part. We would probably deny responsibility on the grounds that we are not directors in the strict sense but the creditors are not aware of the position and I therefore wonder if that particular argument would be effective.'

On Saturday, 25 November 1978 Rochdale lost 1-0 at home to Droylsden in the first round of the FA Cup. The defeat was their fifth to a non-league club in the previous seven years. Droylsden of the Cheshire County League was a team made up of part-time footballers, enthusiasts who trained one or two evenings each week after completing day jobs. They played most weeks in front of a few hundred diehards against similar football journeymen at outposts such as Leek and Darwen. The defeat of Rochdale represented a coup to them and the thousands of 'park' or 'amateur' footballers who, at some point in their lives, had been deemed too small, too slow or lacking sufficient vision, skill or bravery to 'make it' as a professional footballer. When Dave Taylor, Droylsden's young striker, slid the ball across the Spotland mud into the goal, Rochdale suffered abject humiliation; it also meant that they had won only twice in 21 games all season.

## Chapter Six

# An Act Worthy of Lazarus

As an insider of the motor trade, Andrew Hindle had seen the potential in the Lada, an affordable 'people's car' with a boxy design, usually painted in drab colours. The car was mass-manufactured by AvtoVAZ, a company employing more than 100,000 workers in Tolyatti, a city on the River Volga in the east of the Soviet Union. It had become popular with taxi drivers because it was enduring and inexpensive to run. 'It was a cheap car and this appealed to the bloke who normally bought a used car,' said Hindle. 'For roughly the same amount of money, he could now have a new one. It was a hunch on my part really, that they would take off.' The import of Ladas into the UK was controlled by Satra (Soviet American Trade Association), an American-owned trading company based in New York and, bizarrely, Carnaby, a village in north Yorkshire (population: approximately 415). The deep-water ports on England's east coast, principally Hull and Immingham, were perfect for docking the huge containers transporting the vehicles. Carnaby, a couple of miles inland, had a disused airfield with vast space on which to store cars. The airfield had served as an emergency landing site for damaged planes in the Second World War and had an unusually long and wide runway. Satra had located there in 1974 and established production lines where cars were cleaned and, on the MET section (Mechanical, Electrical and Trim), altered to meet British specifications. Every day, the target was to have 120 cars ready to be moved to showrooms around the country.

Hindle had formed a friendship with Nigel Hall-Palmer, the managing director of Satra. 'Nigel had worked at the Lex group and was a really dynamic, youngish bloke. More to the point, he was a thoroughly nice chap and we got on really well,' said Hindle. The pair did a deal whereby Satra granted exclusive rights to Hindle's company, Euroway, to sell Ladas throughout the Midlands and north-west of England, which was 25 per cent of the imported total.

Hindle chose the name Euroway because a few years earlier (January 1973) Britain had joined the European Economic Community and the 'way' element was drawn from 'motorway'. He regularly passed the Euroway Trading Estate near the M606 in Bradford and the word had lodged in his mind. He had set up outlets in Bolton, which became the head office, and then Liverpool, West Bromwich and Prestwich, a small town north of Manchester. While often the butt of jokes (How do you double the value of a Lada? Put a gallon of petrol in it), 350,000 vehicles were sold in the UK between 1977 and 1997. Euroway had a turnover of £1.2 million in 1975/76 and £9 million by 1979. 'It was a slow burner at first but then really took off. I saw an opportunity and I took it,' said Hindle. 'All the various dealers had to come to me for their Ladas and we were quite aggressive with our sales.' He was not overwhelmed by the sudden success. 'I was fine with the dramatic upturn. I was young and daft then and a bit gung-ho,' he said.

Euroway forged a link with the football world through its sponsorship of Bolton Wanderers. In January 1978 the company had offered a Lada to each of the 16 members of Bolton's squad in exchange for having 'Lada' printed on the club shirts. The Football League did not have a policy on the issue and stalled for time, claiming to be 'reviewing the players' contracts'. Hindle, in the press, termed this 'obstructive behaviour'. A year later Liverpool became the first English professional club to have a shirt sponsor – Hitachi. Hindle, meanwhile, still had his Ladas endorsed by the Bolton players. In a press advert, four players were pictured parked in Ladas, waving their car keys. 'Nippy and economical, my Lada averages over 30 miles per gallon,' read the quote beneath the moustachioed Frank Worthington. 'A pleasure to drive and just look at the price tag – four doors, family motoring for less than the price of a Mini,' enthused midfielder Neil McNab. Manager Roy Greaves and winger Willie Morgan were similarly complimentary about their Ladas.

Days after the cup defeat, Mike Ferguson was sacked. It came at a time when the original board was still in place; John Faulks remembers that Fred Ratcliffe took responsibility for telling Ferguson and dealing with the matter. 'Mike was a nice fella and one of the lads, which might not have been a great idea,' said Eric Snookes, the club's left-back. 'What I remember most about him is that he ran us hard but that was how all footballers were treated those days. You ran and ran.' Peter Madden was asked to fill the roles of trainer, coach and caretaker-manager. Madden had previously been a coach at the club, serving under Dick Conner in the early 1970s. He had recently left Darlington after three seasons as manager. Andrew Hindle, still without portfolio but growing in influence, said he had no plans to offer Madden the job on a full-time basis. 'He was more of a journeyman, a good No.2 but not a No.1. He was very much Fred's man – he used to suck up to him a lot,' he said.

One of Madden's first signings was striker Chris Jones, on loan from Doncaster Rovers. He arrived at Spotland a few days before Christmas 1978. 'It was terrible weather, cold and windy. There wasn't a soul around. I remember the gate creaking as I opened it. The whole place was as quiet as a grave,' he said. Jones had fond memories of Spotland while playing for Manchester City's junior and reserve teams in the early 1960s. 'I considered Rochdale a great little club and was keen to play. They didn't have many fans but they knew their football and appreciated players who tried to entertain. I thought I could do a job for them, score some goals.' Jones, then 33, had experienced a typical footballer's life, signing as a youth for a top-level club in Manchester City, playing a handful of first-team games before slipping down the divisions, picking up the usual aggregate of injuries, friends, enemies, signing-on fees, free transfers, promises, let-downs, commendations and criticism. He had played under Madden, again on loan, while he managed Darlington and knew what to expect. 'He was a good bloke. He had been a centre-back as a player and liked to keep a clean sheet. In many ways he was a lot like Malcolm Allison who I played under at City – a disciplinarian who knew what he wanted. You knew there was a bloody big bear hug coming your way if you didn't do as you were told,' he said.

Another visitor to near-empty Spotland in December 1978, stamping down hard to free the snow from his shoes, was John Faulks. In his role as chartered surveyor and partner in the company, Kirkpatrick, Faulks and Co, he undertook a valuation of 'Rochdale Association Football Club Limited, Willbutts Lane, Spotland, Rochdale'. His report was presented to the club's accountants, Stott and Golland. It began by stating, 'Rochdale AFC Limited comprises a Football League ground, together with various stands and usual offices and terracing, extending to approximately 5¼ acres, which in the main is a level site.' It outlined that the social club was held under a lease by Mr K J Leary at a rental of £3,900 per annum on an agreement that could last until October 1993. It continued: 'In the event of the football club ceasing to operate as such, then in our opinion the site would be eminently suitable for re-development purposes. The location is such that it is in a fairly densely developed residential area of town, within convenient distance of the town centre, with made-up highway to both Sandy Lane and Willbutts Lane and bounded on the other sides by local authority development.'

In the report, Faulks stated that he had made enquiries of the planning department of Rochdale Council and been told there was 'no doubt' that permission would be granted for residential purposes. He estimated 'from information available at the present time' that 20 'units' [dwellings] per acre would be permitted, which would produce a total site development of approximately 100 units. He estimated the market value of the site to be £200,000 on the assumption that 'vacant possession would be granted of the football ground'. The valuation, according to Faulks, did not represent anything untoward or underhand but was a routine analysis of the assets and their value typical of any limited company, especially one with a pending new board of directors.

A blizzard swept the country on New Year's Eve 1978. Cars were snowed in. Roads closed. Airports shut down. The average temperature for the whole of January remained below freezing. Snowdrifts were over 20ft deep. More than 100 league matches were postponed and dozens abandoned.

Of the 32 FA Cup third-round ties scheduled for 6 January 1979, only four took place. In one of these, Leicester City v Norwich City, Keith Weller wore leggings beneath his shorts, such was the cold. Many players had taken to wearing training shoes instead of boots to provide a better grip on the ice. Spotland stayed frozen solid for three months.

After the meeting at the Crimble, David Wrigley drew up a 'Heads of Agreement' – a legal term for a 'non-binding document outlining the main issues relevant to a tentative sale, partnership or other agreement'. It was unusually blunt: the 'new' directors were to 'make available sufficient funds' to repay 'capital monies' owed to previous directors who would 'no longer be involved in any way in the control or running of the company [Rochdale AFC Ltd] or the team.' Fred Ratcliffe was to resign as chairman, but remain a director and be appointed life-president to 'bring the benefit of his considerable experience in the football world to assist the new directors'.

The agreement also stated that Andrew Hindle was to become chairman with Sidney Marks as vice-chairman. Hindle promised to make available £6,000 to cover 'pressing liabilities', for which he would have a lien (promise of income) with interest, on a payment due to the club from the Football League. Hindle was also to provide a refundable (with interest) overdraft facility of £25,000 until a similar sum had been negotiated with a bank. 'Unsecured creditors' (primarily ex-board members) had to promise not to press for payment of the £140,000 they were due collectively for one year – after which they would receive a payment on a monthly basis, though it was impossible to state how much in the 'present financial climate'.

As an indication of the upcoming switch in responsibility, the 'new' directors, though not yet formally in place, oversaw interviews for a manager to replace Ferguson. They were held at Half Acre House, the home of David Wrigley in Roch Valley Way, half a mile or so from Spotland. John Tudor, the former Newcastle United striker, was interviewed along with Pat Crerand, who had recently managed Northampton Town after a long playing career with Celtic and Manchester United. There was a prevailing feeling that Rochdale needed a leader on and off the pitch and that a player/manager would best serve the club, specifically a central midfielder to form the fulcrum of the team. The 'new' directors were prevaricating so Fred Ratcliffe contacted his pals across football, as he had done many times before. He spoke to Tommy Docherty, who was managing Queens Park Rangers. Docherty recommended Doug Collins with whom he'd worked at his last club, Derby County. Collins had been a tenacious midfield player, best known for an eight-year spell at Burnley. After a few months in Oklahoma, where he played for Tulsa Roughnecks in the NASL, he had been coaching at Derby. 'Dougie came in and talked a lot of sense,' said Hindle. 'I got on with him and found him quite uplifting. He was smartly turned-out. He looked and talked the part and seemed a deep thinker of the game. I thought he was going to have a bright future as a manager.'

Doug Collins, aged 33, was appointed player/manager in January 1979. 'There were two reactions when I came to Rochdale,' he said. 'Some of my mates said "You must be mad" and others told me I had nothing to lose. But I had plenty to lose. After all, who wants someone who has been sacked by Rochdale?' On the day he arrived at Spotland the club was second from bottom of Division Four and without money to buy new players. 'The only way I can describe my first impressions of the place is that it was like a bankrupt business. It was terribly rundown, and it was then that I realised fully the immensity of the challenge I had accepted,' he said.

Peter Madden remained as his assistant but had difficulty organising training in such wintry conditions. They sometimes cleared a patch of ice on the club car park to set up drills, running around cones or timing short sprints. Madden, then 45, was still extremely fit and joined in many of the exercises. During his National Service he had sometimes misbehaved on purpose to receive the 'punishment' of extra training. The players went on long runs, usually from the ground, up Edenfield Road, across moorland to either Hunger Hill or Knowl Hill, more than 290 metres above sea level, splashing through slushy ice, mud spattering mottled legs. On one occasion Mark Hilditch and Nick Stanley, an apprentice, raced off ahead of the main pack. They were in playful mood and threw snowballs at the senior pros behind. 'When we got back they virtually beat us up,' said Hilditch. 'We stood our ground for as long as we could but they eventually got the better of us. They stripped us naked and threw us in the snow out on the pitch.'

Although Rochdale had a small squad, a stringent hierarchy was in place, similar to most clubs at the time. 'In the summer we forked the pitch and painted the stands. Along with the other young players, I had to clean the boots of the older pros. The boot room was like a cave, a dark place with a horrible pungent smell,' said Hilditch. There was only one sit-down toilet in the dressing-room. 'You can imagine how dirty it was. We had to scrub that as well,' he said. 'Some players grumbled if their boots weren't clean enough and took retribution. I had boot polish rubbed on my balls a few times.' Eric Snookes had spells at Crewe Alexandra and Southport. 'It wasn't just Rochdale – most clubs down the leagues were an absolute mess. You got used to it and made the most of it. You were a professional footballer, a job that most people would give anything to do,' he said. On finishing his playing career, Hilditch worked as a safeguarding officer with young players at Oldham Athletic. 'There would be immediate sackings and probably court cases if anything similar to that went on now. Football is a completely different world, thankfully,' he said.

The freezing temperatures continued and the club was offered the use of Broadwater Youth Centre in Smith Street on the edge of Rochdale town centre. The building was a busy hub, especially in the evenings when it hosted various youth clubs. A section of the former public baths had been converted into a football pitch for small-sided games. 'Peter Madden took most of the training. He was rarely out of a tracksuit,' said Chris Jones. 'Doug would join in with the lads but, to be honest, I think most of us viewed him as a player rather than a manager and it felt as if we were still playing for Pete.' This notion was supported by the fact that Madden used his knowledge of the lower leagues to bring experienced players to the squad, as he had with Jones – Brian Taylor from Doncaster Rovers and Peter Creamer from Hartlepool United.

\* \* \*

In the modern era, clubs are bound by Appendix Three of the Football League's 'Owners' and Directors' Test' which exists to, 'protect the image and integrity of The League and its competitions, the well-being of the Clubs, and the interests of all of the stakeholders in those Clubs, by preventing anyone who is subject to a *Disqualifying Condition* being involved in or influencing the management or administration of a Club.' The appendix runs to almost 4,500 words. In short, it attempts to disqualify from football's administration:

criminals, embezzlers, bankruptees, ticket touts, debtors, sex offenders and anyone with a conflict of interest, such as owning two clubs at the same time.

There was no such test made of the new directors joining the board of Rochdale AFC. No checks were made into their background or financial standing; Appendix Three wasn't applicable back then and, besides, there was nothing to suggest anything untoward about the now not-so-secret five. The signing of the 'Heads of Agreement' by four new directors (Marks and Valentine did not sign but were included in the list of witnesses) and four of the former directors (the signatures of Brierley and Hilton are not on the document) was enough to ratify their position. 'We were a group of mates who had got together and were absolutely taken on face value,' said John Faulks. 'It was very much a case of "Okay lads, you have a go."' At this juncture, they were not asked to introduce money into the club as a statement of commitment; it was enough that they wanted to be directors and appeared to have the club's best interests at heart. 'I did not know what to expect,' said Trevor Butterworth. 'I thought I might have to put money in but I wasn't sure. Not a single element of the club was being well run. None of us had any idea what a shambles it was.' Faulks eventually acquired 3,500 shares at 50p each but this was not until nearly three years after joining the board. Most of the others did similarly over time.

The ever-diligent Les Barlow at the *Rochdale Observer* coaxed a quote from Sidney Marks – possibly the only one he ever made public – and it confounded Rochdale supporters. He told Barlow: 'It is unfortunate that when a club is in a poor position people look for an Elton John type [two years earlier the singer had invested heavily in Watford FC] coming along on a white charger with a bagful of gold. But we have not come to buy Rochdale out of trouble. None of us have the money to donate to charity, as it were. The buying of star players is not on. We have never intended putting money into the club for players.' When pushed, the newcomers said they believed that basic business acumen and pooled contacts would appreciably increase the club's income.

A typical example of their strategy saw Faulks approach his associates at Rochdale Council who gave permission to sell lottery tickets on behalf of the club at the town centre shopping precinct. Sid Marks contacted industry pals at Glasdon, the manufacturers of plastic road signs and street furniture, and they supplied a kiosk. The directors' wives – Stella (Marks), Joan (Faulks), Susan (Wrigley) and Dorothy (Butterworth) – took turns to sell tickets. 'We had the required footfall at the precinct, which was thriving in those days and we soon started to make money,' said John Faulks. Before, the lottery had been particularly badly run and Trevor Butterworth was strung along for weeks before he confronted the agent (who worked outside the club): 'We're not making any money, are we?' The answer, finally, was a sheepish, 'No'. In fact, the club was £6,000 in debt with its lottery after buying a huge amount of scratch-card tickets which had remained unsold. 'To put it in context, Port Vale were making £5,000 per week from their lottery while, somehow, we had been losing £1,500 a week on ours,' said Faulks.

Andrew Hindle, though unaware at the time, had a manifestly different view than the other new directors. He could see the obvious benefits of properly administering and marketing the club, but recognised immediately that they would each have to introduce personal finance. 'I wish I had done my own due diligence and looked at each of the other directors more closely,' he said. 'If I had known it was such a nest of vipers, I would not have got involved in something so problematic. Why would you want to be a director and not put any money in? They each knew that clubs at the bottom of the league were always strapped for cash. I suppose it was the kudos, lads like Trevor Butterworth making a step up from running a sports shop. I'm a big lad, though, and take responsibility for my own actions. I just didn't do enough interrogation.' He said the new board members worked well together and he didn't feel viewed as a 'fairy godfather'. 'To be fair to them, they all had a genuine affection for the club, as much as they liked the social scene around it. They never made me feel like an outsider. It was only afterwards that I became a scapegoat for some of the problems,' he said.

The new board, Andrew Hindle aside, was drawn principally from a clearly discernible professional caste that existed in Rochdale, as it did in most medium-sized towns. Accountants, solicitors, surveyors and estate agents were always in demand, so were largely inured from the recession of the late-1970s. 'We weren't incredibly wealthy but we were earning more than a decent living. We were having good holidays and were pretty successful,' said Faulks. While those from 'older' money, the mill owners and trading class, had tended to build grand houses among the people, perhaps down a ginnel or dirt track a few hundred yards from the terraced houses, the professional clique preferred the outlying districts of Norden and Bamford to the west of the town, sandwiched between the River Roch and rough moorland. The drift towards country life, the Aga and the wellies, had not yet taken hold, so they moved into semi-detached and detached houses that had been built in phases from the turn of the 20th century.

These neat and tidy estates comprised closes, drives, views and avenues with quaint, nature-themed names:

Sandpiper Close, Martlet Avenue, Seven Acres Lane, Keepers Drive, etc. The local sports clubs reflected the social class of the residents – Bamford Tennis Club, Rochdale Golf Club and the cricket clubs of Bamford Fieldhouse and Norden. Rochdale Ramblers and Rochdale Harriers and Athletics Club were also based there. Nearby were the Rochdale and District Riding Club (until 1980) and Rochdale Lacrosse Club. Everything that was wholesome and progressive appeared to spring from this sector of town.

The golf club was a particular hub of congeniality with the requisite air of exclusivity for social climbers. In the late-1970s the waiting list to join was eight years and new members could only sign up with the support of four of the 400 existing members. At 564 ft above sea level, the 100-acre course in Norden was at one of the highest points in town and, according to its handbook of 1932, 'The air is always pure and invigorating and there are glimpses of Rochdale on the left and hills of the Pennine chain in the distance.' Almost all the directors of Rochdale AFC, new and old, were members and, much the same as the Crimble, the Gentleman's Club Room, replete with wooden panelling, was a common rendezvous spot as they mused on the team's last match or the next, or whose job it was that week to find a plumber to repair the leaking tap in the sink in the away dressing-room.

The 'Heads of Agreement' had been unequivocal in divesting the previous board of its power, but little appeared to have changed. The old directors were still attending meetings, having their say and largely carrying on as before. Evidently, it was easy to write down the new 'rules' but much more difficult to put them into practise. The new board resolved to unseat the old-timers incrementally rather than meet the issue head-on. The drinking culture around the Crimble, for example, was deeply entrenched and the new board realised it had to move elsewhere. 'It was a boozing hole for Fred's clique and had become a bit rundown,' said Trevor Butterworth. 'Teddy Lord used to train greyhounds. He ran them in the evenings so was never at a meeting before 10pm. As soon as he came in the Oak Room, Fred would ask him what he wanted to drink. I remember one time he was given a short and he swished it around the glass. Fred asked what he was up to and Ted said he was looking to see if there were any goldfish in it, it was that murky.'

By now, Ratcliffe had sold the Crimble to Rod Brierley who was leasing it to tenant managers, one of whom was the former Manchester United and Wolverhampton Wanderers midfielder Jim McCalliog. He had taken on the lease with a business partner. He was in his early 30s and re-training as a publican after the end of his playing career. 'Fred and Rod were good characters,' he said. 'They were very popular and would help anyone.' Occasionally, Butterworth requested early-morning meetings with Ratcliffe. 'That usually meant noon, for Fred,' he said. 'He was often in the Crimble until 3am. He loved talking to people at the bar until the early hours.' A favourite saying of Ratcliffe's was: 'When there are not enough hours in the day, you pinch some from the night.' Joe Stoney was his regular drinking companion, knocking back pink gins while Ratcliffe preferred Black Label whisky drawn from his own personal optic. Board meetings were switched from 8.30pm at the Crimble to 5.30pm at the football club. This was a considerable concession by Ratcliffe; he liked to sleep in the early-evening before heading out into the night. 'It meant we had more chance of getting on with business and talking sense,' said Faulks. 'They were nearly always pissed by the time we started at the Crimble.'

The dearth of matches because of icy weather seriously affected the club's cash-flow. Trevor Butterworth offered to pay the players' wages for a week. He loaned the club £1,800 on the understanding that he would be recompensed from the proceeds of a league match played away at Portsmouth in January 1979. The rules were that the away team would receive 25 per cent of the gate money, paid within a week. 'Portsmouth didn't pay up until nearly two months afterwards, after we'd been in contact with the FA,' said Butterworth. To help matters, Andrew Hindle made the first of several injections of cash into Rochdale in January 1979. Euroway's ledger showed that £6,000 was transferred to the club from 'A Hindle Limited'.

After the freeze, Rochdale's first home game was on Saturday 10 March, a 1-1 draw with Hartlepool United. The last time they had played at Spotland was three months earlier, a 3-0 defeat to Barnsley. Their form picked up a little, but the defeats continued into spring. On Tuesday, 17 April 1979, the team coach headed east on the M62 across the Pennines, up and over the highest motorway point in England, past Scammonden reservoir and Saddleworth moor. Under the floodlights at Leeds Road, Rochdale lost 1-0 to Huddersfield Town in front of 3,346 supporters. The defeat left Rochdale nine points adrift of 'safety' – 20th place in a division of 24 clubs where the bottom four had to re-apply for membership to the Football League. With seven previous re-election submissions to their name, it was widely held that Rochdale were on the cusp of losing their league status after 72 years.

Only eight games remained. Rochdale needed four wins and a draw – a victory back then was worth two points, not three – to overtake Hartlepool United in 20th place, and that was in the unlikely event that none of the other clubs at the bottom picked up any more points before the end of the season, which, of course, was inevitable. In truth, Rochdale had to win all their remaining games, or close enough. In modern football a small number of hugely monetised clubs in the Premier League regularly embark upon lengthy sequences of consecutive wins but in the lower reaches such hegemony is unusual and results more indeterminate. The task facing Rochdale was put sharply into perspective by the fact that they had not won three consecutive games for nearly seven years. The likelihood of suddenly ending a fixed culture of losing was made even more difficult because they had to play their last eight games in 28 days; a raft of postponements had created a fixture backlog. For once in sporting circles, the hyperbole was a good fit: this would be a miracle, an act worthy of Lazarus.

Rochdale won seven of their last eight matches and finished one place above the re-election zone, two points ahead of Darlington. The media came to town and marvelled. The topographical shorthand was familiar to those already aware of Rochdale and its football club: the cotton industry, foothills of the Pennines, Gracie Fields, rain, Cyril Smith, and, on the pitch, a propensity – until now – to lose frequently. In an attempt to delineate their standing in the football world, 'little' prefixed the club's name in many newspapers. The manager who had overseen the resurgence, Doug Collins, received significant praise and a sizeable number of nicknames – Mr Magic, Houdini, Miracle Man and Super Doug, among them. Even *Shoot!* magazine, which more usually provided updates on Kevin Keegan's form with Hamburg or Kenny Dalglish's favourite television programmes (*George and Mildred* and *Rising Damp*), ran a lengthy piece under the headline, 'The Rochdale Miracle'.

The run of results had not coincided with the introduction of new players or a profound tactical switch. Two narrow home wins against Scunthorpe United and Newport County were followed by a hugely unexpected 3-0 victory against Barnsley at Oakwell who, if they had won, were virtually guaranteed promotion, hence cameras from Yorkshire TV filming the match. 'It's games like that, when you win when no one thinks you've a chance, that really boost your confidence,' said Mark Hilditch. Thereafter, Rochdale 'clicked'. Passes that had previously been 'safe' – sideways or back – were pushed forward, causing opponents to run towards their own goal, made to defend. They ran with the ball. Shots were hit confidently towards goal. Tackles were hard and crisp. They encouraged one another. The final game of the season had been away at Crewe Alexandra, and Rochdale needed a point to avoid having to apply for re-election. They won 2-1 with the winning goal scored by Hilditch. 'I was pleased for Doug Collins. One of the first things he did was to double my wage from £40 to £80 a week. I was like most footballers – if a manager liked me, I liked him,' he said. Eric Snookes had been similarly impressed with Collins. 'He told me, "You can really play" and said he was going to work on me so that I'd be worth a lot of money. I thought Doug was a breath of fresh air and would do really well in management. That run at the end of the season was down to him. He got us playing and gave us all confidence. He got us out of that quagmire,' he said.

Aside from the momentum propelled by confidence, there was another factor. 'I think all the three-a-side football at Broadwater made a lot of difference,' said Hilditch. 'We were much fitter and our technique had come on. It's considered a very modern approach these days, high-intensity training, but we were doing it all those years ago in a youth club in Rochdale because we literally had nowhere else to go.' The players were rewarded for ensuring the club finished outside the bottom four. They each found £50 in notes tucked into their shoes when they returned to the dressing-room at the end of the Crewe match. Afterwards the directors held an impromptu get-together at Norden Liberal Club. 'It was an almighty piss-up,' said John Faulks. 'It was like winning the cup. We'd saved our bacon yet again.'

*Chapter Seven*

# A Tall, Lean Figure in a Trilby Hat

Optimism pulsed throughout the summer of 1979. The unprecedented sequence of wins at the end of the previous season transformed the club. It felt as if all those victories had lifted a curse, an elemental force that had outlasted managers, players and fans, so that everything had seemed coated in failure. The first new signing of the close season reflected this hex-free, hope-dazzled, new-born football club. Alan Weir, 19, and a former captain of England's youth team, was the antithesis of previous signings, who had mostly been either ageing professionals (often carrying long-term injuries) or enthusiastic but callow teenagers, one or two of whom had even been plucked from local pub teams such as the Tim Bobbin or Dicken Green.

The club broke its transfer record when it paid £12,000 for Weir who, such was his capability, could play in either defence or midfield. 'He has a tremendous will to win and is a great competitor,' said Peter Madden, the assistant manager. Weir had also captained County Durham Boys and Sunderland's reserves. He had played only once for

Sunderland's first team, though, against Bolton Wanderers. 'I don't want to wait two or three years for regular first-team football,' he explained. So proud were Rochdale to unveil this ambitious teenager that Andrew Hindle and Fred Ratcliffe, who, as joint vice-chairmen, had divided up the realm between themselves for now, appeared at Spotland for the press announcement. Weir looked the part in a neat tie and wearing a sleek watch. He even had a perm. 'I think this could be a stepping stone for me,' he said.

The squad was treated to a three-day break in Cleethorpes where they played matches against non-league sides Louth United and Skegness Town. Hindle travelled to Lincolnshire in a two-seater plane. Trevor Butterworth, who later became a private pilot, did not view Hindle's mode of transport as necessarily indicative of wealth or ostentation. 'It might have been a club aircraft,' he said. 'You could hire them with a pilot for about £75 per hour back then and you only paid for the time when the engine was actually running.' Hindle has no recollection of the episode. On record in the club's files, however, is that he had introduced £18,000 in four instalments over the summer as 'cash to club' and also £4,000 as 'transfer A Hindle Limited'. These terms would later fall under scrutiny.

Back at Spotland, Tom Nichol announced a trial for local boys and was delighted to find nearly 50 congregated on the club car park, kit bags slung over their shoulders. The avuncular Nichol was typical of the unsung but essential backroom staff at football clubs. Quietly spoken, he did much to forge the club's friendly image. He had first joined Rochdale in 1953 when they were managed by Harry Catterick, later to join Sheffield Wednesday and Everton. Nichol took training sessions for the club's junior sides on Tuesday and Thursday nights. His own career had ended prematurely when he suffered a knee injury while playing in a trial match for Northampton Town. Walter Joyce had persuaded him to work full-time at the club and leave his job as a dyer at Lancashire Tanning works in Littleborough. Nichol's mustard-coloured Datsun Cherry was often seen parked on side streets near amateur football pitches across the north as he sought out players for Rochdale. Sadly, none of the 50 lads at the latest trial were invited back.

Rochdale's squad of 1979/80 was comprised wholly of white, indigenous players of working-class backgrounds from northern England. At a time when the average age of first marriage for a man was almost 27, they had married much younger. This might have been under encouragement of the football fraternity; a married player was perceived to be a happier, more settled and focused sportsman. Dave Esser was 22 with a fiancée, Julie; Alan Weir was 20 and arranging to marry Yvette, a civil servant from his hometown of South Shields; Brian Hart, 20, was married to Cath, a cook, and they already had a daughter, Gemma; Ian Bannon, 20, was planning a summer wedding and a honeymoon in Yugoslavia with Christine, a catering manageress, and Dave Felgate, 20, was also set for a summer wedding, to Lynn, a receptionist. Bobby Hoy, at 29, was the only one without a fiancée or wife. The singularity of his situation saw him referred to as 'Bachelor Bob' in the match programme. He clearly felt duty bound to explicate, in comically world-weary terms. 'I'd like to get married one day,' he said. 'With the right person, marriage should be all right. I've had a couple of broken engagements in my time.'

The players, in physical terms, were difficult to discern from other men of a similar age. Modern footballers are a breed apart, even those with lower league and semi-professional clubs. In a sport where fine margins are understood to be the difference between winning or losing, nothing is left to chance. Players are sculpted until they have the perfect physique to shield the ball, fend off an opponent, but also to sprint away with a burst of energy that appears to swell from beneath the soles of their boots. They eat well. They sleep well. The Rochdale squad of the late-1970s was 'running fit' but not particularly toned. Gym culture did not exist beyond a few old-boys lifting barbells in draughty backstreet gyms. The preoccupation with grooming – moisturising, manicured facial hair and tattoos – was also decades away. The Rochdale players were earthy blokes who turned to their mothers, sisters or girlfriends for haircuts, and fretted that team-mates might consider them effeminate if they took shampoo into the shower. They had workaday professional aspirations – to establish a first-team place, play well consistently and have a 'good career'. Maybe, one day, if they worked really hard, stayed focused and had the rub of the green (their words), they might play at a higher level. On their days off they visited snooker or golf clubs or, in Brian Taylor's case, enjoyed drives from his semi-detached home in Bacup to the seaside with his wife, Teresa. He was 25 years old.

Rochdale's players supplemented their wages with other work, though the club purported to be 'professional'. Ian Bannon and Nigel O'Loughlin were coach drivers. O'Loughlin drove for Les Bywater Ltd, the company which supplied coaches for Rochdale travel. On one occasion he drove the team back from an away match at Colchester United, nearly 250 miles. Two of the more experienced squad members, Chris Jones and Dennis Wann, helped their wives run guest houses, the Saxon Hotel in York and the Kendal Hotel in Blackpool, respectively. This seemed a theme at the club with Brian Taylor revealing: 'I suppose when I do finish football I'll open a little hotel or boarding house at Blackpool. I'd like that.'

In one match programme the precise location of Eric Snookes' new house – Westminster Street, Rochdale – was revealed. This snippet of information inadvertently gave away the social status of a lower-league footballer. Snookes' two-bedroom, terraced house in Brimrod, about a mile from the ground, cost £7,500 and was among the cheapest housing in the town, a place where millworkers or other unskilled workers lived. He moved there with his wife, Jane, and three young children. The players' hobbies were invariably snooker, golf and 'watching television', and several said they enjoyed 'messing about with cars'. Most were unsure of their post-football careers, though Dave Felgate said he would like to open a sports shop and Ian Bannon 'hoped to study at Bolton Technical College'.

Interestingly, none of the players expressed a desire to stay in football once their playing careers had ended, most likely because there were few openings. These days, Rochdale, the same as most clubs, is a mini-kingdom. In the 'Who's Who' section of the official website it lists a backup, non-playing staff of 51. Several are clearly part-time or voluntary – club chaplain, club doctor, etc. – but most are waged and offer employment to former players. In 1979 Rochdale had a handful of remunerated staff with directors and supporters carrying out most roles.

A rare dash of cosmopolitanism arrived at Spotland in the shape of FC Den Bosch. The club from southern Holland played in the second professional tier of their home country and were on a pre-season tour of England. The match announcer, more usually introducing a host of Bobbys, Pauls, Davids and Johns, had to welcome, among others, Hans van der Pluym, Diet Kamps, Chris van de Dungen and

Wim van de Horst. Den Bosch twice took the lead before Alan Weir headed home a Bobby Hoy cross to put Rochdale ahead, 3-2. During the final half hour Rochdale played perfect, scintillating football, barely misplacing a pass or missing a chance. The Den Bosch players barely touched the ball and, much the same as the crowd, were left to marvel at a masterclass where every weight of pass, every flick, every feint, every through-ball, every first touch and every shot was sublime. Rochdale won 7-2 and everyone agreed: this was football, but not as they had seen it before, certainly not at Spotland.

It was difficult, of course, to gauge the standard of FC Den Bosch, but with an average home attendance of almost 4,000 (Rochdale's was 1,700), they were widely assumed to be a superior side. If Rochdale could do this to a team of a higher calibre than themselves, what would be meted out to their equals in the forthcoming season? 'It's almost frightening to say it, but we were brilliant,' said Doug Collins.

In the tiny press box chiselled into the Main Stand, Les Barlow was confounded. Deep within the smog in which he worked – on account of his 40-a-day cigarette habit – lugubrious Les was wrestling for the words. He was more used to summoning the adjectives of defeat. Finally, he gave in to glee: 'If Dale continue to play this way, the missing thousands will soon flock back to Spotland and the coming season will be exciting. Promotion is still a naughty word with some people but the truth is that few Fourth Division teams will be able to live with Dale if they reproduce this sort of form.' The handful of football writers who had made the summer evening journey to Spotland agreed. 'Rochdale on the Rampage' was the headline in the *Daily Mirror*. 'The home side played a brand of fast, fluent soccer not seen at Spotland for years, if ever' – *Daily Star*. 'Rochdale treated their visitors from Holland to a soccer nightmare' – *Daily Express*. 'The Dutch side were competent in every way until Rochdale tore them apart in the second half' – *Manchester Evening News*. Doug Collins had a nagging thought. 'It worries me that everything should go so well. Now I have to bring the lads back down to earth,' he said.

Season tickets, £32 for seats, £20.50 for standing, were selling well and businesses in the town were keen to support the club. Brian Taylor, the new captain, was presented with a car by Lex Motor Company (Rochdale); Taylor's name was painted on to the side. Talks were in progress with companies keen to have their name on the front of Rochdale's shirts. The players, meanwhile, were still set in their asinine ways. Alan Weir was given a crude 'Welcome to Rochdale' when team-mates stripped him on the moors above Spotland and left him with a naked two-mile run back to the ground.

Two new players were added to the squad, both from Darlington, and again at a cost: Dennis Wann, 28, a midfielder, for £8,000 and Jimmy Seal, striker, also 28, for £5,000. Rochdale were granted permission to play home matches on Friday nights. The club was hopeful of attracting supporters of other local teams to witness their brand of attacking, efficacious football. Rochdale was close to the two Manchester clubs, United and City, while two other nearby clubs, Burnley and Leeds United, were also well supported in the town.

Rochdale were knocked out of the League Cup by Blackpool in the first round. The defeat, 2-1 on aggregate over two legs, was viewed as a blip and not entirely unexpected – Blackpool were, after all, of a division above. The first league match of the season, against Bournemouth at home, was the real focus, the start of the sure-fire promotion push. They lost 2-0. After only one league win in the first four games, the headlines in the *Rochdale Observer* reflected a notable change of mood: 'Collins Warns: We Must Get it Right', 'No Crisis at Spotland – Says Collins' and 'Nightmare Start Continues'. The trip to play Torquay United in September was particularly fraught. The team lost 3-0 and there was also a breach of club discipline. The night before the match, Eric Snookes was sharing a room with Bobby Hoy. 'Bobby suddenly decided he was hungry. It was getting late but he said, "Fuck it, I'm going to town." He shinned down the drainpipe on the hotel wall and I followed him,' he said. The pair was joined by others and they had supper in Torquay before heading back to the hotel. 'We were sneaking along this wall, ducked down, when we came to a recess and standing there was Peter Madden. He said, "Go to bed" and we all did because we were terrified of Big Pete.'

There had been other issues with Hoy, who did not appear to grasp the commitment required of a professional footballer; as a teenager he had played in the top division for Huddersfield Town. 'He was a terrific player but a bit daft,' said Snookes. 'He took his guitar everywhere with him. I remember once when all the players were having a briefing from the manager and Bobby asked if it was okay to leave the meeting early. The boss asked him why and he said, "It's just that I'd said I'd meet my sister in town."'

Hundreds of Rochdale fans made the 23-mile journey to see them play at The Shay, home of Halifax Town, on Tuesday, 18 September. Rochdale and Halifax were almost the mirror image of one another, separated by a range of hills forming the last fragment of the Pennines. They were two northern clubs that shared the same history of getting by, making do, struggling on. Most Rochdale fans saw the match as the categorical gauge of the club's true standing.

Was Rochdale really born afresh to a new positivism, an ethos of winning, and had the first eight games (which had garnered one win) been merely a settling-down period into the new season? Or had the curse returned and were they about to return to the village of the damned, that communion of clubs – Darlington, Hartlepool United, Crewe Alexandra, Aldershot, Scunthorpe United et al – who, it seemed, spent season after season clinging to their Football League status?

Rochdale lost 1-0 and had only one shot in the entire match. That solitary effort, from Ted Oliver, was high and wide of the crossbar. The defeat took Rochdale into the re-election zone for the first time in the 1979/80 season. The despondency bled to anger for many fans. At the final whistle they were marched to Halifax train station, flanked by barking dogs and police officers. Scores of agitated supporters were shepherded on to the train heading to Rochdale. They let loose their rage, severely vandalising four carriages. As it passed through Sowerby Bridge station, toilets, fire extinguishers, basins, shards of glass and sections of seating were thrown on to the platform. The emergency cord was pulled several times. Police boarded the train at Hebden Bridge and took 97 Rochdale fans back to Halifax on buses where they were detained until 7am. Nine supporters were charged with offences relating to the damage. The episode was, and remains, the worst ever behaviour by Rochdale fans.

Doug Collins spent a great deal of time pondering on how a group of footballers could play so outstandingly at the close of the previous season, then so badly a few months later with, in his opinion, an improved squad. Unusually for a football manager, he delved deep into ancient Greek history, mentioning the Battle of Thermopylae where, in 480 BC,

7,000 Spartans outfought an army from the Persian Empire which was at least 25 times the greater number. 'I suppose that was the sort of situation which we faced last season,' he told the press. The subtext of the analogy suggested that, much the same as the Spartans' victory, Rochdale's incredible run of form had been a one-off, a dredging up of superhuman effort and resolve which, by its very nature, could only be counted upon in very special circumstances. So now, Rochdale had returned to type.

* * *

The main intermediary between the new and old board was Trevor Butterworth. 'I think I was the only one who Fred Ratcliffe really trusted,' he said. The two had much in common. They were both self-made men from working-class backgrounds with a lifelong support of Rochdale. They had also done business together for several years. Butterworth's store had provided, among other items, match balls, usually Mitre Maxs. They had an agreement that the club would pay for these twice a year, at Christmas and in May. Butterworth had been impressed that despite the club's financial problems, Ratcliffe always honoured this pledge and supported a local business. On a deeper level, Butterworth, the same as most Rochdale supporters, had been imbued with the legend of Fred Ratcliffe. His was a name passed down to fans from almost their first visit to Spotland. The small man stood taller than any players. All this around you, the stands, the pitch, the players, the club, was at the benevolence of a fellow sitting over there in the shadows of the Main Stand. And he was an unassuming, quiet, modest man (he was excused the Rolls-Royce) who would do anything for a fellow Rochdale fan. This saintly status was without tarnish, and this made it as good as impossible to chase him out of a boardroom and a football club which was as good as his own.

Andrew Hindle was not clouded by such sentiment. He'd already navigated himself through the sharp elbows of the motor trade. He'd met men similar to Fred Ratcliffe before. He'd showed them respect, genuflected when necessary, but had also steel-eyed them, done the deal and shook hands. It was business, nothing personal. Fred was similar. He didn't suffer fools or fanny about – if there was a better deal to be had, more money to be made, he got on with it. The two men, Hindle and Ratcliffe, spoke civilly for several weeks. Ratcliffe was still conflicted, reluctant to let go of his club and concerned for its future, but aware that he lacked the energy of these upstarts or, indeed, his former self. 'They had a bit of a barney,' revealed Judith Hilton, Ratcliffe's daughter. 'I don't know what exactly went on apart from the fact that Hindle had told my dad that money talked.' Indeed, since the summer, Hindle had put in an additional £16,000, listing it in Euroway's accounts as either 'cash to club' or 'transfer A Hindle Limited' – these descriptions, as before, were significant.

A year after the secret six had first formed, it was announced that Andrew Hindle had replaced Fred Ratcliffe as chairman of Rochdale AFC. Ratcliffe, who had held the position for 33 years, became club president, an honorary title with limited dominion. Hindle said there was no lasting ill-will between him and Ratcliffe. 'We felt a bit stymied while Fred was there. Our philosophies were beginning to grind,' said Hindle. 'I always liked Fred, though. He was a real card. He'd done extraordinarily well for the club. He wasn't forced out. To put it frankly, he was past his sell-by date. The club was stagnating, much like Fred. His daughter was a bit snotty with me at the time. She said something to me along the lines that I'd ruined her dad's life – maybe not quite that bad but something similar. I told her I was doing my best for the club. The former directors were very old-fashioned in their approach, not dynamic at all. It was an all-lads' club and I had the impression Fred was putting most in, by a country mile.' David Wrigley felt similarly about the previous board. 'I do not want to throw brickbats, but they were all quite elderly and it was a struggle for them. It was time for a change,' he said. 'They were asleep, just muddling along.' Judith Hilton had seen closely the dynamic of Hindle and Wrigley and felt the latter had a particular aim. 'I think Wrigley, in his own way, wanted to be another Fred Ratcliffe. He bought the Egerton Arms [a country pub on the outskirts of Rochdale of which Andrew Hindle was a co-owner], didn't he? It was as if Fred had owned the Crimble so he had to have somewhere similar,' she said.

Many questioned why Hindle, a relative outsider and not previously an ardent Rochdale fan, was keen to take the helm. '*I* could understand it,' said Trevor Butterworth. 'His company was growing at a fast rate and it was another feather in his cap to strut around as chairman of a Football League club. Remember, there are only 92 people in the whole of England who can hold such a position at any given time. Maybe he had visions of using the club to promote himself. You're bound to think there must have been other motives when he had no interest in the club beforehand.'

Fred Ratcliffe and fellow director, Harry Carter, were served notice of their new reduced standing when they travelled to Vale Park, home of Port Vale. After traversing the pot holes on the car park and brushing themselves down from dust – it was a dry late summer's afternoon in September – they reported to the directors' entrance, as they had done many times before. The home directors welcomed them to the boardroom and they partook in the usual chatter, helped down by a shot of whisky and one or two sandwiches. A few days later both Ratcliffe and Carter received a letter on Rochdale AFC notepaper informing them that they had 'caused some embarrassment' and, in future, they should inform Jack Butterfield, the club's general manager, if they intended to avail themselves of directors' privileges at away grounds. Rochdale lost the game 5-1.

* * *

The defeats continued to pile up and fans wrote letters to the club and the *Rochdale Observer* implying that Collins had acted duplicitously by joining as player-manager but not actually playing. His last run of consecutive league games had come at Plymouth Argyle more than two years previously, which meant he was considerably short of match fitness. His mental state was similarly depleted. 'I will be perfectly honest and say that after some defeats I have not slept a wink. I have worried all night about what has gone wrong,' he said. After a 1-1 draw away at Hereford United on 17 November 1979, an emergency board meeting was called for the following day. The match result was creditable enough but Rochdale had won only twice in the 21 games played that season. They were second from bottom and already six points adrift of having to make another re-election application. Doug Collins was summoned and told he was being sacked because of poor results and his reluctance to combine the roles of management and playing. 'It was so disappointing having to sack Dougie. I don't think it was a majority decision,' said Hindle. 'I sacked him. It obviously wasn't very pleasant but they know what they are getting into when they become managers.'

Collins's ten months in charge had been the shortest of any Rochdale manager since the war. As a player he had made six full appearances and two as a substitute, all during the previous season. The players had been surprised that he had not played more often, noting his obvious talent in training. He confided to one or two that he suffered pain in his knees. The same as hundreds of footballers in the 1960s and 1970s, he had received regular doses of cortisone, a pain-suppressing steroid. An injection into the seat of an injury had an almost miraculous effect, masking the pain initially but causing long-term damage – more than half of all ex-players were diagnosed with arthritis before the age of 40. Collins was also reminded by the board that he had the 'largest playing staff in the Fourth Division', which seems unlikely, though, with 18 senior professionals, it was a good deal more than previous Rochdale managers had been able to call upon.

'It had got bad under Collins,' said John Faulks. 'The directors' box was positioned among the fans in the stand and I remember at one game we won a free kick. About half a dozen of our players ran up as if they were about to take it and jumped over the ball. Finally, one of them took it and kicked it over the stand behind the goal. This fan turned round and shouted to us, "Fucking hell – I'll work that one out when I get home!"' Peter Madden questioned whether Collins had the necessary experience to work with lower-league players. 'I never felt that he was particularly committed,' he said. 'He was signed as a player but on cold days he didn't want to come out training with us.' Collins later claimed unfair dismissal. His counsel said he had been sacked on 'team results' and not on 'his ability to do the job as a manager' and was therefore due compensation. The tribunal agreed and he was awarded £3,555. Afterwards,

Collins said he was happy with the outcome and that it had 'cleared his name'.

* * *

Bob Stokoe, a tall, lean figure in a trilby hat, had been seen in and around Spotland for a couple of months. A week before the start of the new season he had resigned as manager of Blackpool when, without his knowledge, they had spent £52,000 signing midfielder Brian Smith from Bolton Wanderers. He left with a broadside to the Blackpool board, referring to them as 'the most unprofessional group of buffoons I have ever worked for'. He had acted similarly when leaving Charlton Athletic before joining Rochdale for the first time, in October 1967. As he left the Valley, he met two directors in the club car park. 'Go fuck yourself and your inflated egos,' he told them.

He had been a regular visitor to Spotland in his capacity as a scout for Carlisle United, assessing Eric Snookes. Some of the players felt this was 'cover' and his real intention was to ingratiate himself with the board, should a managerial vacancy arise. 'I think it created unrest,' said Chris Jones. 'He was at so many games, hovering up in the stands. It wasn't fair on Doug Collins and affected our team spirit.' Eric Snookes (the surname is thought to be of Dutch origin) was one of few Rochdale players with genuine transfer value. He had left Smethwick, four miles west of Birmingham, to join Preston North End as an apprentice at the age of 15. He lived in a shared house owned by the club and broke into the first team a few weeks after his 18th birthday. In the summer before the 1973/74 season, stories appeared in the local and national newspapers linking him with a move to Liverpool. 'It frightened me to death,' he said. 'I was only a kid and I've never been the most confident person anyway.' Still, he settled his nerves and knocked on the door of the Preston manager, Bobby Charlton. 'I was in awe of him because he'd been one of my favourite players when I was growing up. I told him I'd read all these pieces in the paper. He told me outright that there'd been no interest in me and, what's more, why would I want to leave a great club like Preston anyway? I came out of his office apologising.' A few years later, Snookes learned that Liverpool *had* made a bid for him.

Carlisle were mid-table in the division above Rochdale and had offered £60,000, but Rochdale, Snookes was told, were holding out for £90,000 – a risky piece of brinkmanship, if true, for a club so short of funds. The deal appeared in doubt when Snookes injured his Achilles tendon in a 3-2 defeat at York City in October 1979. Carlisle reiterated that they were still interested in signing him despite the injury, though matters became further complicated when their part-time scout became Rochdale's full-time manager.

The appointment of Bob Stokoe as manager of Rochdale on Monday, 19 November 1979 was the first public piece of club business handled exclusively by Hindle, with Fred Ratcliffe nowhere to be seen. Hindle said Stokoe had been taken on because he was a 'proven motivator'. Stokoe's return to the club was marked with a suitably grand PR stunt. The 'press' – on this occasion Les Barlow and local freelance reporter, Jack Hammill – was invited to a special unveiling at Euroway's sales office in Prestwich. The name of the new manager was thought to be a closely guarded secret. The door opened and Hammill, without turning round, said, 'Morning Bob, nice to see you again.' Everyone in and around the club had known for a good while that Stokoe was on his way back.

The consensus among the board was that they had made an exceptional appointment. 'Bob Stokoe had managed at a higher level and was a well-known name in football. It was a bit like, "Crikey, we've got Bob Stokoe",' said John Faulks. The departing Doug Collins, who had moved house from Burnley to Rochdale to be closer to Spotland, told the press: 'Whoever gets my job has got it made. If only the board had been patient. I would have given them what they wanted.' As the season progressed, Collins's 'got it made' comment would irk Stokoe immensely and he returned to it many times.

Stokoe had been impressed with the new chairman, Hindle, then aged 34. 'He was a fair man. He asked me to go in for a season and see how I felt,' said Stokoe. 'He told me I would have to be ruthless but whatever decision I made he would back, so long as I kept him informed.' Hindle returned the compliment. 'I liked Bob,' he said. 'He was a mature thinker and never got rattled. He was thoughtful and measured, a thoroughly nice bloke.' Stokoe was disappointed with the squad he had inherited; he felt several players were not of Football League standard.

The directors soon became used to what they referred to as Stokoe's catchphrase, as he spoke-sang in his north-east brogue: 'They canna' play.' He told confidantes that Collins had bought 'unwisely' in signing the likes of Alan Weir, Dennis Wann and Jimmy Seal for relatively high fees. He also questioned the acquisition of two of Collins's former Burnley team-mates, Colin Waldron and Eddie Cliff. He said it 'smacked of desperation'. Stokoe's greater sadness, he claimed, was for Rochdale on a broader level. 'I could have cried. The Rochdale I knew so well from my previous time at the club had gone,' he said. 'It didn't look as though anyone cared about it. The ground needed more than a lick of paint to make it respectable. The supporters' toilets were unclean and stunk to high heaven and there were gaping cracks in some of the concrete terracing. Rubbish was strewn about and building up behind the perimeter fence around the pitch. The place had been unloved for too long.'

The appointment of Stokoe was viewed ominously by Chris Jones. Four years earlier Jones had played in a fractious Boxing Day match for York City in front of 35,000 fans at Sunderland, then managed by Stokoe. Barry Swallow, York's captain, had been involved in an altercation with Stokoe in the tunnel after the game. 'It was a nasty affair both on and off the pitch. Bob Stokoe never forgot and he carried that grudge on with me when he became manager at Rochdale,' he said. Jones felt the antipathy also stretched to Jimmy Seal and Dennis Wann, who had also played for York in the mid-1970s. Whether their misgiving about Stokoe was valid or not, the ex-York contingent had expected to be 'frozen out'. In the event, they played as regularly as any other player. All the same, Seal's antipathy was such that he offered to pay £5 to anyone who could knock off Stokoe's bobble hat with a well-disguised shot or chip during training.

* * *

In January 1980 Rochdale Council revealed that it had spent £10,000 on a machine called a 'word processor'. A press release was sent out to mitigate why so much *rate-payers' money* (standard journalese at the time) had been invested in this new equipment. Malcolm Duffield, administrative assistant in the architects' department, said a letter could be written, printed off within seconds and stored on a disk which could hold as much information as 100 sheets of writing paper. 'Using ordinary telephone lines, information fed into one word processor could be typed out on another in a different office. It could also be used to send electronic mail between different council departments,' he said. Jacqueline

Pickering was photographed tapping away at a keyboard. In case the Rochdale public remained unconvinced by such space-age technology, Duffield added that one word processor would allow the council to make two members of staff redundant and so effectively pay for itself.

* * *

Stokoe's first training session was held on a misty midweek morning at Firgrove, a collection of council-owned playing fields framed by terraced houses on one side and Rochdale Canal, the other. The players, 18 of them, were photographed standing dutifully in a line, Peter Madden and Bob Stokoe (with bobble hat), far right. They looked as if they had been transplanted from a boys' comic, a collection of misfits and misshapes rounded up from all corners of town to make up the numbers in an impromptu football competition. They each wore different clothes: jeans, rugby jerseys, T-shirts, undone tracksuit tops, zipped-up tracksuit tops, socks either rolled down or pulled up, tight shorts, long shorts, slack shorts, short shorts. Some were hunched, others rigid. Arms were limp at the side or fastened across the chest, as if keeping out the cold. They were all physically different to one another. Bobby Scaife had legs like oil drums, a big pirate's face and straggly beard. Ted Oliver was as thin as the goal-line and almost as white. Dave Esser, a small, compact figure in jeans, was standing as if queuing patiently at a bus stop. Alan Weir's perm had collapsed. Anyone passing, walking their dog or on their way to the newsagents in Milnrow Road, might, at best, have thought they were a pub or works' team.

*Chapter Eight*

# A Dangerous Precedent

Rumours began spreading. They caught fire easily in a town such as Rochdale where hundreds of people worked in the same factory, mill or warehouse and often socialised together after work. Pints were downed and empty glasses steadied on Formica-covered tables at the Brickcroft Social Club, Kirkholt Working Men's Club and all the pubs and clubs in between. They asked: have you heard the news? The football club was up for sale. It was a half-truth. The football *ground* was for sale, but not the football club per se. David Wrigley revealed that the club was looking for a buyer on the proviso that the ground was leased back to the club on a 99-year agreement. 'The hope is to raise money for ground improvements and the purchase of players,' he said. He acknowledged that the facilities at Spotland were 'among the worst in the country' and that 'very substantial' sums were required for improvement. 'This is a perfectly normal commercial transaction, where a person or company owning property wishes to raise money on the security of that property,' he said.

Wrigley's assertion was true, of course, but football clubs were not strictly and solely commercial entities. If, say, an engineering company sold the space on which it stood, relocation was relatively easy and a move could be made without consideration of emotional, social or cultural impact. A football club – tightly bound to a particularly dedicated community – was very different. Fans understood and accepted the board's motives (to secure funds quickly) but divorcing the ground from the club and introducing a third party to whom the club might one day be beholden felt questionable, at the very least. Between pints, fans muttered that it sounded too much like 'free money'. And that didn't exist.

The plan to sell the ground had not been discussed at board level, at least as far as anyone could remember. 'Andrew Hindle and David Wrigley had hatched the idea between themselves,' said John Faulks. 'I think the rest of us thought it was necessary to keep the club going and perhaps we deferred to what we considered at the time to be their greater knowledge of these kind of arrangements.' Trevor Butterworth saw it as a positive move. 'It didn't really matter who owned the ground as long as it said in the deeds that it was for the use of the football club,' he said.

Around this time, Butterworth made a visit to Vaux Brewery in Sunderland. The company held a charge on the social club at Spotland and he wanted to negotiate a settlement. 'I went all the way up there and was shocked at the reception I got. They started mentioning all these debts we owed them,' he said. The incident marked the first time Butterworth had felt animosity towards a fellow director. He claimed: 'Wrigley knew all about this and let me go up there and embarrass myself. What a shithouse, I thought.'

Within a few weeks it was announced that the directors were in negotiation with an unnamed company interested in buying the ground. The sum offered for Spotland was not revealed officially, but was thought to be between £150,000 and £200,000. Jack Butterfield, the general manager, introduced another caveat to the sale – the club would be able to buy back the ground at a later date when 'the financial situation made it possible'. Ominously, Butterfield added: 'Obviously a lot could depend on what happens at the end of the season in the Fourth Division.' Understandably, fans were confused. Butterfield was clearly referring to whether the club was re-elected to the Football League, should it finish in the bottom four. Why had he seemingly conflated these two issues – the ground sale and the club's on-field fortunes? No one could quite work it out. All they knew for sure was that there was a lot going on up there on that hill – the 'going on' in plain sight, as relayed faithfully in the *Rochdale Observer*, and another to which they weren't privy, hidden from view.

Perhaps predictably, given that Bob Stokoe was synonymous with the competition, his first game as Rochdale's manager was a first-round FA Cup tie. Despite being depleted by injuries, Rochdale beat Scunthorpe United 2-1 at Spotland with Chris Jones scoring the winning goal. The next evening, Sunday, 25 November 1979, Stokoe was guest of honour at a banquet to celebrate the centenary of Sunderland, the club he had managed from 1972 to 1976. The main speaker at the event held in the Mayfair Suite, Sunderland, was the television presenter, Frank Bough. He announced the club's player of the century as Charlie Hurley, the Irish centre-back who played for Sunderland from 1957 to 1969, and then referred to Stokoe as 'the Messiah'. The ovation from the 700 people in the room was long and loud. Sunderland would later install a bronze statue of Stokoe outside their Stadium of Light ground bearing the inscription: 'The Man The "Messiah" The Moment...'

Rochdale's league form remained mixed but after drawing 2-2 with Tranmere Rovers in the second round of the FA Cup, they won the replay 2-1 at Spotland. Stokoe's appointment had no immediate impact on away performances. Three days after beating Tranmere in the cup, they lost 5-1 at Huddersfield Town; it meant Rochdale had failed to win any of their 15 away games during the first five months of the 1979/80 season.

On New Year's Day 1980, another defeat, most likely heavy, was expected on the 30-mile journey to Valley Parade, home of Bradford City. One of the best-supported clubs in the division, Bradford were particularly strong at home.

Rochdale's start to the game was unusually sprightly and they scored goals on their first two attacks, through Dave Esser and Jimmy Seal, giving them a 2-0 lead after seven minutes. Thereafter, Bradford attacked relentlessly and Rochdale were barely able to get out of their own half. The pressure was so sustained that, for Rochdale, the game was stripped back to merely a dogged exercise in containment, defence above all. Les Barlow noted that, 'Rochdale hammered the ball into no-man's land on numerous occasions.' Bradford twice hit the crossbar but managed just a single goal, from a Steve Baines header a few minutes after half-time.

At last, an away victory. At the end of the match the Rochdale players clenched their fists and punched one another playfully on the shoulders, as if to check it hadn't all been a dream. The effervescent Dave Esser led the team across the snow-smattered pitch towards the band of supporters, zipped up in snorkel jackets and blowing hard into cupped hands to stay warm. The group of lads gathered behind the goal on the open terrace started up: 'Jingle bells, jingle bells, jingle all the way, oh what fun it is to see Rochdale win away.' Players clapped fans, fans clapped players. In the press box, Les Barlow, as the sole journalist with Rochdale affiliations, received commendations on the team's behalf. As the last of the supporters left the ground, all quiet now, the communion of the match over, Barlow composed his 'pay off', the last sentence of his match report: 'If medals were awarded for heroic defences in football these players would be in the reckoning.'

The win meant Rochdale were five points behind Scunthorpe United, the team directly above the re-election zone. Rochdale had a game in hand, too. Win that, and the gap was a mere three points. So, three wins would see them right, see them safe. The talk on the way home across the dark, dark Pennines wasn't about a lucky, desperate win but of the heroism of these free-transfer players and greenhorns, how they had fought for the cause and the shirt. It was a new year, a new start. Spirits soared. Up the Dale, down the ale.

Hindsight lends the Bradford result its true, atypical nature and the folly of the hope it inspired. Afterwards Rochdale failed to win away for almost a year, taking in 24 matches. Bradford City, meanwhile, lost only one other home game all season and missed out on promotion on goal difference. In the short term, if the plan was to build on the Bradford result, forge a new confidence and re-set the heartbeat of the team, it went disastrously wrong. After their next away league game Rochdale were to find themselves on the national sporting agenda, their woes and ineptitude laid bare before all – across newspapers, on radio and television. Before that, they had a cup tie scheduled against a local rival.

Snow fell heavily on the first few days of the New Year. The ground staff at Spotland – largely youth players and volunteers – worked hard to ensure the FA Cup third-round tie against Bury would go ahead. While they were working on the pitch, the club had a visitor from a local firm of surveyors, much as it had done 13 months previously. This time it was Barry Dean of Morris, Dean & Co. His report, dated 4 January 1980, said that he was acting upon instructions from John Faulks. Dean wrote that there were several ways of valuing the property (by which he meant the area on which the club stood) but he considered 'the most beneficial to be as a cleared site'. He reiterated that enquiries to the Planning department had indicated that there would be 'no objection to redevelopment'. There were only slight differences to Faulks's report: he considered the site to total almost six acres to Faulks's 5¼ and he envisaged 16 terraced dwellings per acre, compared to Faulks's 20. He agreed with Faulks's valuation of £200,000. Dean closed with, 'I trust this limited report is sufficient for the Directors' present requirements.'

A roller was hired to make the snow compact. The lines were marked out in blue dye to create a pitch that was both visible and, by chance, themed in the club colours. Temperatures increased through the week and snow was replaced by rain which formed a messy blue collage of the previously straight or curved lines. In a typically homespun attempt at branding, the club announced that the pre-match and half-time records would all be by Gracie Fields to give the game 'an added Lancashire flavour'. Fans readied themselves for the caterwauling of *Rochdale Hounds*, *Sally* and *Pass Shoot Goal!* with its inapt refrain of 'Come on Oldham'.

As match day approached the rain continued to fall. Jack Butterfield was adamant. 'We are not even thinking of a postponement,' he told the press. The referee, Peter Willis, a police officer and a Freemason, arrived unusually early at Spotland on Saturday morning, before 9am, and said the pitch was playable. He retired to his hotel but, as the rain lashed against the windows, decided to return to

Spotland two hours later. He made his way gingerly across the soggy pitch. He returned to the touchline, squelch, mud up to his ankles, squelch. Much shaking of the head: match postponed.

The game was quickly rearranged for three days later. The delay served to burnish a remarkable fervour. The focus of media coverage was primarily Bob Stokoe who was perceived to embody the magic, the folklore and the romance of the FA Cup – three adjectives splashed liberally across the sports pages of local and the northern editions of national newspapers. Seven years earlier Stokoe had featured in one of the most iconic sporting freeze-frames of the age. As manager of Sunderland, who had just beaten Leeds United 1-0 in the 1973 FA Cup Final, he ran across the Wembley turf at the final whistle to embrace goalkeeper, Jim Montgomery. The dash was accompanied on television by a fevered staccato commentary from Brian Moore: 'Stokoe can't believe it. Sunderland, from the second division. Where's he going? Bob Stokoe. To Jimmy Montgomery.' In the years afterwards, the 12-second gallop had come to represent the sheer unabashed joy of the underdog having his day, with the episode lent a madcap element by Stokoe's outlandish apparel – red tracksuit bottoms, a cream-coloured raincoat (buttoned up, in May) and a trilby hat.

The football reporting pack was clearly hoping for more of the same at Spotland, albeit on a wet Tuesday night in January. Incidentally, on the evening of that FA Cup final win, Fred Ratcliffe had attended the official 'celebration buffet and dance' held at the Park Lane Hotel, Piccadilly, London. Afterwards, he carefully affixed the menu into his scrapbook: Consomme Xavier en Tasse, Cotelettes d'Agneau a l'Estragnon (sic), followed by Timbale de Fruits Rivera.

Back home in Rochdale, he told everyone he'd had soup, lamb and fruit.

Thousands converged on Spotland, but only 12 of the 18 turnstiles were operational. The cost of repairing them – on average £500 each – was beyond the club's finances. Queues formed and snaked across the car park, down the street. A decision made in good faith, to maintain the usual league admission price of £1.10, rather than charge more and appear opportunistic, caused havoc. Turnstile operators, working in poorly-lit recesses with out-of-date equipment, had to constantly count out 90p change when presented with two £1 notes and, consequently, often ran out of coins. Children were expected to gain admittance via specially nominated turnstiles, but parents were understandably reluctant to deposit them at the back of a long queue, to be reunited in the ground later at an arbitrary time. Police estimated that 2,000 fans were still outside the ground at kick-off time. Many drifted off to their cars or to catch buses and head home.

The match ended 1-1 and was played out in front of Rochdale's biggest crowd for almost a decade, 10,739. The debacle at the turnstiles caused a furore that lasted several weeks, calling into question the commitment of the club's personnel and the state of its infrastructure. The sole outlet for public complaint was the *Rochdale Observer* and the volume of letters revealed the depth of dissatisfaction. M Hoyle of Bury wrote that it took him more than an hour to enter the ground and there had been 'bedlam' at the turnstiles. On finally gaining entrance, he said the place was a 'death trap'. John Dyson asked: 'Could the directors not have rolled up their sleeves and helped out?' Someone writing under the pseudonym of Not Just a Cup Tie Supporter continued the theme: 'I condemn the club directors on the deplorable arrangements for

*Spotland, mid-1970s, 'unloved for too long' – Bob Stokoe.*

*The Main Stand at Spotland with Dronsfield Gate (far left).*

*Gasometer looms over streets close to Rochdale's training ground.*

*Dexine Mill, another bites the dust, just a few hundred yards from Spotland.*

*Rochdale, built from bricks and millstone grit.*

*Townhead Mill, early 1960s, pressed up close to the houses.*

*Young Fred Ratcliffe, dreaming of springs and Dale.*

*The Spring King – Fred Ratcliffe.*

*Dark days. Rochdale v Cambridge United, Tuesday, 5 February 1974. Lowest post-war league attendance.*

*Willbutts Lane Stand, aka 'the scratching shed'.*

*Fifty pence to upgrade from terraces to the Main Stand.*

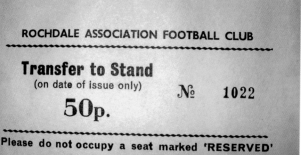

ROCHDALE ASSOCIATION FOOTBALL CLUB

**Transfer to Stand**
(on date of issue only)

№ 1022

**50p.**

Please do not occupy a seat marked 'RESERVED'

*David Wrigley, handsome solicitor-about-town.*

*John Faulks – social butterfly.*

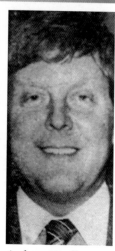

*Andrew Hindle – fairy godfather? Philanthropist? Asset-stripper?*

*Big Pete (Madden), a man for a crisis.*

*Smoke and mirrors. Les Barlow, Rochdale* Observer *sports reporter.*

*Mark Hilditch slots home.*

*Peter Madden (right) on the moors with Reg Jenkins.*

## ROCHDALE ASSOCIATION FOOTBALL CLUB LTD. (2½ mths ESTIMATED)

### INCOME AND EXPENDITURE ACCOUNT FOR THE YEAR TO 31ST MAY, 1980

| | 1982 | 1980 | 1979 |
|---|---|---|---|
| **Receipts:** — TV 1092.46 | | | |
| Football League, English and Lancashire Cup Pool, Broadcasting and T.V. Fees, etc. 59,711.47 | | 51,411 | 42,145 |
| Football League Pool—FL 18326.46 + 74,904.37 82,377.91 | | 82,668 | 32,667 |
| Percentage from other Clubs 18,168.21 | 24,168.21 | 18,920 | 17,600 |
| | 166,257.59 | 152,999 | 92,412 |
| Less Percentage to League 2935.23 | 1,796 | | 1,155 |
| F.A. Cup Pool and Percentage to other Clubs 20609.58 | 20,968 | | 12,229 |
| 23544.81 | 142,712.78 | 22,764 | 13,384 |
| | | 130,235 | 79,028 |
| Ground Advertising | | 2,365 | 784 |
| Sundry Receipts 1248.03 | | 1,306 | 1,415 |
| Sale of Programmes 3026.85 | | 18 | 1,070 |
| ~~Football League Grant (for Ground Improvements)~~ | | 4,900 | 1,495 |
| Social Club Rent Receivable 5133.79 | | — | 3,900 |
| Open Day 5333.30 | | | |
| Sportsman's Dinner 957.66 | | | |
| | | 138,824 | 87,692 |
| Wages, Salaries, Benefits and Pension Scheme Payments 172961.32 | 164,403 | 98,692 | |
| Transfer and Other Fees (Net) | 23,444 | 1,091 | |
| Travelling and Refreshments 20067.80 | 21,525 | 13,845 | |
| Stores, Clothing and Laundry 1639.10 | 2,904 | 4,070 | |
| Gatekeepers and Police 7244.64 | 5,484 | 3,788 | |
| Referees and Linesmen 2305.43 | 871 | 253 | |
| Rent, Rates and Insurance 6420.60 | 4,453 | 2,642 | |
| League and Football Association Fees 150.85 | 399 | 384 | |
| Postages, Advertising and Stationery 1858.00 | 2,707 | 2,984 | |
| Office, Medical Expenses and Telephone 494.58 | 3,040 | 1,819 | |
| Electricity, Fuel and Water Charges 3276.07 | 3,989 | 2,744 | |
| Ground Maintenance & Improvements 578.66 | 9,750 | 3,129 | |
| Lease of Seating | 1,879 | — | |
| Bank Interest and Charges 438.30 | 4,271 | 1,741 | |
| Mortgage Interest 1497.42 | 1,398 | 1,493 | |
| Hire Purchase Charges — | — | 135 | |
| Incidental Expenses legal fees 710.00 2372.52 | 660 | 1,451 | |
| Audit and Accountancy Fees 400.00 | 500 | 500 | |
| Interest on Paving Charges 5.06 | 5 | 5 | |
| Depreciation and Amounts written off 117.30 | 23 | 260 | |
| Compensation for wrongful dismissal | 731 | — | |
| Bad Debt | 906 | | |
| 222,757.65 | | 253,342 | 141,026 |
| | (63,645.84) | 114,518 | 53,334 |
| Donations from Development Association | 19,900 | 19,641 | |
| Other Donations & Sponsorships 18885.02 30349.48 | 2,662 | 2,452 | |
| | 22,562 | 22,093 | |
| Net Loss for the year before tax 40,747.04 | £ 91,956 | £31,241 | |
| (£24,898.20) | | | |

*Profit and loss sheet – replete with annotations by Graham Morris.*

*Realm of the gods. The directors' box at Spotland.*

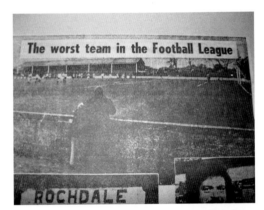

The worst team in the Football League

ROCHDALE

*Telling it straight – typical coverage of Rochdale's plight.*

*Owning a little piece of Rochdale AFC – share certificate.*

*Rochdale's social club – Les Barlow's home from home.*

# THE JOB'S TOO BIG, SAYS STOKOE

*Bob Stokoe bows out in unequivocal style.*

*Bag packed, Bob Stokoe exits Spotland.*

# Receiver takes over soccer-ground 'asset'

# SPOTLAND UP FOR SALE BUT SOCCER 'SAFE

'Spotland Up For Sale' – fans begin to worry.

Rochdale stalwarts, a generation apart. Trevor Butterworth (left) and Fred Ratcliffe at Spotland.

*Cyril Smith kisses a reluctant Gracie Fields.*

*Graham Morris, the young overcoat-man-to-be: not fond of nippy little wingers.*

ROCHDALE FOOTBALL CLUB

## Garden Party Luncheon

SUNDAY, 19th JULY, 1981 from 12 noon

Tickets: £3 - Children £1-50

*Fundraising, the Rochdale way. Ron Atkinson may appear.*

*Peter Swales (left) and David Kilpatrick celebrate the re-opening of the social club.*

*All set for a good tuck-in. The social club finally re-opens.*

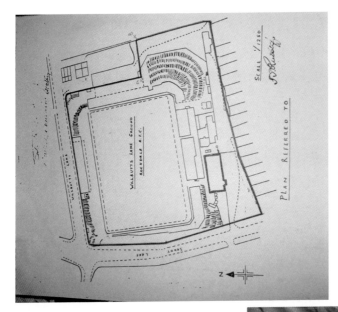

*Spotland, the surveyors' version.*

*Lord Kitchener enlisted to rally support.*

*High-flyer. Trevor Butterworth, private pilot.*

*Trouble brewing. David Wrigley (far left) and John Faulks (far right) meet with Fighting Fund volunteers.*

*David Wrigley still looks out for Rochdale's results.*

*'I should have stuck with rugby' – Andrew Hindle.*

*John Faulks. Rochdale – we've got it covered.*

*Trevor Butterworth. Catalyst in forming the new regime.*

*Rod Brierley, Spring King-ally,*
*Rochdale lad done (very) well.*

*Eric Snookes, irascible defender.*

*Graham Morris (left) and David Kilpatrick – Overcoat Men incarnate.*

*David Kilpatrick (left) and Graham Morris, the Overcoat Men in situ at Spotland.*

*Rochdale AFC, nearly 40 years on, thriving. The club built by Overcoat Men.*

*Job done! Spotland owned by Rochdale AFC once more. The first day of summer.*

*Fred Ratcliffe, cast in metal.*

spectators entering the ground.' Peter Hunter of Newhey felt similarly and made reference to a looming issue: 'When the new board of directors took over at Spotland, I, along with probably most supporters, expected great things from them. Unfortunately they seem content to let things drift along without doing a great deal to improve the playing staff. With the BBC extolling the virtues of Altrincham FC at every opportunity, to finish in the bottom four again could be fatal.' Another fan was piqued by the behaviour of some of the 'supporters': 'Don't come to Dale in your time off from watching the so-called bigger teams in Lancashire and laugh and shout at our players.'

There were no queues at the next home match; 1,697 saw Rochdale draw 2-2 with Darlington. The cup replay at Gigg Lane was twice postponed because of a frozen pitch. Officials at Bury assured fans there would be no congestion at the turnstiles when the game finally went ahead on a Monday night, three weeks into the New Year. The draw for the fourth round had already been made, with the winner due to play Burnley of the second tier. This time, Rochdale were keen to reveal that preparations were underway to deal with another large crowd. Jack Butterfield announced that it would be an all-ticket game with an attendance limit of precisely 15,480. He had done his sums; the match would generate £24,000 in receipts. 'This shows why it is so important for us to beat Bury,' he said.

Entry into Gigg Lane was, indeed, achieved without difficulty and a thrilling match was played in monsoon conditions – many feared it might be abandoned at any minute – with Bury winning 3-2. Steve Johnson, later to play for Rochdale in three spells, scored twice for Bury. The well-fed 22-year-old had a distinct advantage. His sheer bulk allowed him to heave through the quagmire, often, it seemed, with two or three Rochdale players either brushed aside or hanging forlornly on to his torso.

* * *

Among those who attended the cup-tie at Spotland and the replay at Gigg Lane was Graham Morris, an accountant based in Rochdale. He had been invited by Philip Jackson, a partner of John Faulks at Norford Estates, who had helped Morris buy a new house in Bamford. 'He asked me to go, I went, and I quite enjoyed it and that was that,' said Morris.

It was the first time he had seen Rochdale play since an infamous FA Cup defeat against Colchester United, nine years earlier. On that occasion he had become aware of Rochdale's FA Cup run of 1970/71. They had beaten Coventry City, then of the top division, 2-1, at Spotland in the third round. The game was played on a Monday afternoon because of power shortages caused by the miners' strike; it meant the floodlights could not be switched on. Schools closed down, offices and workshops shut early and the chilly, dim January day became a festival of the underdog, talked about for decades afterwards in the town. Morris had missed that game but, catching the enthusiasm, attended the fourth-round tie at Spotland against Colchester in January 1971. He had moved with his young family to the town two years earlier from High Crompton, Oldham, and passed the ground most days on his way to and from work. He had entered through a turnstile on the Willbutts Lane side. 'I remember thinking, "This is a funny football ground." I was standing on mud and cinders,' he said. More than 12,000 packed in to see the tie and Morris found himself beneath a stand that was referred to by locals as the 'scratching shed', presumably because of its similarity to a hen coop. Ray Crawford, the Colchester striker, scored after three minutes.

This was particularly annoying, remembered Morris, because the home fans had been teasing Crawford about his gargantuan sideburns, shouting out that he had two ferrets stuck to his face. Rochdale equalised and scored two more to lead 3-1, with minutes remaining. But Colchester scored two late goals and the match ended in a 3-3 draw. The replay was held two days later. Colchester won 5-0. Graham Morris was destined to make many more visits to Spotland.

\* \* \*

Four days after the replay at Bury, Rochdale travelled to Birkenhead to take on Tranmere Rovers in their first away league match since the victory at Bradford City. In a bid to attract fans of Everton and Liverpool, Tranmere, the same as Rochdale, had adopted a policy of playing home games on a Friday night. While attendances had increased slightly, an unforeseen benefit had seen Tranmere winning more regularly because visiting players were caught out of routine, their weekly pattern shifted to accommodate travelling and playing on a Friday. Rochdale didn't have this excuse.

The match started badly when Mark Hilditch was injured soon after kick-off. 'Their centre-back, John Bramhall, raked me down the back of my leg all the way to the ankle. It came up like a balloon. I asked the physio whether I should take off my boot so he could treat it, but he said if I did I probably wouldn't be able to get it back on again,' said Hilditch. Minutes later Dennis Wann pulled a muscle and was substituted. Eric Snookes was left hobbling when he was tackled hard from behind. All the while, Tranmere were dominating the game. 'It was always a hard place to go to,' said Hilditch. 'You had to stand up to them physically or they'd run all over you.' Rochdale lost 5-1 and had only one shot on goal from open play during the entire match;

the solitary goal had come from a penalty taken by Dave Esser. It was Rochdale's fourth defeat of the season by a four-goal margin.

Bob Stokoe was subdued afterwards. The players were aware of his explosive temper. They had witnessed it after a few home games. A trestle table was positioned in the dressing-room at Spotland, a few feet inside the entrance. Before games it would be decked out with plasters, liniment, tie-ups, Vaseline, a handpump, bootlaces, shin pads – the routine football paraphernalia. Afterwards, the volunteers who worked on a match day (often the directors' wives) replaced these with a buffet for the players. 'I'd seen him give out a few bollockings,' said Hilditch. 'The contents of the table would be thrown around, so the next minute you've got half a loaf and some lettuce perched on your shoulder. The older pros would have a go back. It never came to actual physical confrontation but Stokoe could let rip,' he said. The expected outburst had not come in the dressing-room at Tranmere, or on the coach trip back to Spotland. All was quiet. The card schools soon began shuffling packs. Conversations broke out about what they each planned to do over the weekend, or the next match, nothing in particular. At the front of the coach, still hushed, Stokoe was forming a plan.

Les Barlow had made pages of notes and was still scribbling on the way home. Sports reporters, especially those from local newspapers, had to be diplomatic, obsequious even, when assigned to cover specific clubs. They had to ensure continued access to personnel and facilities. They also had to mingle with players on a regular basis, in the corridors and outside dressing-rooms, and were directly accountable for any criticism they might level. After the Tranmere debacle Barlow was true to the maxim of showing first loyalty to the reader. 'I always had a policy that if it was shite, I had to say it was,' he said. In his match report he wrote that it had been a 'pathetic display' and the players had 'not shown one bit of fight'. The hundred or so Rochdale supporters who had made the trip to Tranmere had been cheated, he wrote. He pondered on the club's future: 'Unless Dale produce much better form in the games that are left this season they will have as much chance as a snowball in hell of avoiding having to apply for re-election.' All these years on, he can still recall the game vividly. 'It was bloody embarrassing. The Tranmere fans were laughing at us. We'd run with the ball and when we got anywhere near the goal we'd panic and fall over,' he said.

Despite appearances, Bob Stokoe was livid. He was steeped in football. A miner's son, he had signed for Newcastle United as a 16-year-old and played more than 250 times for them through the 1950s. As a centre-half he was at the heart of the action, a definitive hobnail, tin-bath footballer who tackled hard and brave in leather boots on muddy pitches. Famously, towards the end of his career while playing for Bury against Sunderland on Boxing Day 1962, he had scolded an injured Brian Clough. While Clough writhed on the icy pitch after colliding with Bury goalkeeper, Chris Harker, Stokoe stood over him and yelled: 'Get up, you bastard. There's nowt the matter with you.' Clough had torn medial and cruciate ligaments in his knee. The injury, though he played a few more games, effectively ended his career. This episode formed the other prevailing snapshot of Stokoe's football career, the snarl to the smile of his Wembley congeniality. Before rejoining Rochdale as manager, Stokoe had served in the dugout at five other clubs. He thought he had seen or experienced all that was possible in football.

It was only an idea. It might have stayed that way – unspoken, passed over and quickly forgotten. But Stokoe was boiling, teeth clenched, furious but, perversely, made still and catatonic by his wrath. He could accept the limitations of his players' ability, individually and as a team, but not what he perceived as lack of effort. How could they have scrapped so hard for him at Bradford and in the cup against Bury but then capitulate so meekly against Tranmere? He'd had enough. The idea was about to become an act. He'd thought it through again and again, how it would impact on his players. But he had not considered how it might reverberate across the football world. Why should he? This was personal, a feud between him and his players; fuck all to do with anyone else.

On the Monday after the Tranmere game, Stokoe called the players into Spotland and told them he was going to fine each member of the team that had played at Prenton Park half a week's wage – an average of £35. 'I have shouted at the players, kicked them up the backside but I feel I have to go further,' he told the press. He did not exonerate himself from the performance and said he would fine himself the same amount. He was backed by David Wrigley, who had just been announced as vice-chairman to share the workload with Andrew Hindle. 'Bob Stokoe was appointed by us to manage the players and if he has seen fit to act in this way then he has our full backing. I saw the game at Tranmere and it was embarrassing,' said Wrigley.

In the pre-internet age, without Twitter, Facebook and fans' on-line forums, it was more difficult to gauge the mood of supporters, but it appeared Stokoe had widespread support of those writing letters to the *Rochdale Observer*. 'The team appeared determined not to play, almost as though there was a conspiracy,' wrote Nevermissamatch. 'For some reason the players did not seem interested and the match was Tranmere's – on a plate. I do not think I have seen that kind of disinterest in about 20 years of watching Dale,' wrote Ian Nigel Parker. 'I, and a few thousand more, get fined £1.10 every two weeks, because this is what it costs us to watch poor displays at Rochdale,' wrote Mrs C Fielding of Spotland. Another, calling himself Dale Fan, said the players only deserved half a wage because they tried for only half the time in most games.

The players were spoken to on an individual basis over a four-hour spell and each given a letter in which they were told they were being fined, 'for not performing in an efficient manner and to the best of their ability'. 'We were at a low ebb anyway,' said Eric Snookes. 'Dave Esser went ballistic, saying "How dare he accuse us of not trying." It hurt, both in terms of insulting us and we were also worried about how we were going to pay our mortgages.' Stokoe clearly wanted to agitate and admonish the players publicly with a view to improved performances but he underestimated the level of media interest. He had naively believed that his players would accept the censure and keep the matter 'in house'; perhaps in his time as a player this would have been the case such was the deference to managers and clubs. Seven Rochdale players contacted their trade union, the Professional Footballers' Association (PFA) and lodged formal complaints.

Stokoe's action was immediately viewed as a test case that could impact at all levels of football, if not the whole of sport. 'If Bob Stokoe is allowed to get away with this it would set a dangerous precedent for footballers all over the country. There could be terrible consequences,' said Gordon Taylor, the chairman of the PFA who, at the time, was closing his playing career at Bury.

Unknown to almost everyone but a few insiders, 13 years before, in early December 1968 when he was just six weeks into his first spell as manager of Rochdale, Stokoe had suffered a near-identical ignominy at Prenton Park. Rochdale lost 5-1 in the first round of the FA Cup. Afterwards, he had been so incandescent that he could not bring himself to speak to the players. As 'punishment' he devised a gruelling schedule for their next training session. He made them run until they were 'fit to drop' and then held a lengthy seven-a-side game followed by relentless gym work. 'I wanted to teach them a lesson – let me down and you will suffer,' he said. A few weeks later they had lost again, at Lincoln City, and Stokoe was incensed once more. He threatened his playing staff with dismissal. 'I will embarrass them. I'll shame them and I will do anything to get from them the response I think they should give on Saturday afternoons,' he said at the time. He added: 'I told every player that unless he was prepared to stand by the manager and fight for the manager every week, then he could have his cards.'

In the event, only one player was dismissed in such an arbitrary manner – the left-back, Brian Eastham, who had previously played nearly 200 games for Bury. After one particular match Stokoe had accused him of 'not marking and tackling', but he was given another chance in a Manchester Senior Cup replay at Old Trafford, a tournament in which United routinely played reserve players. Rochdale lost 7-0, conceding the first goal after 15 seconds. 'My team simply capitulated,' said Stokoe. 'Up to that time in my career I had never seen a team of players put in such an inept performance.' Eastham, a team-mate of Stokoe at Bury, was blamed for five of the goals. After the game they had a row and Stokoe claimed he was told to 'fuck off' by Eastham. Stokoe ordered him, 'not to come near Spotland again'.

A deadlock set in between Stokoe and the various football bodies over the issue of fining the players. Cliff Lloyd, secretary of the PFA, and Gordon Taylor could see the obvious implications of setting a precedent whereby wages or a fine system was linked to performances. Stokoe, meanwhile, was affronted that an outside body could intervene in a relationship he considered sacrosanct, that of a manager and his players. 'I resent the remarks of these PFA men,' he said. 'I'm really not concerned with their feelings on the matter. I was ashamed and embarrassed by the defeat.'

Throughout football Stokoe was known for his impetuous nature. He famously hated losing and played combatively in five-a-side training matches, even as a manager. His team talks, similar to many managers of his generation, were peppered with the vocabulary of battle. They were to fight, scrap, get their retaliation in first, let them know what's what, get their foot in, swap a few bruises, have a dig, make the first tackle a bloody hard one. He also went in for mind games, imagining himself as a general and ascertaining those upon whom he could trust in the white heat of a match day. On his first day in training as Rochdale's manager, back in October 1967, he held a meeting with the players who were expecting praise after beating promotion-chasing Barnsley two days earlier. He accused them of being 'wimps and cowards'. He wanted them to argue, stand their ground. 'Not one of the buggers said a word and I thought to myself, "Christ, what have you taken on here, Bobby?"' Stokoe, paradoxically, could also be extremely sensitive and considerate of others' feelings, sometimes reduced to tears. While he managed Charlton Athletic in the mid-1960s he once failed to turn up for a game because his dog had died. He was sacked soon afterwards. Along with poor results, missing a match because of his dog's death was cited. 'It's the way I am,' he said.

Interestingly, and almost lost in the hullabaloo, was the revelation that Rochdale players received a wage of about £70 per week. Presumably this was the basic figure before extra was added for wins, points, cup runs and attaining certain positions in the division. All the same, it was low when the average wage across the UK was £115 per week. Peter Shilton was thought to be the best-paid footballer in the English game, earning £1,200 per week at Nottingham Forest. Rochdale players were paid considerably less than local secondary school teachers, who received £120 per week, and builders, who earned an average of £105 per week.

The appeal against the fines was heard by a management commission of the Football League in London. It comprised three of football's most established aldermen – Dick Wragg, chairman of Sheffield United; Bob Lord, chairman of Burnley, and Jack Dunnett, chairman of Notts County and former chairman of Brentford. The hearing lasted two hours with Bob Scaife representing his team-mates, along with Cliff Lloyd of the PFA. Bob Stokoe and David Wrigley put forward the club's case. 'Bob was absolutely disgusted with the performance and said in his opinion they had not tried,' said Wrigley. 'As a board we have decided to back our manager and trust that he knows best.' The commission upheld Rochdale's right to fine the players, claiming they had breached Clause One of their contracts which stated that they must 'perform in an efficient manner and to the best of their ability'. In hindsight, establishment figures such as Wragg, Lord and Dunnett, drawn deep from old-school football-club propriety, were highly unlikely to return any other verdict. The PFA staff who accompanied the Rochdale players at the hearing went further, claiming the panel were 'friends of Stokoe's'. The PFA appealed immediately. 'Fining players for bad results could lead to an impossible situation,' said Gordon Taylor. 'This action smacks of the Dark Ages. I know Rochdale have financial problems but they're not cutting their wage bill at our expense.'

While legal matters proceeded, Stokoe and the players agreed a training ground and match-day truce so that the league programme could continue. The impact of the story was such that one of the country's leading sportswriters, Alan Thompson of the *Daily Express*, accompanied the team on their journey to take on Portsmouth, who had lost only twice in 19 home league matches all season. Thompson's piece, 'The Open Road with Rochdale', made reference to the fact that the club was at 'rock bottom' and that 'resentment, anger and frustration filled the air'. Colin Waldron, at 31, made the case for the players. He was playing out the final days of his career after spells at Manchester United, Chelsea, Burnley and several seasons in the United States. 'We are not where we are without a reason,' he said. 'This is the bottom of the well, but the £35 is irrelevant. It is the stigma attached to it. Low as we are, we try.'

Injuries and suspensions meant Stokoe had just 12 players able to travel to Portsmouth. They kept out the home side in the first half but conceded three goals afterwards. Rochdale did not have a single shot on target. 'Frankly they were short on skill but I saw no evidence of lack of effort,' wrote Thompson. His article provided a fascinating insight into the life of a lower-league footballer. The players had lunch on the coach while they travelled south – pieces of cold chicken, a pickled onion, crisps, an apple and a can of pop. They stayed overnight in a 'plush' hotel, followed by a team stroll on Saturday morning. On the return journey Peter Madden gave each player £2 and told them to buy 'bangers, hamburgers and mash' at a motorway service station. When they returned to the coach, the engine would not start. The players pushed it about 100 yards from the car park to a forecourt area where the air lock in the fuel pipe was cleared. They arrived back at Spotland at 1am. As they disembarked, Stokoe had good news for them. He'd done his maths. They had avoided falling to the bottom of the Football League by a single goal. Crewe Alexandra had the same number of points but had a goal difference of minus 32, to Rochdale's minus 31.

The appeal by the PFA on behalf of the Rochdale players took place at the Football League headquarters in Lytham St Annes. During the hearing the PFA representatives said it would have been more appropriate for Stokoe to terminate the players' contracts or suspend them, rather than issue fines. After 90 minutes of evidence, the club announced that it wanted to withdraw from the appeal. 'We always intended this to be a domestic matter which should have been confined to the dressing-room,' said Stokoe. Later he added: 'I had to explore every avenue. I tried with the threat of fines and it went further than I intended. I'm glad it is out of the way, but it served its purpose and will never happen again.' Gordon Taylor called it 'a victory for common sense'. He said: 'It could have led to anarchy in the game with players reporting for Monday training not knowing what to expect.' He revealed that if Rochdale had not backed down, the PFA was considering a strike, an action never taken en bloc in the English game. In a final twist, Stokoe revealed that the players had not actually been fined at all. It had been a ruse, an empty threat, in a desperate bid to motivate his players and make them aware of the gravity of the club's situation.

A film crew from the BBC visited Spotland for a news report on the affair reaching its finale. Stokoe was still smarting and repeated his claim that the players had not tried against Tranmere. 'I, along with the rest of the squad, felt insulted by his attitude,' said Chris Jones, who had been dropped for the infamous match. 'I have given everything in every game in which I've played for various clubs over 17 seasons.' Stokoe was asked why his strikers had not scored many goals. In earshot of the players, he answered: 'Ask them, maybe they can tell you.' The camera panned to Mark Hilditch and Jimmy Seal, but they shrugged, nervous in the spotlight. The question was put to Jones, who answered that he had scored seven goals in 16 games before the end of November. 'That's a good ratio until then, but what since?' asked the reporter. Jones pointed at Stokoe: 'You'd better ask him – even I find it difficult scoring from the fucking bench.' This section was not broadcast.

After leaving Rochdale, Jones played a few games for Bridlington Town before becoming a PE teacher at Tadcaster Grammar School. Along with his wife, Therese, he has owned and run hotels in York. His attitude towards Stokoe has not softened. 'He really should have packed in after winning the FA Cup with Sunderland,' he said. 'He was always chasing that dream, trying to get back in the limelight where he'd been in the early-1970s. He played up to the television cameras. It's probably not a coincidence that the fining nonsense came after we'd been knocked out of the cup at Bury. The lads were not well paid as it was. I heard later that Stokoe suffered from migraines. Maybe that's what caused him to have such mood swings.' Jones is adamant that the team was playing to its utmost on that fateful night. 'It was an insult. There is no question that they tried. They were good quality bread-and-butter players,' he said. Mark Hilditch, now a custodial manager in the prison service, is less certain. 'Stokoe probably had a point. There were times when one or two players gave up. When you know a team is better than you and is stronger physically and more determined you try your best for a while, but it eventually takes it out of you,' he said. Hilditch felt Stokoe's actions were motivated principally by self-interest. 'I don't think he was overly bothered about Rochdale. By blaming the players he was diverting attention away from himself and his own failings,' he said. Eric Snookes also felt Stokoe put himself ahead of the club. 'He loved himself. He had pictures on his office wall from his playing days,' he said. 'A few of the lads spoke to players who had been with him at other clubs. They said he had a love-hate relationship with them. He liked to argue with them, put pressure on them and then he was sometimes all over them. He believed in this approach because it had worked for him with that FA Cup win.'

The fines debacle did substantial damage to the reputation of Rochdale AFC. The club had made national news over several weeks when it was most often ignored by the media or, at best, formed an occasional footnote. Across a single episode – the fines threat – the club's abysmal playing record, hardship, disunity and calamitous administration (a hand on the shoulder from Wrigley or another director might have been a better palliative to Stokoe's ire rather than wholehearted support) was revealed to millions. During a season when Altrincham were petitioning strongly to join the Football League, mounting an adversarial campaign against Rochdale, the timing was disastrous. And Stokoe's crude plan to galvanise the players also failed on the pitch. After the threat of fines they won once in their next 17 games.

Rochdale fell to the bottom of the Football League after a 2-0 defeat away at Peterborough United in February 1980.

Attendances were dropping and a fundraising 'Sports Forum' planned for Whitworth Civic Hall had to be cancelled when only 20 of 250 tickets were sold. Duncan McKenzie, then of Blackburn Rovers, was due to be one of the panellists. Brian Clough, vice-chairman of the supporters' club, said: 'We should all be rallying round to help in any way possible. Something like this does not help when people are queuing up to take every opportunity to knock the club.' Bob Stokoe expressed his concern, too: 'There is apathy in Rochdale and people don't lean to something like this. I would have been on the panel and willing to answer questions about the club. But apparently people do not seem interested.'

The indifference to a sports forum and, on a wider context, the football club itself was perhaps explainable; the people of Rochdale were having a hard time of it. The textile and engineering industries were being ravaged. There was little white-collar work in the town and scant investment in new enterprise. The North West Industrial Development Association revealed that unemployment in Rochdale was increasing 30 times faster than the national average. During a six-week period in 1980, 400 jobs were lost at various mills. No company was safe. Long-established firms such as John Ormerod & Sons and Eli Sutcliffe & Sons closed in the same week, at the cost of almost 200 jobs. Cheap imports, as ever, were to blame: from Taiwan and Brazil in the case of Ormerod's, where leather had been tanned since 1868. Thickset men, for they were mostly men made strong from the graft, were laid off and instructed to 'sign on' every other week to receive unemployment benefit from the DHSS (Department of Health and Social Security). There was an implicit acceptance that there would no longer be any jobs for them in the tanning industry or an allied trade. Their time had been and gone. Memories and stories were all they had left, about the soaking, liming, unhairing, fleshing, tanning, samming and the myriad other processes that turned an animal skin into a leather jacket.

The deal to take Eric Snookes from Rochdale to Carlisle United had remained intact since first mooted. Although still carrying the injury, he had returned to the team fortified by cortisone injections. Trevor Butterworth had organised for these to be administered at Highfield Hospital, a private hospital a mile or so from Spotland. 'I was told to turn up at a certain time and the surgeon would sort me out between operations. I was on a trolley bed on the corridor and he'd give me an injection,' he said. A few years later, his Achilles would be so sore after matches that he had to descend the stairs at home one step at a time in a sitting position. Rochdale were obviously keen to bring in what would have been a considerable sum for them, but the deal was finally scuppered when Bobby Moncur, the Carlisle manager, left to join Heart of Midlothian in February 1980.

Les Barlow was charged with relaying the club's ill fortune to the wider public of Rochdale. 'It had got to the stage with away matches that there was no hope of a win and little hope of a goal, so it became a sort of day out above everything else, albeit spoiled by the football,' he said. 'I used to travel with the supporters' club on a coach. Well, I say a coach but there were only about 20 of us and we fitted into a minibus.' Aside from a press box usually positioned among home supporters, there were seldom bespoke facilities for journalists. Managers would chat to anyone with a notebook, whether in the dugout, by the dressing-room door or out on the pitch. Barlow had grown accustomed to home managers patronising Rochdale. 'They'd go on about it being a tough game, how they'd worked hard for the victory. Fuck that – we'd usually lose 4-0 and it had been a stroll!' The defeats were starting to impact in the boardroom. 'You go into these things with enthusiasm, thinking you can make a change but it soon wears you down,' said John Faulks. 'I quickly realised the players had no commitment to the town – they were only interested in their wages. We had players no one else wanted, the bottom of the food chain if you like. I didn't want to put my own money in, but I suspect we all did at times. I had quickly become disillusioned.'

The match between Rochdale and Crewe Alexandra at Spotland, the two teams at the bottom of the Football League, finished 0-0 and afterwards a group of about 100 Rochdale supporters gathered outside the main entrance shouting 'Stokoe Out'. 'I feel I am taking the stick for someone else,' said Stokoe. 'I inherited a situation that was none of my making. Doug Collins said that the man who followed him as manager "had it made". He must have been joking. If the players haven't got it, I can't put it there. In fact, some of them couldn't care less about Rochdale Football Club but what can I do?' Peter Madden, his assistant, was close to Stokoe, but it was very much a working arrangement rather than friendship. 'I have nothing but good to say about Bob as a player and later as manager of Sunderland,' he said. 'But I don't think he was really interested in Rochdale. He struggled to work with the level of players we had. He seemed unhappy a lot of the time and starting coming into work late.'

Madden was often disapproving of Stokoe's man-management. In one game they were losing at half-time and as the players made their way into the dressing-room, Stokoe clapped sarcastically and said, 'Well done lads, you nearly won a corner.' Another time, Stokoe was briefing the team on the opposition players, extolling their virtues, when he broke off and said: 'To be honest with you lads, I can't see you getting much out of today's game.' Stokoe seemed resigned to the fact that the club would once again finish in the re-election zone. After another 0-0 draw, this time away at Northampton Town, he said: 'It's going to take a minor miracle to pull clear.' He was a little premature; 13 games were left in the season and the club was only seven points from safety.

\* \* \*

The plane in which Hindle sometimes travelled was offered to the board to attend an away match at Aldershot. 'I think it was something to do with someone who worked with Andrew at the Liverpool branch of Euroway,' said Faulks. The party – Hindle, Wrigley, Marks, Faulks and his business partner at Norford Estates, Philip Jackson – duly assembled at Manchester Airport. They christened the pilot 'Captain Beaky' and climbed into the skies in the single-prop plane heading to an airfield near Aldershot. On landing, they were desperate to use the toilet. 'It was a field in the middle of nowhere and for a bit of cover we dashed over to this Dornier, a German plane, and had a piss against it,' said Faulks. Rochdale lost the game 3-0. Before the return flight, Wrigley stocked up on cans of beer at an off-licence which was a bad idea because they ran into turbulence.

\* \* \*

Much as he had done at Bolton Wanderers, Andrew Hindle was keen to forge a link between his business and the football club. He celebrated the union of his Lada franchise with Red Rose Motor Company in nearby Royton by inviting Bobby Charlton to make a personal appearance at the showroom. 'Have fun and meet Bobby. You might even get him to talk a bit of football,' read the leaflet. In March 1980 Hindle organised a fleet of Ladas to be put on sale on the car park at Spotland. 'Lada Comes to Rochdale' was the headline on posters which continued: 'Euroway, Europe's biggest Lada dealers, are making room for new stock and are holding at Rochdale FC an unrepeatable two day give-a-way [sic] sale. This offer will not be repeated.' P-registered Lada 1200 saloons were priced at £795 and P-registered Lada 1200 estates, £695. Staff at Euroway were clearly still learning their way around the new association – press adverts said the sale was due to take place on Saturday and Sunday from 10am until 6pm at *Spotlands*, Rochdale.

Stokoe maintained a bizarre dialogue with the press, with no apparent regard to its impact on the players. His candidness might have been refreshing to some, foolhardy to others. Before the 2-0 home defeat to Huddersfield Town, he said: 'Some of the players have been consistent – consistently bad. Six or seven of them should not be in the team, but they know I can't leave them out because of injuries. They have been playing so badly and it makes me wonder what you have to do to motivate them. I don't think a 10-ton crane could lift some of them at the moment. I have tried to get things through to them but in some cases I have been met with blank stares.' Eric Snookes had at least showed passion and aggression in the Huddersfield game. Unfortunately it led to him being sent off. Still fuming, he kicked a hole in the dressing-room door. Unable to free himself from the splintered wood, he had to shout for help. After another defeat, Stokoe issued a dressing-down to the players in particularly grave terms. Peter Madden, believing Stokoe had left the room, informed the players that they would not have to suffer this for too much longer because their manager was soon to take up another job – he was replacing the laughing clown in a glass case at Blackpool Pleasure Beach. Unknown to Madden, Stokoe was standing behind him.

## Chapter Nine

# A Hypothetical Scenario

During the latter part of the season a forbidding metaphorical drum beat could be heard emanating from a few miles south of Manchester, especially after the tumult over the threatened fines. And it was growing ever louder. Officials at Altrincham had noted Rochdale's abysmal form and the dilapidated state of the ground. They were also aware of the seven previous re-election applications and that Fred Ratcliffe was no longer chairman, potentially robbing the club of 'personality' votes (though he was still in and around the club, contrary to the wishes of the new board). Altrincham was a PR-savvy, go-ahead club based in an affluent town in Manchester's commuter belt. It could call, if needed, on obliging local professional help – in law, accountancy and the media, for example – but the strategy was simple and obvious: target Rochdale. While previous league applicants had focused on their own merits and shied away from overt denigration of their 'rivals', Altrincham saw an all-out adversarial stance as their ticket to the Football League. They could hardly be blamed. Scores of previous applicants had shown themselves to be well-funded and successful, but had been passed over.

The Alliance Premier League (APL) had been launched in 1979/80. It had nationwide membership which meant, unlike previously, clubs from different regional leagues were no longer sub-dividing each other's vote by vying for a Football League place. In essence, the APL was a step towards greater access to the Football League – automatic promotion would come six years later. There seemed a tacit agreement that the first APL champions would be elected to the Football League, justifying its very existence. All the same, since January, Noel White, Altrincham's chairman, and his fellow director Raymond Donn had been travelling up and down the country visiting Football League chairmen, canvassing votes for their club. White had formed White and Swales in the 1950s, a chain of 15 shops in the Cheshire area specialising in renting televisions. He owned it with Peter Swales, later chairman of Manchester City. The pair had taken over Altrincham in 1961 with Swales leaving the club six years later. Donn was a smart, streetwise lawyer, specialising in personal injury claims. He was the first lawyer to open a practice in an NHS hospital and to advertise his services on commercial radio.

As the season wound down, Altrincham's campaign intensified with directors forming a 'flying squad' and each given a specific task. They called on support for their nomination chiefly among the first and second division clubs who controlled the majority of the votes in the ballot. Over a cup of tea and slice of cake, chairmen were told that Altrincham's average attendance was already almost 2,000 – imagine how it would increase on entry to the Football League. The club had returned a record profit of £53,971 and planned an investment of £100,000 into its Moss Lane ground, which included the extension and refurbishment of the dressing-rooms and club offices; a gymnasium; a new reception lounge and the installation of new turnstiles. And, of course, they were duty bound to mention: Rochdale were applying for re-election for the second time in three years. They had recently played 15 matches and scored once – a solitary goal in 22.5 hours of playing time. They had reported a loss of £91,956 on the trading year and were losing £2,000 a week. 'This is the best chance and the strongest case that we have ever had,' said Noel White. 'The club is geared for Fourth Division football. The only thing that can defeat us is sympathy for the clubs who have finished in the bottom four again. On merit, we should get in.' White and Hindle went head-to-head on BBC North West in a piece presented by David Davies, later to become executive director of the Football Association. Hindle referred to his appearance on television as 'a bit fraught'.

Rochdale went into the away match at Newport County on Saturday, 12 April 1980 knowing that a defeat would condemn them to another re-election application. They had gone 11 games without a win. Newport were on course for their tenth consecutive victory. In the final minutes of the match, with Rochdale losing 1-0, Brian Hart raced through on goal but shot into the side netting. Rochdale would have to seek re-election again.

Many supporters felt the board had been exaggerating the parlous state of the club; they had heard it many times before. The new board, however, was very much of the mind that the club was on the brink of folding. They had given it their best, made changes, increased revenue and yet they were in much the same place as before – in a shabby ground with a losing team, debts mounting. A meeting was arranged for the Sunday after the Newport game, when the five directors would vote to either continue or resign from the Football League. Sidney Marks had already played his hand, stating that he believed the club was trading fraudulently by continuing to incur bills it could not pay. The club was, he said, therefore obliged to cease trading. Trevor Butterworth and John Faulks wanted the club to progress to re-election and let its peers decide its fate. Wrigley had intimated that he too felt the club should resign, though the other directors weren't sure this was his definitive standpoint. 'This meant it would be left to Andrew, as chairman, to have the presiding vote,' said Faulks. 'And I felt sure he would vote for us not to seek re-election.'

Wrigley and Faulks were the only Rochdale directors to make the trip to Newport. On the way back, the gravity of the situation and the importance of the next few hours weighed heavily on Faulks. He was convinced he had to persuade Wrigley to change his mind and vote to continue. 'I was saying to David that we owed it to the people of Rochdale to seek re-election. We'd done all we could and to not even try to be re-elected would be abdicating our responsibilities.' Faulks was also worried that Rochdale supporters and others across town might assume he was culpable if Spotland was later replaced by a housing development. As both a surveyor and estate agent he had much to benefit from such an outcome. Faulks, who was driving, remembers well the journey through the rolling countryside of the Wye Valley, the spring sunshine lighting the way. 'It was an emotional plea, really. By the time we got back to the Blue Ball in Norden I like to think he'd been persuaded by my argument,' he said. Wrigley cannot recall Faulks's petition, but remembers the mood in the car. 'I was pretty miserable. It wasn't the happiest journey – it's a long way. You feel that supporters only make comments about directors if things are not going well. I was always going to vote to carry on,' he said.

The next day, Sunday, 13 April 1980, each board member travelled to Andrew Hindle's home in Mirfield, West Yorkshire. John Faulks could see why Marks felt as he did and understood that perhaps Wrigley and Hindle would also want to bring the fiasco to an end – the club was draining them of energy and funds, especially Hindle who had already paid £58,000 into the club in instalments, though whether this was a gift or loan and from which source, later became a point of contention. It might have seemed obvious to wait a few more weeks and let the league chairmen decide the club's fate, but debts were increasing every day and all manner of business was outstanding in preparation of another season. 'It was another beautiful spring day,' said Faulks. 'And we all assembled at Hindle's place.' Faulks was worried that Wrigley may have changed his mind overnight. Although the other directors often assumed Hindle and Wrigley were in cahoots, they were not particularly close friends, according to Hindle. 'David and I did not get on that well,' he said. 'We have a family relationship through our wives but I wasn't closely involved with him.'

Rochdale AFC had been in existence for 73 years. Faulks and, even more so, Butterworth were lost to reverie on the drive over, thinking of long-gone Rochdalians such as Harvey Rigg, the man who had first formed the club at a public meeting in 1907. And Herbert Hopkinson, a local referee and early advocate of 'Association football' who became the club's first secretary. And famous ex-players they had been told about by old-boy supporters. The likes of Tommy Tippett, who scored six goals in one match against Hartlepools United; Albert Whitehurst, 44 goals in a single season; Reg Jenkins (who they remembered well, of course), with a shot so hard it was said he sometimes burst the netting. And players who became famous after starting at the club, most recently David Cross and Alan Taylor. And, off the pitch, the magnanimous, if occasionally infuriating, Fred Ratcliffe, dipping his hand into his pocket again and again. And the odd sprig of glory, the League Cup Final of 1962 and the promotion season of 1968/69. And important social milestones – the club appointed the first black manager (Tony Collins, 1960–67) and was the first to include three black players in a starting line-up (Leo Skeete, Stan Horne and Tony Whelan, against Shrewsbury Town, in August 1974). And, most of all, those fans who moaned and groaned but bled the blue of the club colours, trudging up to Spotland every other week, holding on to hope. Wrigley voted that the club should carry on trading and the motion to seek re-election was carried. Oddly, Andrew Hindle has no memory of the meeting but concedes that it 'sounds logical' that it would have occurred.

On the drive back to Rochdale, Faulks wondered if it had been little more than a reprieve and that the Football League would turn its back on the club a few weeks later. He realised, too, that Wrigley and Hindle might sense this, so the vote around the dining table at Hindle's pile had been largely immaterial. In fact, allowing the club's fate to rest with the wider football world was perhaps a wiser political move because it absolved the board of responsibility for a final closedown, should it occur. Interestingly, there had been no discussion of the possible ground sale and the implications of a scenario where the club went out of business and a third party owned Spotland. Although unspoken, a good portion of the board thought a sale unlikely and, if it did occur, trusted that Hindle, as an experienced businessman, could handle all the necessary bureaucracy.

Rochdale's long and arduous season finished on Tuesday, 6 May 1980 when they were beaten 2-0 by Hereford United at

Spotland. Bob Stokoe, a man who had previously left several clubs of his own volition, immediately told the press: 'I'm not running away.' Three days earlier, Altrincham had clinched the APL title with a 2-0 win at Gravesend and Northfleet. The Football League management committee visited Moss Lane and undertook a thorough inspection, which the ground passed. They were now authorised to proceed as the sole non-League club nominated for election to the Fourth Division at the Football League's forthcoming AGM. The match of the day, of the year, was now on: Altrincham v Rochdale; it felt as if Rochdale were the metaphorical away team such was the weight of evidence in Altrincham's favour and the force of their campaign.

'We have finalised our re-election strategy,' Andrew Hindle told the press. 'Obviously we have to rely on our friends in the game and in this respect we have the services of our president, Mr FS Ratcliffe.' Any antipathy between the new and old boards was put aside immediately to deal with the crisis facing the club. Ratcliffe may well have stood back and gloated at the mess the *new lot* had made, but his love of the club superseded such peevishness or *Schadenfreude*, however bruised his ego: Rochdale AFC was greater than any individual. Hindle said the club would write to every League chairman and 'fight tooth and nail' to get re-elected. By coincidence, that month the Football Writers' Association held a special dinner in Manchester in tribute to Ratcliffe. He was given an inscribed clock and Football Association cufflinks for his services to football. The timing was perfect. Between and after the three-course meal he was able to petition players and managers: don't forget, lads, put in a good word with your chairman.

The village of Rochdale AFC was fast emptying. Bob Stokoe released or transfer-listed most of the playing staff;

only six were offered new contracts. He revealed that he would resign if Rochdale failed to be re-elected. Jack Butterfield announced that he was leaving to take up a similar position at Tranmere Rovers. He said he was 'tired of banging his head against a brick wall'. The *Football Pink*, the sports paper produced by the *Manchester Evening News* on Saturdays, ran a piece about the re-election dogfight in which it noted, 'The Rochdale directors have seemed strangely reluctant to defend themselves and the club.' Such was the forcefulness of Altrincham's PR, some claimed it amounted to a 'smear campaign' and might prove counter-productive if it inadvertently engendered sympathy for Rochdale. On their part, Rochdale's negligible 'campaign' was to point out that two of the clubs also seeking re-election, Crewe Alexandra and Darlington, had applied several times before, four times in ten years in Darlington's case.

If so inclined, Rochdale might have pointed out that Altrincham's 2,000 average attendance was not overly impressive considering their high standing in the APL. People tended to 'buy into' success, to winning teams, so the fall-off should Altrincham join the Football League and win less often would most likely drop below Rochdale's. They might also have argued that Altrincham's success was based principally on the patronage of Noel White and, for a good while, Peter Swales. In 1961 Altrincham had themselves been on the brink of bankruptcy and only a loan of £6,000 – a huge sum in those days – from the two businessmen had kept the club solvent. What would happen if White moved on and with him his money (he did five years later, when he became a director at Liverpool)?

The most poignant and heartfelt plea for Rochdale to remain in the Football League came from the pen of Brian Clough, the vice-chairman of the supporters' club. A big chap with a huge beard, Clough was a familiar figure around Spotland, serving in the club 'shop' (a hole in the wall behind the Main Stand, complete with a flip-open counter) or selling raffle tickets by the turnstiles in his best anorak. He was asked to produce a letter for distribution among football club chairmen and wrote: 'For a football club to lose its League status means far more to its supporters than simply changing a name on a pools coupon. For Rochdale Football Club it would mean the end of continuous membership of the Football League, but more importantly for the supporters it would mean a loss of identity which could never be replaced by the offer of League football in neighbouring towns and cities. The standard may be higher but the involvement and sense of belonging would always be lacking. It is with this in mind, coupled with the knowledge that the supporters are fully behind the directors in their efforts to ensure the future of the club, that the supporters' club asks for a positive response to Rochdale AFC's re-election application.'

* * *

Amid such turmoil, Spotland was reported to have been 'sold' for between £175,000 and £200,000 to Euroway Car Centre of Prestwich (Euroway was registered at Companies House in various guises). Andrew Hindle told the press that Euroway was a company with which he was 'associated'. In conversation, he had always referred to it as 'my' company. He said the purchase was a philanthropic gesture and Euroway had initially been reluctant to make public its involvement. He provided a long-winded, ambiguous statement to the *Rochdale Observer*: 'The reason that the board of directors of that company [Euroway] wished to remain anonymous was that this action hardly made commercial sense and did not reflect in a good light the sound business acumen of the directors of that company. In other words, it was a philanthropic gesture initiated by genuine affection for Rochdale Football Club, without thought for hard-headed businessmanship.' In the finer detail, he revealed that the ground would be leased back to Rochdale for 99 years at a rental of £35,000 per year (almost £3,000 per month) with the first year's rent waived. 'I had to do it [use the ground to underwrite the money he had introduced],' said Hindle. 'I had to satisfy the Euroway group that I had some security against the money I had put in. They thought I'd lost my marbles, with good reason. It was an exercise to satisfy our bankers, a gesture I would have never called in.'

Hindle had realised that practically the only guaranteed substantial income into the club on an annual basis was the 'television money' – Rochdale's share of the deal done each year with the BBC and ITV. In the early summer of 1980 the Football League (at that point including all 92 clubs) received £2.4m to be shared among clubs. Hindle had negotiated with the board for this money, approximately £25,000, to be diverted immediately to Euroway on an annual basis to cover most of the ground rent. Although trifling by today's standards, the television money was vital to Rochdale and enabled the club to pay wages through the close season and beyond.

Stirred by the news from Spotland, the previous board of directors became concerned about money they had invested previously in the club. Several years before, the six former directors had put up £60,000 to clear an overdraft called in by the bank. One or two said they had taken out personal loans to secure this money. Hindle reportedly paid each ex-director £10,000 and promised them an additional £1,000 on an annual basis in perpetuity. 'That means I would have to live for another 50 years to get my money,' said Ratcliffe.

He was 66 at the time. He also queried how the ground sale had gone through when he and his fellow ex-directors had not signed over the deeds. 'They are still lodged with our solicitor,' said Ratcliffe. David Wrigley, whose firm, Wrigley & Co, had overseen the deal, was adamant: 'The sale has been legally completed.'

In his role as a surveyor and valuer, Faulks was asked, once more, to value the 'hard' assets (which excluded players, though most had little sell-on value anyway) for the club's annual financial report. This was, apparently, completely unconnected to the ground deal. He arranged to visit the planning office to discuss a hypothetical scenario – or so he assumed – of what Spotland might be worth should a change of use be approved, and it be given over to, say, a housing development. He met John Pierce, Rochdale Council's chief planning officer, at the Black Box, the nickname given to the 12-storey council building standing tall above the bus station in Rochdale town centre. Unbidden, he was handed a sheet of paper. 'It was a sketch of how Spotland could be developed for houses, covering about seven and a half acres of land,' said Faulks. 'I was surprised, to say the least. I was only going there to present something to them which was hypothetical but this was something beyond hypothetical.'

Whoever had lodged the plan had done so as part of a formal procedure whereby any new development or change of use of private land required consent from the council at a later date. Introducing it in such a way was to see if it fell within the Town Development Plan and how it might affect highways and utilities if given the go-ahead and also whether there were enough amenities to serve the houses and increase in population. 'There are always off-the-record discussions with developers and planning officers,' said Faulks. 'They need to know that there is a good chance that they will get the green light before they make a formal planning application.' After seeing the document, Faulks was confused. 'It didn't cross my mind that anyone might be acting deviously or planning for the club to fold,' he said.

Only one other witness – a director who joined the board at a later date – saw this sketch of Spotland as a housing development. It now appears to have either gone missing or has been destroyed. Hannah Lomax, communications officer at Rochdale Council, said in 2019: 'I have carried out a full search of our off-site records and unfortunately cannot find anything for the period [late 1970s/early 1980s]. Legal files only have to be retained for six years and as such I can only presume that any files from that time have been destroyed. The officers in Legal who dealt with the matter at that time have left the Authority and there is no one in the present team who can provide any background historical information to assist with this request.'

Others, sure of the authenticity of the 'housing' story, advise to check with HM Land Registry with the assertion, 'It's all lodged down there.' It is a misconception that every piece of land or potential change of use of land has to be registered with this national body. In practise, registration comes later, often when a builder has redeveloped land. The HM Land Registry has nothing on file for this period relating to GM660018 (the reference number of the land occupied by the pitch at Rochdale AFC) and there was no record until 1994 of it ever being registered at all, even as a sporting venue.

\* \* \*

As the Football League AGM approached, and with it the vital vote, a narrative developed in the national newspapers. The *Daily Mail* depicted the 'battle' as Cheshire Affluence v Lancashire Austerity. Another referred to Altrincham as having 'pulsating vitality' while the vocabulary fastened to Rochdale, the club, the town and the people, was habitually glum: long-suffering, beleaguered, impoverished, bleak. And, in almost every article, it was *little* Rochdale, once more. In the final days, the repeated theme from the Rochdale camp was the potency of the Ratcliffe-Stokoe axis. These were two men, one of the boardroom, the other of the boot room, who personified all that was authentic about football. Les Barlow, who came as close as any reporter to Ratcliffe, was in the social club one evening when they were about to show a live World Cup match on television, featuring Brazil. 'Are you going to stay and watch?' he asked Ratcliffe. The chairman shook his head. 'I'm only bothered if it's Dale playing,' he said. Stokoe, despite how he was perceived by his players and the Rochdale fans, was still Mr FA Cup to the rest of the country – a passionate, galloping, crying, laughing, shouting mix-up of a man. This was the kind of commitment, defiant and daft, the Football League chairmen were up against. Could they really rob them and a rain-soaked town of their football club?

The Café Royal at 68 Regent Street, Piccadilly, London ('Where the elegance of Mayfair, energy of Soho and sophistication of St. James combine') had been a meeting point for the rich and famous since first opening in 1865, from Oscar Wilde to Winston Churchill. Every June, usually on the first Friday of the month, it hosted the annual general meeting of the Football League. On the letters of invite it was referred to as a ceremonial event but to the chairmen and their guests, the term most commonly used was 'beano' or 'piss up', depending on their social class – the community of football club ownership was a rich assortment, from the Cobbold family, landed gentry, who provided five chairmen of Ipswich Town, to a handful of felons whose stewardship tended to be much shorter. There was the obligatory official business to deal with – a tweak of the rules perhaps, a new addition to the management committee – but mainly it was a chance for these men of means to talk shop, smoke a cigar or two, enjoy a tipple or three. Routinely, as they visited each other's clubs, they were forced to meet before, during and after matches. Such encounters were a little rushed, compromised by etiquette and dependent on the resources of the host club, which were sometimes basic. They did their best to hide the fact but dry triangular sandwiches served on chipped plates in what resembled a waiting room at a taxi office, had only a limited appeal. This was better, more fitting. They were under the chandeliers at the Café Royal, treading the thick, plush carpet, bathed in opulence. Staff in smart uniform handed out canapés from silver trays. The Overcoat Men took off their overcoats, loosened their ties and rolled up their shirt sleeves. It was summer, after all.

The various Football League chairmen convened on Friday, 6 June 1980 with the re-election vote scheduled for 2pm. Altrincham had six representatives, although only two were allowed into the meeting room where the vote was due to take place. The Rochdale party comprised three – Fred Ratcliffe, Bob Stokoe and David Wrigley; Andrew Hindle was unable to attend because he said he had to attend a business arrangement elsewhere. Lord Westwood, Newcastle United's chairman, presided over the meeting as president of the Football League. David Wrigley found himself sitting next to Harold Shepherdson, trainer of the England World Cup-winning team of 1966. 'It was a tremendous honour to find myself next to him,' he said.

Few Rochdale fans believed the club would be re-elected. Regardless of Altrincham's campaign and manifest vitality, what did Rochdale have to recommend it, aside from tradition? On and off the pitch it was in disarray, shin pad-deep in debt and rising. The fan base was minimal; it had barely any players. Further, the fines issue had brought ignominy to the club, and God knows what was happening with all this selling-the-ground business. And if Fred Ratcliffe's force of personality was the last-gasp factor in lending the club support, he was halfway through the out-door anyway, replaced by a bunch of blokes no one knew outside of Rochdale and who had no experience of running a football club. This was a club lying face down in the mud, waiting for the stretcher-bearers to shift it to one side and have done with it.

The votes cast in the Football League re-election poll for the 1979/80 season were Darlington 49; Crewe Alexandra 48; Hereford United 48; Rochdale 26 and Altrincham 25. If Altrincham had received one more vote and tied with Rochdale, a second ballot featuring only those two candidates would have followed in which the chairmen would cast a single vote for the club of their choice. In the two preceding instances when this had happened, the non-League club had prevailed, namely Hereford United (1972) and Wigan Athletic (1978). 'The idea of going out of the League had been absolutely terrifying. You can only do your best, but I thought the club was doomed. It was a considerable relief when we were re-elected and I headed straight to the bar to get myself a large brandy,' said Wrigley.

Within minutes of the vote being announced and Rochdale's survival confirmed, a phone call supposedly took place between an unnamed club 'official' – of which there were very few – and Andrew Hindle. The 'conversation' has been relayed, presented as fact, no doubt expanded upon, down two generations of Rochdale supporters, directors and staff. The story goes that Hindle took the call at his house, possibly a palace, in the Isle of Man (emphasising both his outsider status and excessive wealth). When he was told the outcome of the vote he fell silent for a minute, maybe several. He was rendered catatonic, it was said, because he was crestfallen. He had purposely carried out what would later become known in economic circles as a 'managed decline' of Rochdale AFC but the plan had been thwarted. Football had won. He couldn't build houses on Spotland. There would be no Reg Jenkins Avenue or Tommy Tippett Close (rumours had got so far as to suggest street names would commemorate the players who had once skittered across this piece of land, back when it was a football pitch). 'It had never occurred to me to do anything like that,' he said. 'I would have been strung up. Imagine how I would feel as a local bloke doing such a thing as that. The stigma would have been horrendous. The last thing you would have wanted to be associated with is a club going out of the league. I wanted Rochdale to succeed.'

Most clubs that had not been voted back into the Football League – Gateshead, Bradford Park Avenue, Barrow, Workington, Southport, etc. – continued regardless, accepting their new non-League status but dreaming of returning, usually after a period of restructuring. It was widely held that Rochdale would almost certainly have wound up had they not been re-elected; there was no contingency plan to enter the APL. The debts were too substantial and the board disillusioned, exhausted.

The accusation that Hindle had designed a cynical and concerted plan to wind down the club seems unlikely. Viewed from a different perspective, it might be said that he was, as Wrigley claimed many times, the club's saviour. The other directors had put in many hours and dedicated a good portion of their lives to the club but in terms of hard cash, they were lapped numerous times by Hindle. Many hold that the measure of the man was in his willingness to take money from his pocket and put it on the table. Here, Hindle was a titan. Over an 18-month period he had introduced more money into it than anyone had done before, notwithstanding Fred Ratcliffe. The nature, terms and extent of this funding, how it was sourced and what he expected in return, was open to question but his overall intentions would appear principled. His claim that it was a series of philanthropic gestures was perhaps rich considering it came with caveats (the yearly rental charge, for instance) and that he later tried to retrieve the money. Although it wasn't intentional, the ground-purchase plan created a morass of complications that took several years to resolve and almost sounded the death knell for the club.

Afterwards it emerged that two clubs had failed to vote at the Café Royal. This, or similar, might have been a regular occurrence each year and habitually gone undetected, but Altrincham's six-man team and their associates were resolute in unravelling any possible iniquity. Denis Mortimer, chairman of Luton Town, was the first to admit he had missed the vote, claiming he had been held up in traffic. 'To be fair to everyone involved, I am not going to reveal who we would have voted for,' he said. Richard (Dick) Kitchener Middleton, the chairman of Division Three champions, Grimsby Town, and owner of a successful window company, said he had been unsure whether to assemble with the chairmen from the top two divisions or take his place with the others. Consequently, he found himself in the wrong part of the building and did not hand in the ballot paper.

Many half-truths, theories and suppositions were brewed up subsequently to add drama to this tipping point in the lives of two football clubs, and, on a wider level, two towns. An Altrincham player alleged that one of the missing chairmen had 'got pissed and fallen asleep' while Noel While, Altrincham's chairman, said officials at both Grimsby Town and Luton Town had said categorically that they would have voted for his club. Rochdale, safely re-elected, had no need to forensically examine the events of the day. If they had mounted a counter-campaign, they might have questioned the veracity of Altrincham's claims. How would a player who had not been there know of the state, inebriated or otherwise, of another club's chairman, and didn't people often say they would vote a certain way but then secretly vote another? Still, year on year, Rochdale fans would be told that Altrincham had been duped out of a place in the Football League and Rochdale filled a space which was rightly theirs.

On the train back from London, Fred Ratcliffe was suspicious that Stokoe had not been acting in the best interests of the club. 'I heard that while Fred was going round the room pleading with the chairmen to vote for Rochdale, Stokoe was telling everyone to throw them out,' said Les Barlow. Stokoe wasn't assumed to be acting maliciously, but felt the time had come to effectively put the club 'out of its misery'. As he saw it, the few people who had put so much time, effort and heart into the club were worn out. They needed to give up the fight, move on. Ratcliffe was not of this conviction. He was affronted. When Stokoe left the group to visit the buffet carriage, he reportedly snapped: 'He goes on Monday morning.' 'I think it shows that Fred was still pulling the strings,' said Barlow. 'He was getting to the end of his time at the club and had more or less had enough but he didn't want it to go to the wall after all those years. Rochdale should have been voted out, really. The team was awful, the ground was a mess. There were buckets everywhere catching the water. Good old little wizened Fred had saved the day.'

Bob Stokoe's version of that afternoon at the Café Royal differed radically, spelled out in a biography published in 2009, five years after his death. In an interview for the book, he referred cryptically to the two 'missing' chairmen. He said one had been directed to the wrong room and the other was 'chasing around after a mysterious phone call.' He appeared to be suggesting that he, or an accomplice, was behind this subterfuge. 'At least I achieved one thing at Rochdale, keeping them in the Football League,' he said.

Three days after the vote, Andrew Hindle wrote a letter to 'The Directors, Rochdale AFC, Sandy Lane' tending his resignation as chairman. 'I do so because I feel the precarious financial situation that prevails at the club leads me to believe that our chances of survival are slight,' he wrote. 'Therefore, knowing the enthusiasm and conviction of other members of the board, I think it is only right that someone else should have the Chair.' He said he felt strongly that the club ought to be led by local people 'who have a closer affinity with the town of Rochdale'. David Wrigley told the press that 'there had been nothing unsavoury in the ground sale and lease back'. 'In my opinion Andrew Hindle has performed a tremendous service to the club, not only by the financial support he provided during his chairmanship, but also by the act of purchase and lease back. I have said on previous occasions that without him there would not now be a football club, and I still hold that view,' he said.

*Chapter Ten*

# The Local Ruling Class

The club had maintained its League status but was still in disarray, lacking funds and personnel to properly function. An appeal for help brought forward about 30 fans to meet Bob Stokoe and the directors at Spotland on a Sunday morning. Several said they would sell lottery tickets on behalf of the club, while others planned jumble sales. Two donations 'in their hundreds' were made on the day. Later that week, Graham Morris, the local accountant on nodding terms with John Faulks, called at the club with a cheque for £50. He posted it after finishing work one evening. 'I wasn't a fan,' he said. 'But it was the town's club and I didn't want it to go out of business. It's no good when you lose a club – you never hear of the place again.' David Wrigley both comforted and discomfited fans with his pronouncements. 'I can see no reason why there will not be League football at Spotland in August,' he said. Ominously, he mooted the possibility that a team 'made up of amateurs' might have to represent the club if finance was not found.

Proceeds from the ground sale had been quickly used up and there was no money left to buy players. Almost £10,000 was still owed to the Inland Revenue. The club turned to the most charismatic and well-known man in town to front their public appeal for funds: Cyril Smith, MP. Fred Ratcliffe knew Smith well. He had employed him at his spring works in 1960 and quickly made him production controller. Three years later, Smith, then aged 35, was sacked. 'At the time he told us it was because Cyril was on the phone doing a lot of council business,' said Judith Hilton, Ratcliffe's daughter. 'But I've sometimes wondered whether there was more to it.' Smith took with him five members of FS Ratcliffe's staff to form Smith's Springs (Rochdale). They worked out of a former joiner's workshop in Flannel Street and, with £4,000 capital, made springs using second-hand machinery. Later, more than 70 people worked at the company. Although not a Rochdale AFC supporter, Smith had been secretary of the club's Improvement Fund from 1959 to 1962 – he was astute enough to know where votes might be harvested. 'I have certainly no reason to believe that there is any cause for panic at Spotland,' he told the press. 'The directors have asked me to meet them to see if there is any way I can help or advise. This I have readily agreed to do, as I would with any Rochdale organisation making such a request.' Cyril Smith was extremely popular. He'd 'put Rochdale on the map'. He was often seen at the market, jolly and chatty. One or two people had reservations, but they were often shouted down: why do they have to knock him? As time would show, there were plenty of reasons.

Bob Stokoe told directors and fans that he needed £50,000 to raise a team for the forthcoming season. John Faulks revealed that Manchester United had said they would play a friendly at Spotland. The negotiations were being carried out by Cyril Smith, who claimed to be a friend of Martin Edwards, the Manchester United chairman, and Sir Matt Busby, their former manager and now a director at Old

Trafford. West Ham United and Manchester City were also invited to play friendlies at Spotland. None of these matches took place.

The new directors had specific roles to reflect their areas of expertise. Trevor Butterworth handled most of the commercial operation, overseeing the lottery and ensuring the club shop was stocked and running at a profit. He called upon a contact at Buckley Hall, a young offenders' institution in Rochdale, and a number of inmates were 'loaned' to the club each Sunday. They carried out various chores, such as clearing the terracing of weeds and litter. The board organised several fund-raising events, including sponsored walks from Spotland to Halifax Town and Wigan Athletic. John Faulks held a garden party on land attached to his home in Norden, while David Wrigley opened the doors of his house for a fund-raising party attended by the players. The constant need for funds had started to drain the energy of the directors. 'It was all work and there was no bloody fun trying to raise money all the time,' said Butterworth. 'Spotland was a shit-heap but, all the same, walking into that main entrance and knowing I was a director meant I had achieved a boyhood dream. I always wanted to play for the club but to be a director was the next best thing and that feeling never wore off.'

The friction between the old and new board continued. In a piece strategically placed in the *Rochdale Observer*, Ratcliffe asked the new board: do you want to own a ground or run a football club? In the article he expressed surprise that the new board had not called on the experience of its predecessors. 'I have worked for 33 years to keep League football in Rochdale because I believe a League club is an asset to a town,' he said. 'I worked damned hard for 48 hours before the League's annual meeting, asking other clubs to vote for Rochdale's re-election. What I want to impress on everyone is that the club is bigger than any one man. There are those of us with experience which can be of great value at this time.' Ratcliffe was upset over rumours that the old board had departed leaving behind 'massive debt'. He revealed that the debt stood at £22,000. The club's running costs of £2,000 per week had risen to £4,500 per week under the new regime, he said.

Fred Ratcliffe had not been able to fathom Andrew Hindle. He grumbled to his pals that he thought Hindle was 'too quiet' and 'kept himself to himself'. He knew Hindle had 'a fair bit of brass' but he was unnerved because it wasn't accompanied by swagger. Ratcliffe had a natural suspicion of discretion; years in business had taught him that it was usually a tactic of concealment. He seems all right to us, the former directors assured Fred. He's just been to a posh school, they said. They're like that, educated lads. He's Rochdale, underneath. As might have been expected, Ratcliffe had looked at the figures. He wanted to know how this Hindle fellow was acting the philanthropist. If he had paid top whack for the ground, £200,000 – which Ratcliffe very much doubted – he'd have all his money back in seven years, charging £35,000 in rent per annum. No wonder he was offering a year's free rent! Ratcliffe also worked out how much the club – should it continue – might end up paying over 98 years (the presumed term of the agreement) in rent: £3.34 million. His maths, if not done by the company accountant, tended to be scribbled down on the insides of ripped-up cigarette packets. It didn't take long for him to see the obvious: Rochdale could end up paying nearly £3.5 million for the privilege of an immediate cash injection of £200,000 (though, he'd had word it was actually £150,000). Ratcliffe pondered on how the daft buggers on the board had fallen for this and also how Hindle could claim to have Rochdale's best interests at heart – he knew full well that the club could not afford to pay such a high rent to play on its own pitch. He's just covering his back, the other ex-board members told Ratcliffe. He's not going to draw off it for the next hundred bloody years. He'll sell it back to the club at a fair price when he's covered his costs and maybe made a few bob for himself, don't worry.

The exodus from Spotland continued with the announcement that Sid Marks was to leave the board. Marks said he was too busy at work to devote enough time to the club.

As the mid-summer of 1980 approached, the club finally announced that it had bolstered its resources. Jack Connor, aged 60, who had played as a striker for the club from 1948 to 1951, returned as promotions manager. His main role was to oversee a lottery which had been launched a few weeks earlier and was already bringing in £1,000 a week in profit.

\* \* \*

Graham Morris was invited by John Faulks to a meeting at David Wrigley's office, though he wasn't sure of the reason. The pair had been alerted to Morris through his £50 donation. 'Once I got there, it was only the three of us and they started talking about the football club. They were telling me that Fred [Ratcliffe] had moved on and there was an opportunity to have a fresh start,' he said. They asked Morris if he knew of anyone who could help the club with its accounts. He said he didn't. They circumvented the issue for a while and then Morris realised they were proposing that he join the board. 'I said, "Bugger off, you must be joking."' The pair continued with their lobby. 'There are a lot of slime-balls who end up as directors and we wanted decent people you could trust,' said Faulks. Wrigley confirmed that Morris had been a clear and singular target. 'We wanted Graham because he had a reputation for sorting things out,' he said. Morris departed, saying he would 'help out' by taking a look at the club's accounts. 'By the time I got back to my office that afternoon my staff said the *Rochdale Observer* had been on the phone asking if it was true that I'd joined the board,' he said.

Morris, by virtue of his occupation, was at the epicentre of a social circle of professionals in Rochdale. His company did the books for many local businesses, often working alongside solicitors. He also knew most of the senior staff at the banks, building societies and estate agents. 'It wasn't like today where everyone is e-mailing one another or they answer somewhere in India when you ring the bank. We used to talk on the phone and actually meet up,' said Morris. Most days, at lunchtime, he ambled down from his office at the 'business end' of Drake Street – where the accountants, insurance companies, GP surgeries, dentists and satellite council offices were bunched – and headed to the Broadfield Park Hotel. The bar in the hotel was a popular haunt for solicitors and staff who worked at the nearby Rochdale Magistrates' Court. At other times, he'd have a drink at the Flying Horse, close to the town hall, or nip around the corner, along South Parade, to the bottom of Drake Street for a pint in the former coach house, the Wellington Hotel. 'I never drank in the evenings but, aside from impromptu gatherings at lunch, we'd see one another at golf open days or various functions in and around the town. They were mostly reasonable blokes and easy to get on with,' he said.

On a more formal basis, many were members of Rochdale Round Table. During the 1970s and 1980s it was a ready assumption that most businessmen under the age of 40 (later extended to 45) would be members of their local

Round Table. This non-political, non-sectarian association aimed to 'encourage high ethical standards in commercial life, the promotion of fellowship amongst young professional and business men, and the quickening of individual interests in everything affecting the public welfare.' On reaching the age threshold, most moved on to either the Rotary Club of Rochdale or the Rotary Club of Rochdale East – known colloquially as 'the Bosses Clubs'. Interestingly, a political dimension was revealed in January 1980 when Rochdale East hosted Enoch Powell as its after-dinner speaker. His 'rivers of blood' speech had occurred 12 years earlier but Powell, by then an MP for the Ulster Unionist Party, was still considered an incendiary figure of the political right. Most Rotarians, however, principally sought out the camaraderie: the firm handshake, the chin-chinning, the tall tale well told in the lounge bar. There was much to celebrate, for these former grammar and private schoolboys were fulfilling family expectations of professional and social furtherance. After the bonhomie, they would pull out their diaries and arrange to meet, business to business, or share a contact – someone who might supply typewriters at a cheaper rate, or a decent joiner to fix the jammed door in the back office.

Another favourite haunt of the Bamford and Norden set, and particularly the directors of the football club, was the Masonic Hall, close to Rochdale train station. Fred Ratcliffe was a prominent Freemason. He was a member of the Veneration Lodge in Manchester. The square and compasses, the symbol of Freemasonry, stand high above the stone-fronted building in Richard Street, Rochdale, which was built in 1926. Although largely unknown (reflecting its clandestine ethos), Rochdale has a rich history of Masonry. In the early-1980s it had almost 2,000 members. The town had 12 lodges, each comprising 20 to 40 men. A mile or so from

Spotland stands St Edmund's Church in Falinge, England's only church dedicated overtly to Masonic symbolism. Nikolaus Pevsner, the famous writer on architecture, described it as a 'Temple to Freemasonry.' The Masonic Hall in Rochdale was soon to provide the venue for a notable episode in the club's history.

Retail parks fastened to dual carriageways had yet to reach Rochdale in the early-1980s, though 'superstores' had arrived a few years earlier. The town's well-heeled professional community was served principally by family-run, town-centre stores where their parents and grandparents had also shopped. They bought furniture from Lovick's in Yorkshire Street, established in 1919. They shopped at Iveson's, a department store in Drake Street dating back to 1810 with its own turret, complete with flagpole. The store was publicity savvy and organised in-store photo shoots with reigning Miss Cotton Queens, local girls who had won beauty competitions held at the mills across town. At the corner of Drake Street and Fleece Street was the jewellers, Butterworth, which dated back to 1901, while, a few hundred yards up the street, stood Denis Hope, a gents' outfitter specialising in weddings. Other well-established businesses included Bateson's, an ironmongery; Samuel Williams, glass and china; Wilson Brothers, paint and wallpaper; William Pilling and Son, furniture; Shorrock and Shorrock, musical instruments and records; Ashton, Leach and Cumberbirch, carpets; Hough Electric Motor Company, televisions and radios; Halfpenney's, ladieswear, and Diggle and Taylor, another gents' outfitters. The cars of choice for Rochdale's professional elite, perhaps a BMW 3 series, Ford Sierra or, ideal for carrying golf clubs, a Volvo 740, were purchased from car dealerships such as Motorama in John Street or Tom Mellor Ford in Oldham Road.

*RAP* magazine, ever keen to cock its political rifle, ran a cover piece noting that a new Establishment had formed in the town during the 1970s and early-1980s. They identified estate agents, solicitors, accountants and business owners who 'set the rules, made the money and pulled the strings'. They had replaced a syndicate of families – the Turners, Brights, Tweedales, Lyes, Tathams, Riggs, etc. – who had risen to eminence in the previous 200 years, principally owning mills and engineering works. Back then, seven families owned 24 companies between them, employing thousands of people. Typical of the new breed, according to the article, were local estate agents Graham Anderson, Peter Smith and Keith Mosley, but its epitome was said to be David Wrigley. 'He has slipped readily into the business and social world of the Bamford generation,' it read. 'I've no idea why *RAP* was so interested in me,' said Wrigley. 'They rang me up on a couple of occasions. The football club board would have meetings at my house and they'd find out whose car was seen on Roch Valley Way and put it in the paper.' The social conventions supposedly carried over from the age of the mills were said to include nepotism and inter-marriage between what *RAP* referred to as the 'local ruling class'. The archetype of this newly-identified social animal was male, white, in his late 30s or early 40s, working in a profession, a resident of Bamford or Norden, a Mason, a Methodist, a member of Rotary, a Conservative voter and a member of Rochdale Golf Club. Most of the board of Rochdale, past and present, fitted this description, as did the boards of most English football clubs at the time.

*Chapter Eleven*

# Oh, Graham – What Have You Let Yourself in For?

John Faulks and David Wrigley were unaware of the fact, but Graham Morris had been involved in football two decades earlier. He had formed a team based at a youth club affiliated to St Peter's Church in Blackley, north Manchester, where he lived. 'I liked soccer, we needed a team and all the lads fell in behind me when I suggested it. We won a lot of cups for sportsmanship, which isn't the same as winning medals for playing well,' said Morris. 'I was crap. I started off as right-half but ended up right-back. I just enjoyed being there. I'm tall, which helps, but once you come across little lads who are quick, you've bloody had it.'

He undertook most of the roles for the club – collecting subscriptions, paying referees, attending league meetings and presentation nights – but it folded after five or six seasons.

'I think we suffered for not having a bar which would have made us money and also forged a wider social scene. After a match we'd adjourn to the nearest pub but it wasn't the same as having our own place,' he said.

His time running St Peter's FC was scant preparation for what he had committed himself to at Rochdale. His tenure began with an immediate shock – three days after Morris had joined the board, Bob Stokoe announced that he was leaving Rochdale. Stokoe obliged the press, with whom he generally had a good relationship, by allowing himself to be photographed marching away from Spotland on Monday, 23 June 1980, a bulging holdall in his hand. 'The reason I held back [before leaving] was that I didn't want to hinder the club's re-election application,' he said. He had also wanted to see how much was raised by the public appeal for funds. David Wrigley conceded that, 'the number of donations received has been disappointing'. Stokoe had told the board that, while he wished for £50,000, he could have brought in enough players with £30,000. The appeal had fallen considerably short of this figure. 'The last few months have been a nightmare,' said Stokoe. 'I am not a miracle worker. I hope that Rochdale find the miracle they are looking for, but I know in my heart that I cannot do the job they require. I don't think there is any doubt that it will be the end if they have to apply for re-election again next season.'

Stokoe revealed that he had been working without a contract. 'I have no other job lined up, as some people might think, and at the moment I am not bothered about another job. This is such a sickener,' he said. Les Barlow was sad to see him depart. 'I got on okay with Bob. He had a difficult time of it,' he said. 'He came in and was viewed as the saviour of the club but it never took off for him. He had a poor squad to work with. I heard he had a breakdown after he left Rochdale, which wouldn't surprise me.' David Wrigley had also been fond of Stokoe, with whom he sometimes played golf. 'I liked Bob very much. The relationship between a manager and directors is always a difficult one to steer but I found him to be a delightful man,' he said. At the meeting a few days earlier, Graham Morris had not been forewarned of Stokoe's intention. 'I saw Stokoe in the paper walking out and I thought, "Oh, Graham – what have you let yourself in for?"'

On the other side of Manchester, the prosperous side, the officials of Altrincham were seething. They felt Stokoe had deliberately misled League chairmen into believing he would stay at Spotland, when he had already decided to move on. Their case was taken up by Jim Thompson, chairman of the APL. 'I would seriously pose the question to those in the higher echelons of football as to whether Mr Stokoe's behaviour is not tantamount to bringing the game into disrepute,' he said. He called on the Football League to take action. Typically, Stokoe gave a firm rebuttal to the allegation. 'This chap is totally out of order,' he said. 'He has made a slur on my character and I shall have to consider legal action.' He said he had not done any lobbying on behalf of Rochdale and always intended to see what budget was available before resolving to stay on or not as manager. The Football League did not take any action against either Rochdale AFC or Bob Stokoe. After leaving the club, one of the few people Stokoe kept in touch with was Andrew Hindle. He sent his former chairman a pair of FA Cup final tickets every year.

A shortage of money at Rochdale AFC had been a theme covered ad nauseam in the *Rochdale Observer*, back to the club's formation in 1907. The articles in the summer of 1980, however, had more urgency, more anxiety, than ever before. The opening paragraphs in front-page lead stories running over two consecutive issues told it straight: 'Rochdale soccer club's precarious hold on Football League status slipped nearer the brink when Bob Stokoe quit as manager on Monday' and 'A question mark hangs over Rochdale Football

Club's ability to survive without the support of Rochdale people.' Elsewhere, Rochdale was referred to as a 'crisis club' and 'debt-ridden'. Rochdale, the town, was similarly on its knees. Round-the-clock working in the mills had become a four-day week, to three, two, one, gone. The town's other main source of work, the engineering industry, was just a few years behind textiles in its sharp spiral downwards. The men in blue overalls no longer did overtime and there were constant whispers of redundancies. The club, with its various if fluid board members, had already mined the handful of people in the town with enough surplus wealth and interest in either football or Rochdale. There was no more to be had.

Les Barlow regularly saw his stories running on both the back and front pages of the *Rochdale Observer* as he combined the roles of a news, business and sports reporter to relate the discord at Spotland. His job was made easier by the fact that he had literally become embedded at the club. A former railway booking clerk, he had started out in journalism working part-time for a freelance based in Heywood. Until the advent of the internet and closure of hundreds of newspapers, most towns had a freelance who could eke out a living covering sports, magistrates' courts and tip-offs from emergency workers. He joined the *Heywood Advertiser* before a move to the sports desk at the *Rochdale Observer*, reporting primarily on Rochdale. His stint covering the club coincided with a period of homelessness when dry rot was discovered at his house in Heywood and it had to be virtually rebuilt. In his mid-30s, he began living in the social club at Spotland, bedding down each night on the bench seats in the concert room. 'It made sense, really. I was up there such a lot anyway. No one bothered me. I just got on with it.' He became de facto steward and was at the club on memorable nights such as the wedding reception when the bride left with the best man. Another time, a function described by Barlow as 'a dirty do' was held at Christmas by a local building firm. The police arrived and he thought he was going to be admonished for staying open all afternoon. Instead, they inquired as to the 'quality' of the strippers and thanked him for housing most of Rochdale's ne'er-do-wells in one place rather than having them dispersed through town centre pubs.

Most nights Barlow ambled round to Cockley's Chippy in Willbutts Lane, the street adjacent to the ground, for his evening meal before moving on to The Church pub for a pint or two. Inevitably, he soon found himself in several semi-official roles at the club. He was caretaker. He helped run the supporters' club. He edited the match programme. He didn't drive, so had to catch a train to Todmorden, ten miles away, to leave copy with the printer. 'You can't avoid it at a small club, you just get on with it,' he said.

When fans called at the ground answering the various pleas for help, Barlow was often the first person they met. 'Despite the club being in the shit on and off the field, it felt like a family club with a real sense of camaraderie. The ground was a mess but people mucked in and carried out repairs,' he said. One ill-founded assignment saw volunteers dig over the pitch and remove loose stones ready for the arrival of topsoil and grass seed. The stones were bagged up and left behind the away end at Pearl Street. 'The police turned up and asked us if we'd all gone mad,' said Barlow. 'We were due to play Blackpool and the police said we'd kindly prepared a load of missiles for them to chuck at the Dale supporters. We had to shift every single bag.'

Within days, a replacement for Bob Stokoe was announced. Peter Madden, who had assisted Doug Collins and Stokoe, stepped forward. The rhetoric matched the size of the man. 'There is no question of us not starting the new season in the Football League,' he insisted. He was a fighter, he said, and determined to 'have a real go'. Madden, born in October 1934, had been raised in a deprived area of Bradford. One of six siblings, he was streetwise and as a teenager had hustled at snooker halls, passing on winnings to his parents. His father, a mill worker, suffered stomach ulcers and was often unable to work, so his mother did three jobs to support the family. Madden joined Rotherham United. On one of his first days at Millmoor he mistakenly walked into the first team's dressing-room. He was told to clear off but, as he did so, he told them to save a peg for him because he would be back. He made his debut in April 1956 and played more than 300 times, mainly as a centre-back, before closing his career at Bradford Park Avenue and Aldershot.

Most match reports from Madden's playing days make reference to his physique. 'Tall and built like the side of a house' reads one, and another, 'he enjoys a hard game of soccer like most people enjoy a thick steak'. Among the football fraternity he was regarded as a man of integrity, a gentleman, but still willing to stand his corner if picked upon. As a player he was regarded as much more than a mere 'stopper'. He had good technique and was strong with both feet. During his decade at Rotherham United he had been linked with several top clubs. He had a deep affection for Rotherham United – which rankled with some at Rochdale who felt he expressed it too often – but still had regular disagreements with the board when his desire to move to bigger clubs was thwarted.

He was sent off only once in his playing days, in what Bryon Butler of the *News Chronicle* dubbed the 'Clash of the Beefy Six-footers'. Madden had been marking Alfie Biggs of Bristol Rovers in a league match in September 1960. The players clashed and Madden took hold of Biggs in a headlock. As he set about him, Madden fractured a bone in his right wrist. Butler wrote that, 'This was the worst brawl I have ever seen mar the good name of football. Fists, one or two lesser known wrestling moves and even heads were used.'

Madden, while manager at Darlington, had a similar clash in the early-1970s with Harry Gregg, the Swansea manager and former Manchester United goalkeeper. The match had become heated and Gregg was calling on his players to play more aggressively, to the point of recklessness. 'Calm down, you mad Irish bastard,' shouted Madden. Gregg was furious and, after the match, kicked in wooden panels in the away dressing-room. He then hunted down Madden, who was enjoying a Mackeson in the boardroom. Madden asked him to wait until he'd finished his drink and then the two men set about each other in an anteroom. Madden landed the first punch and was quickly on top of Gregg. George Tait, Darlington's chairman, beseeched them to stop but it was Madden's wife, Christine, who dragged him away. Gregg, widely regarded as one of football's hard men, phoned Madden on the Monday afterwards and apologised.

Madden revealed that he would be shopping around for 'free transfers' but they would still incur a cost. The players would receive a £250 signing fee and another £250 was required for administration and insurance. He signed Eugene Martinez and Alan Jones from Bradford City; Peter Burke from Halifax Town and Barry Wellings from York City. Madden expected to lose Eric Snookes to Torquay United, who had offered £25,000 for him; money the board was keen to acquire. Snookes spent three days in Devon, meeting club officials and viewing potential houses to buy. He had asked for a £5,000 signing-on fee and £200 per week, almost double his wage at Rochdale. 'It seemed a lot to ask at the time,' he said. 'But it was a different world down there. The houses were two or three times more expensive than they were in Rochdale.' He was offered a signing-on fee of £2,500 and advised by the chairman to convert a room in the house to rent to lodgers or tourists; it would help pay the mortgage. Madden phoned him the next day and Snookes made a gentleman's agreement to re-sign for Rochdale. The phone rang immediately afterwards. It was a director of Torquay reporting that the board would meet Snookes's terms. 'I told him it was too late and I'd agreed to sign for Rochdale. Well, to sign for Peter Madden. He was straight as a die, Pete, and I had a great loyalty to him. He'd done things he needn't have done, like taking me in his car to visit my wife in hospital after she'd given birth.'

## Chapter Twelve

# A Hammer and a Bag of Nails

'New face on the board' whispered the three-paragraph news piece in the *Rochdale Observer* of 13 August 1980. A man who was to play a huge part in the future of Rochdale AFC was revealed beneath the smallest font size appropriate for a headline. He was David Kilpatrick, aged 36, a 'granite merchant of Littleborough'. He had been persuaded to join the board by the social butterfly, John Faulks. 'David has a hell of a personality and is a very astute businessman. I knew he would be ideal for the board,' said Faulks. The pair had met when Faulks acted on behalf of the Kilpatrick family in the sale of land close to the family home. 'John and his pal David Wrigley kept asking me to join the board but I wasn't interested. As a Manchester United fan, I thought I'd have no credibility with Rochdale supporters,' said Kilpatrick.

He was eventually stirred by their enthusiasm. 'The club was clearly dying on its feet. The ground was an absolute disgrace and John was among this group of relatively young people anxious to do something about it. I don't think John and the rest of them were in a position to stand their corner financially, which is why he wanted others to help. He was a likeable bloke who you knew, straight off, would never be anything other than honourable,' he said. Kilpatrick did not sense that Wrigley had the same emotional attachment to the club. 'He was more measured than John. He weighed things up and if he got an opportunity, he went for it. Don't get me wrong, though, he did his bit for the club,' he said. Kilpatrick was soon privy to Wrigley's capacity for drinking. 'He could drink but so could I, back then. He was good fun. He had a sense of humour and was very personable. He never got silly or antagonistic in drink.'

Kilpatrick enjoyed their stories of life at Spotland. 'They were telling me they were planning to put concrete terracing in front of the Main Stand. It was something I knew a little bit about, so I asked how many cubic yards they'd ordered, how they were going to shift it and how long they thought it would take to set. They didn't have a clue. I thought, "If they can't sort out something as basic as putting in some concrete, what the fuck are they going to do with the club?" To their credit, they had seen that the old board had allowed it to fall apart and decay, and things needed changing.'

His first visit to Spotland had come at some point in the 1960s. One Saturday afternoon Manchester United were playing away and Kilpatrick was anxious to know the score. 'It wasn't like today when you can find out on your phone or the telly. On this particular day, I couldn't get near a radio. I realised Rochdale were at home and decided I'd drive there at half-time and find out the score.' He assumed, much as they did at most grounds, that there would be letters on the perimeter fence corresponding to particular games, showing the scores underneath. He paid at the turnstile but could not see any of these letters, once inside the ground. 'I asked someone and he said they used to do it but not anymore. Bloody great, I thought, they do it everywhere else but not at fucking Rochdale.' He left the ground immediately and has no memory of who the opponents were or even the year.

He had next returned in January 1976 when Rochdale played Norwich City in an FA Cup third-round replay. The match ended as a 0-0 draw, but Rochdale played with great heart against top-tier opponents, mounting wave after wave of attacks on a muddy pitch. More than 8,000 had turned up – almost five times greater than Rochdale's average league attendance at the time – with everyone packed tightly together and singing themselves hoarse. The game became part of local sporting folklore for many years afterwards, fans rueing the missed chances and recalling the great saves made by Kevin Keelan, the Norwich goalkeeper. Kilpatrick, although he enjoyed the match, had felt no emotion or connection that would compromise his allegiance to Manchester United. He continued to watch United through the 1970s, but became slowly disillusioned. 'I was walking out of the ground one day and all these fans were spitting on everyone below, including fellow United fans. They were doing it for the "fun" of it but it was absolutely appalling. I used to leave my car on a car park at White City and when I got back to it after one match, it had been damaged,' he said. He also witnessed hooliganism several times in the vicinity of Old Trafford. 'The whole image of football in the 1970s was awful and I decided I'd had enough,' he said.

Kilpatrick agreed formally to join the Rochdale board after he and his wife Gillian had spent an evening out with John Faulks and his wife Joan at the Old Bridge Inn, Ripponden, just over the Lancashire–Yorkshire border from Rochdale. 'It was a rather smart place and we'd downed a few tonics when I finally said I'd give it a go,' he said.

\* \* \*

After taking a family holiday in Saint-Raphaël on the Côte d'Azur, Graham Morris returned to Rochdale with renewed energy to set about the club's accounts. Most nights after work, he drove to Spotland and carried boxes of files and folders into his car. 'The books were okay in that nothing untoward was going on. The problem was that hardly any money was coming in,' he said. 'We'd sold a few season tickets and had a little bit from the lottery, but that was about it. It's always difficult in the close season when you're not getting any income from matches.' He could see immediately that the club had received regular amounts of money from Andrew Hindle, usually as payments of £5,000 or £10,000. Importantly, there were no asterisks against such entries or accompanying letters of condition that might indicate that they were loans or involved caveats. They had stood purely as donations and the club had used the money to pay creditors.

Rochdale drew their opening game of the 1980/81 season away at Stockport County. Kilpatrick, for better or worse – he's not sure – caught 'the bug' that afternoon: the condition whereby one's mood, sense of wellbeing and outlook on life is fastened to the fortunes of a football club. He had long been a Manchester United supporter, of course, but this was different – all the more intense for being smaller, more personal than anything offered at Old Trafford. He remembers the banter with 'a couple of characters' – Alan Kirk, Stockport's president, and Dragan Lukic, the chairman, and feeling immediately at home in the boardroom. Rochdale had played well, twice taking the lead. Mark Hilditch scored after being put through by Eric Snookes, and Dave Esser restored the lead a few minutes before half-time.

'I remember it clearly. Getting a draw at Stockport then was quite an achievement and it made me feel tremendous,' said Kilpatrick. 'It wasn't quite a Damascene moment but my absolute passion catapulted into the Dale. I recall the feeling I had when Mark Hilditch scored. It was as if someone had suddenly switched on a light.' That evening, he went with friends to an Indian restaurant. 'I couldn't stop talking, telling everyone what a fantastic day I'd had,' he said.

Although he was only eight years old, Michael Kilpatrick began accompanying his dad to games at Spotland. 'My early memories are of the general air of dilapidation,' he said. 'The buckets placed in the reception area to catch water leaks were particularly striking. There was a lady who used to operate a big tea urn via a hatch. The boardroom always seemed a busy, boozy, smoke-filled place. There was an ice bucket in the shape of an old-style lace-up brown football on the bar. The directors' wives had a separate ladies' room for socialising in. I used to watch games from the paddock to the left of the tunnel and dugouts. Most of all, I remember it being a friendly place with people wanting to muck in and keep things going.'

Another child who visited the club regularly with his dad was Mark Brierley, the son of ex-director, Rod Brierley. 'I always enjoyed being able to get into places that fans weren't able to go. There was a distinctive smell to the place, a mixture of liniment and cigarette and cigar smoke,' he said. Christian Morris also began accompanying his dad, Graham. 'If I'm being honest, it was boring. I was football mad and keen on playing. Sitting down watching was not really on my agenda,' he said. 'I used to sit with my mum because dad was in the directors' box. My first experience panned out pretty much like every experience week after week. I had to sit in the ladies' room which, as a young boy surrounded by old women, was completely tedious. The football was always terrible and we lost game after game. There was definitely a drinking culture where the directors, home and away, all tended to stay for a session after the match. Obviously, I can see the appeal now, but for a young lad I wanted to be running around playing.'

Christian's sister, Helen Morris (now Thompson), remembers being under strict instruction to be on best behaviour, which meant no shouting or cheering from the directors' box, only polite clapping. 'We accessed the box via a rickety wooden staircase which would undoubtedly be condemned by health and safety these days. The box itself was equally decrepit but it didn't deter us. We were proud to be there,' she said. 'I attended home and away games with my parents and even worked voluntarily during school holidays in the club's commercial department. That sounds very official but, in reality, it consisted of a pokey back office.' Occasionally, the directors were the subject of hostility from supporters. 'I found this very hurtful and wanted to defend my dad but, of course, couldn't,' she said. 'I accepted that it was to be expected given he had assumed responsibility and was therefore accountable. But it struck me how little fans realised what hard work went on behind the scenes, which was obvious to us when dad was away from home night after night at board meetings.'

Rochdale began the season well and after six games had a chance to go second if they could win away at Hereford United. They lost 3-0 and it was the first time Kilpatrick had felt the cold, harsh shock of a Rochdale defeat. A few weeks later he was lifted again when Rochdale recorded the same score-line, but in their favour against Wigan Athletic. Freddie Pye, the scrap-metal millionaire, was Wigan's chairman at the time and Bobby Charlton, a director. 'After the game the pair of them had faces like slapped arses. It was great,' said Kilpatrick.

The departing chairman Andrew Hindle asked if he could meet the two newcomers, Morris and Kilpatrick. They agreed to see him before a Rochdale home match, at the Tim Bobbin, a shabby pub on the outskirts of the town centre. They assumed there was less chance of being seen by fans away from the Spotland side of town. 'I thought Hindle was a very cold fish,' said Morris. 'I did not take to him at all. He wasn't like the others on the board who were more sociable and easy-going.' Hindle was obviously concerned about the money he had invested in the club, but admits he travelled to see them 'more in hope than realism'. 'Hindle asked us, "What are you going to do financially?"' said Kilpatrick. 'I didn't know whether he was asking for his money back or wanting to know if we were going to put anything in. Either way, the answer was, "not a lot". He'd obviously started putting money in and realised it was a great big bloody colander. I can imagine him thinking that we were a pair of upstarts and what had we done at that point for the club, compared to him?' said Kilpatrick. Morris, having perused the club's accounts, was aware that Hindle had paid around £75,000 into the club on a drip-drip basis. 'I think he'd realised it was goodbye to that money and he wasn't going to get it back. Once you start putting money into a football club, you have to keep pedalling. I think he'd seen how much Fred [Ratcliffe] had put in over the years, panicked and bailed out.'

Kilpatrick had no doubt that the ground sale amounted to a de facto insurance policy for Hindle, which had created a clear conflict of interest. As chairman of a football club he would want it to remain in the Football League, but had Rochdale not been re-elected and gone out of business,

Hindle had a mandate to sell the ground, most likely at a reasonable profit. 'It was noticeable that Hindle did not canvass for us to get back in the League [Hindle did canvass on behalf of the club, though it is impossible to gauge to what degree and is ultimately subjective] – it was Freddie who did that,' said Kilpatrick. He could understand why Hindle, probably with the support of Wrigley, had acted in such a way. 'They had done quite a lot and it was getting more and more depressing. The ground was an absolute disgrace and gates were down to about 900. They probably thought, "If this was a horse, we'd shoot it." I don't think for one minute that Hindle set out originally to make money from seeing Rochdale go out of the League and then selling off the ground. He might have been drawn closer to the idea as time went on, I suppose. Initially, he had probably wanted to make a name for himself as a football person. I think he wanted to do okay at Rochdale, to use us as a stepping-stone, and then get on the board at, say, Bolton Wanderers. Manchester United may have been on his horizon. In his mind it was a quick fix – move the job along and then get out. I have no doubt whatsoever that on Day One his plans were absolutely honourable. There was nothing philanthropic about it, though. He was putting money in and realised it was a never-ending hole and was trying to salvage something from a disaster. They wanted some security on their money. Hindle had no great loyalty to the football club, why should he? The one asset was the land and in some ways I'm not knocking it. If I had put £200,000 into Rochdale I would want to cover my arse. Taking ownership of the ground made commercial sense even if it was wrong for Rochdale AFC,' he said.

On his part, Hindle insisted he had no designs of a life in the boardrooms of football clubs. 'It wasn't in my mind at all. I didn't have any delusions of grandeur. I was not a soccer man [he later became chairman of West Hartlepool rugby club]. Rochdale was different because it was my hometown club,' he said. He had built up a relationship with Bolton Wanderers because the head office of his business was in the town. 'They asked me along two or three times a season. George Warburton from the famous baking family was chairman at the time and it was very much a closed shop.'

While Hindle's period at the club would later be viewed by some fans with scepticism, Kilpatrick offered a different opinion. 'He was possibly at the vanguard of your commercially-minded entrepreneur looking at a football club from a totally different perspective – no longer an institution. Why should football clubs be any different to a normal commercial proposition, subject to the vagaries of the market? He may have been before his time. He might have had contingency plans had the ground been sold, having us playing at Bury or somewhere like that,' he said. Only two English clubs, Port Vale (1950) and Southend United (1955), had moved to new grounds in the 30-year period up to 1980. 'You just didn't do it at that time,' said Kilpatrick. 'But it has happened many times since and it's no longer a big deal. No one could have imagined Arsenal leaving Highbury, the Clock End and all that crap, but now everyone is used to them being at the Emirates. And no one mentions Maine Road anymore when they talk about Manchester City,' he added.

Unknown to everyone, though Graham Morris had suspected it, Hindle's company Euroway was in financial trouble which was why he no longer had the funds to underwrite a football club. Hindle's principal contact at Satra, Nigel Hall-Palmer, had suffered a heart attack and been forced to leave the company. His replacement – 'an unpleasant bloke' in Hindle's words – changed the policy and rather than 'warehousing' cars with Euroway, he went direct to dealers. 'I had a rolling deal with Satra and in my naivety I thought this meant it was an ongoing arrangement but when it suited them they brought it to an end. I was obviously shattered,' said Hindle. 'It didn't quite happen overnight. They told me it was coming. I tried to cut down overheads but I had all these rented sites on long-term leases. It upset me and I was depressed for a while but I'm the type of person who gets back up again.' The manufacture of Ladas had also been hit by a range of issues at the AvtoVAZ plant in Russia including strikes and rumours of corruption stretching to the Kremlin.

On 27 November 1980, it was announced that a receiver had been called in to Euroway Car Centre. Grahame Watts of Touche, Ross and Co revealed that Spotland was listed as one of the company's assets. He said Euroway was being sold as a 'going concern' but any such deal would not include the ground (it clearly had no use in the trading of cars) which meant it was technically up for sale and the proceeds might be used to pay creditors. 'I am exploring all avenues to find a buyer for the ground,' said Watts. David Wrigley reminded worried fans that whoever bought it was subject to the term of the lease which stipulated that the club could play on the pitch and have use of all facilities for 99 years in exchange for an annual rent. 'They were worrying times, all the same,' said Kilpatrick. 'We didn't know whether the administrator or someone else was going to turn up with a hammer and bag of nails, board the place up and close us down.'

\* \* \*

A few weeks before Christmas 1980, half the workforce of TBA Industrial Products, 700 people, were put on short time.

Brook Motors, an electric motor manufacturer based in Queensway, Rochdale, closed down with the loss of 100 jobs. 'With this rate of engineering redundancies in Rochdale, one wonders what the future will be for the town,' said Jim Calverley, Rochdale secretary of the Amalgamated Union of Engineering Workers.

\* \* \*

The board of directors at Rochdale AFC was increased once more to six in January 1981 when Cyril David Walkden (usually known by his middle name, David) and William (Bill) Alfred Carlisle Dronsfield joined. Walkden, nicknamed 'Woggy', was well-known in lacrosse circles, and had played for Great Britain in the 1948 London Olympics. He later captained and managed the England lacrosse team. He had revealed more home-spun skills to the Rochdale contingent at a garden party held at the home of John Faulks when he won the welly-throwing competition. He was a Manchester City fan and had organised testimonial seasons for several of their players. A cricket lover, he supported Lancashire and played for Sale Cricket Club. He was a director of the family firm, Walkden, Son & Co, which manufactured tin boxes at Atlas Works in Moston, north Manchester. He had recently moved to Castleton in Rochdale. Friends described him as 'cheerful' and 'enthusiastic' and said that he was 'a great organiser'.

Bill Dronsfield was another brought to the fold by John Faulks. He was managing director of Dronsfield Bros but made for a reluctant industrialist. 'He preferred the rural life,' said Faulks. 'He was living over Skipton way and was much happier in the countryside.' Dronsfield had inherited the company, which had been set up in 1860 in Oldham, from his father, James Dronsfield. Among its patents was a device for milking cows and a lawnmower known as 'the Swallow' but its core business was the manufacture of textile machinery. At its height in the early-1960s it had employed more than 300 people. 'The family owned property in and around Oldham and I was involved in selling it off for them,' said Faulks. 'I think James wanted Bill to be a captain of industry but he wasn't interested. I suppose he was the black sheep of the family.' Before Dronsfield joined the board, Faulks had spied him standing among the fans in the enclosure in front of the Main Stand; it made him an obvious candidate for directorship.

Both Butterworth and Faulks were delighted to see new additions to the board; they wanted to spend less time at the club. Butterworth would soon find himself in the midst of a 'messy divorce' which inevitably sapped his energy and resources. A few weeks after the appointment of the new directors, Joe Stoney, the club's vice-president, died at his home in Bamford, aged 68. He had been ill during the Easter period but had still managed to see Rochdale beat York City and then lose away at Halifax Town. He had been a director for 25 years. During the Second World War he had served in Italy and North Africa and had risen to the rank of major.

The main aim of the 1980/81 season – to avoid having to apply for re-election – was achieved with four games remaining. Madden had assembled the squad over a few weeks when, before the season began, there had been mention of Rochdale possibly not fulfilling their fixtures or fielding a team made up of amateurs. Attendances had risen to more than 2,700 per game and they finished in a creditable 15th place, seven points above the re-election zone. As recognition of his achievement, Madden was granted a three-year contract, an unusually high level of commitment in lower-league football. 'What he did for Rochdale and with that side was genius,' said Kilpatrick. 'He deserves every credit. I did not realise at the time how well he did with just 14 professionals. He was fit and looked after himself and was an honest, trustworthy guy.' Kilpatrick can still name the regular team that turned out for Madden.

* * *

Graham Morris approached the accounts of Rochdale AFC as he might any of his company's clients. He painstakingly set up a balance sheet in longhand, jotting down every payment (referees and linesmen, gatekeepers and police, laundry, etc. and receipt (transfer fees, ground advertising, sales of programmes, etc.) The statement of accounts for the year ending 31 May 1980 – figures were routinely released a year in arrears – showed a loss of £91,956. The main increase on the previous year had been spending an additional £65,000 on wages and £22,000 on transfer fees. When these figures were made public, Wrigley told the press: 'Following the Great Escape in the 1979/80 season, the club was flushed with a small amount of success and decided to take a gamble on more success by spending money on players. Unfortunately the gamble failed and consequently there was more expense than ever on salaries and expenses.' On a more optimistic note, Morris reported that the figures up until May 1981, although still to be finalised, would show a loss of 'only' £35,000.

A social scene fell together comprising the directors, their wives and friends. David Wrigley held a party at his house to mark Pancake Day. Graham Morris hosted garden parties at his home in Bamford. Ron Atkinson, the manager of Manchester United at the time, was a near-neighbour and sometimes called round with his wife Maggie to help raise funds. 'One time, we all got round the piano and

Ron was singing for us. He has a lovely voice,' said Beryl, Morris's wife. Two well-known musicians were also living in Bamford – Lovelace Watkins, the American singer dubbed 'the Black Sinatra', and Graham Gouldman of 10CC who wrote the song *From Rochdale to Ocho Rios* about living there. 'There was a good team spirit. All the players seemed to be genuine people and Peter Madden got the best out of them,' said Morris.

John Faulks and David Wrigley were asked to try to secure loans for the club from banks in town. The pair was granted appointments with bank managers but a pattern soon emerged. The meetings seemed extremely positive but, within a few days, the loan was invariably refused. 'We were finding it impossible to find banking facilities. I remember we went to this peculiar Middle Eastern bank on Drake Street and even they wouldn't take us on. I started to ask around and was told that so long as David Wrigley was on the board, we would not find a bank,' said Faulks. He was hearing rumours across town, from the Blue Ball in Norden to the bar of the Broadfield Hotel, that Wrigley was not as honourable as might be expected of someone in such a respected profession. 'A friend of mine worked in a bank in town and he told me that one day he'd gone in to see the manager and he had his head in his hands and his elbows on the desk,' said Faulks. 'My pal asked him what was wrong and he said, "David Wrigley has just been in."'

Faulks arranged to meet Wrigley for lunch at Rochdale Golf Club, hoping for a candid talk where Wrigley might reveal all. 'I told him he'd have to resign from the football club and he just said, "Why?" I told him the reason we were having all these doors shut in our faces was because of his reputation.' Wrigley responded blithely, unable to see that there was an issue. 'That was David, very ostrich-like,' said

Faulks. 'He didn't think he was doing anything wrong. He seemed to think that it would all work out fine in the end and what was the fuss about.' Faulks was worried, too, that his professional standing might be tarnished if he continued to associate with Wrigley. 'I'd never doubted him until then. Then again, I believe people and don't expect them to be ducking and diving,' he said. 'He was my friend. I was not joined at the hip to David but we were close. We went on holiday together and played golf a great deal.'

Trevor Butterworth, much the same as Faulks, was becoming uneasy. 'I was hearing stuff about David,' he said. 'The manager of a local building society came into my shop and said he was having trouble with him, something about the payment of a house being bought by a young lady not going through. Looking back, I never tried to read anyone back then. I just got on with it. I think there might have been a lot going on behind the scenes.' He appreciated it might be merely rumours about Wrigley but there seemed rather a lot of them; they were starting to add up. Butterworth was also becoming disillusioned with other board members. 'I was a novice as a businessman compared to Wrigley and Faulks. I thought I was going to learn a lot from them, but they disappointed me. They didn't seem to have any common sense. I remember John Faulks got someone in to fix the leaking roof over the dressing-room. The builder said £1,300 and Faulks said that was fine. It was way too much and they had to stop the job halfway through. I don't think he would have done that if it was his own money he was spending.'

Morris and Kilpatrick, who had not known each other before joining the board, found themselves increasingly drawn together. Their personalities were disparate, but they held similar views, though reached in different ways. Kilpatrick liked to sound off, test an argument and hunt down the opinion of everyone in the room, even if contrary to his own. He usually ended up back where he had started, even more convinced of his own rightness. Morris was more reflective. He spoke in shorter sentences or, as if saving energy, would make a facial expression instead, a wince to show disagreement, a small smile to assent. They put the work in, delivered, and quickly formed the heartbeat of the club. Between them, they identified three areas that required immediate attention – reconciling the old board members financially, resolving the issue of ground ownership and levering David Wrigley from the board. And then they had to resuscitate a near-dead football club.

## Chapter Thirteen

# Team Ethic, Structure and Discipline

All the various board members and ex-board members (now given honorary vice-presidential status) mixed well on match days but there were still niggles, disagreements and wrangling over power and control. Teddy Lord of the original board was known for straight talking. He had something on his mind. He put it to Kilpatrick: 'When are you lads going to put some money in?' The newcomer was flummoxed. 'I gulped and walked away, looking for another drink,' he said. 'Teddy was right. I can't knock him or any of the old directors on that score. That's what they did in their day – they divvied up for players' wages on a Thursday or Friday. That was, in its way, a policy whereas ours was to look at ways we could generate money commercially, so we didn't have to do that.'

Supporters assume that directors gift money to football clubs. In fact, this is a factor in forming a threshold, a 'them and us' situation. Fans imagine that they are barred from the boardroom and a greater stake in their club because they have insufficient funds to contribute. They are unaware of the sums involved, but assume them to be substantial. In practice, certainly in the lower divisions, directors, as a rule, do not donate as they might to a charity. The complexity of ownership is the principal reason for this. At most clubs it remains difficult to substantiate overall ownership because shares are distributed widely among fans or factions. Under such an arrangement, why would anyone or a group of individuals wish to invest heavily in a business over which they did not have ultimate control? Directors more usually issue loans or buy shares which, although unlikely, might one day pay a dividend should there be an upturn at the club. The *possession* of wealth, if not the actual spending of it, is a prime factor in boardrooms because it provides brokerage with banks. Most clubs routinely sense that they are on the cusp of a windfall, whether from a cup run or league success or selling a star player. A metaphorical bridge stretching from now until then – a loan, in other words – might be required to cover the workaday running costs until that pay-day arrives. Wealthy directors are able to offer either personal or 'joint and several' (where responsibility is shared) guarantees on the club's behalf and secure that vital loan.

Many assumed that Hindle, in the guise of Euroway, had bought the ground with a one-off sum, distinct from previous cash he had put in. Graham Morris, after examining the books, saw that Hindle had included all previous injections of cash against the purchase. Behind the scenes, Hindle was still hopeful of retrieving the money he had put into the club. Solicitors were instructed on both sides to explore how this finance had been introduced. Nightingales, of Deansgate, Manchester, represented the club; an out-of-town company was chosen specifically to minimise rumours circulating within Rochdale. In a letter from Nightingales to Hindle of June 1981, it was pointed out that the initials B.A.H (Brian Andrew Hindle) were placed next to most of these cash introductions as if they were personal, rather than payments from a company account. The letter read: 'We can only presume that after Mr Hindle's dismal failure at running the club and his financial difficulties he found it to his advantage to change the facts and state that Euroway Car Centre had loaned money to Rochdale AFC.' A loan rather than a donation would have meant the club was obligated to return the money. Nightingales also argued that these tranches of cash were 'past consideration', a legal term defined as an act done before a contract was made which, therefore, could not be introduced later as a valid concern.

The bills had started to mount again and the new directors realised they would need to inject cash into the club, after all. Graham Morris recognised that this might form leverage with Fred Ratcliffe et al and help wrestle power, finally, from the old boys. Ratcliffe had been imploring everyone to 'get round the table and sort the job out' so Morris appealed to his vanity and called a meeting at the Crimble, returning the original board members to their favourite haunt.

Graham Morris spelled out the situation in grave terms. Tall, upright, dressed in a dark suit and capable of a sigh or two, Morris played the undertaker well. He said the club was struggling under the onslaught of debts and on the brink of closing. The only way to save it was an immediate input of cash. He said the current board members were willing to do this on the proviso that the old board wrote off the debts they were each owed by the club. In exchange for this magnanimous gesture, he said the club would issue each of them with shares to the value of £5,000 or, in Ratcliffe's case, £10,000. In all likelihood – if the club continued to perform badly – these shares would be of no value, paying nil dividends. Still, they were, in effect, raffle tickets should the club improve and move to profitability.

Morris had undertaken a masterful piece of brinkmanship. By insisting the old board write off their debts before the new board introduced extra money, he was shrewdly placing responsibility for the club's survival with the old board. Would they really want to close down a club they had tended for all those years? 'They didn't jump at it,' said Morris. 'It took a lot of persuasion. Maybe they took the view that if the club did fold they definitely wouldn't get anything, so it was in their interest to get at least something.' In exchange for the shares, each director agreed to write off approximately £50,000 or, in Ratcliffe's case, almost £200,000. Rod Brierley took the longest to agree. He issued the club with a writ for the money he was owed. Morris explained to Brierley that if the club paid him, it wouldn't be fair on the other former directors: they should all be paid too, but that would bankrupt the club. Brierley, Rochdale through-and-through, wouldn't stand for that: he accepted the deal. As promised, the new board pooled their money and raised £17,000 to put into the club's account, for which they received the requisite number of 50p shares. 'The old directors were still offered boardroom facilities, so they could eat and drink with us all but it meant we no longer had this problem of historical debt hanging over us – money we'd always have to find at some point,' said Morris.

On the eve of the 1981/82 season, another new director joined the board: Christopher Martin Dunphy, aged 30. 'If you put your hand up back then, you were in,' said Graham Morris. 'Chris had staged an Elvis Presley memorial night or something like that at the social club. And I think he'd also organised for one of Lisa Stansfield's early groups to play.'

The first game Dunphy had attended at Spotland was as a ten-year-old when he saw them play Peterborough United. The match was abandoned after 33 minutes – he can recall the exact time – because of fog with the score at 1-1. 'I should have got the message there and then,' he said. He was drawn resolutely to the club by the League Cup run of 1961/62 which saw Rochdale reach the final, losing 4-0 to Norwich City on aggregate over two legs.

He became formally involved by organising events at the social club. He held sportsmen's dinners and quizzes. He booked comedians and singers. Tribute acts had not yet been established but Dunphy promoted 'An evening in the memory of John Lennon'. A ticket cost £1.25 and also included an appearance by Phil Sayer of Piccadilly Radio. 'Dale Discos' were held every Wednesday and Saturday through the winter of 1981. The social club was also a regular venue for 'Public Sales'. One of them, held in November 1981, was of ex-rental, refurbished colour televisions. A Grundig 22in cost £79 and a Bush 20in, £49. 'The events earned a lot of revenue for the club. I had no experience at it, but it just takes a few phone calls and you're away,' said Dunphy. He had a shop in Yorkshire Street in the town centre, The Hotspot ('For all your central heating requirements'), from where he sold gas fires and ran a small domestic heating firm. He was also branching out to provide bespoke heating for churches as Christopher Dunphy Ecclesiastical. 'He put in thousands of miles chasing business. He'd sometimes try to tie in visiting churches with our away games,' said Morris. Along with Trevor Butterworth, Dunphy was the only other member of the board who had been a lifelong fan. 'We heard a lot about him walking to matches with a packet of crisps in one hand and a Wagon Wheel in the other,' said David Kilpatrick. Perhaps to his own surprise, Kilpatrick had found himself enjoying life at Spotland. 'It was quite exciting. I remember a night in the Sun Hotel in Littleborough, a good session, with the lads from the supporters' club, Brian Clough, Trevor Lorimer and Colin Smith. It was great fun and I recall thinking we might be on to something here.'

A boardroom shake-up saw Kilpatrick replace David Wrigley as chairman. 'The others didn't fancy it for various reasons and I'm someone who always likes to be in charge of everything, so it made good sense,' said Kilpatrick. Fred Ratcliffe was pleased and told Kilpatrick that he was 'just like him'. 'I was probably a foot taller and wider than Freddie and certainly didn't drink anywhere near as much Scotch or go out as often, but I knew what he meant and took it as a compliment.' Les Barlow noticed an immediate upswing in the mood around the club. 'With Killy, it was, "Come on, we've still got a pitch and a few players, let's get on with it." It was a noticeable contrast from what had gone on before,' he said. John Faulks became vice-chairman and Wrigley remained as a director, albeit on a nominal basis.

David Frank Kilpatrick's background was typical of those who often rose to boardroom level. He had been a boarder from the age of ten at the prestigious Rossall School based on the Fylde Coast, Lancashire. A sister school to Marlborough College, it was established in 1844 to 'provide, at a moderate cost, for the sons of Clergymen and others, a classical, mathematical and general education of the highest class, and to do all things necessary, incidental, or conducive to the attainment of the above objects.' The 'moderate cost' in 2019 for a child from a UK-based family wishing to board at the school on a full-time basis was £35,000.

Despite being among mainly working-class children at his junior school in Littleborough, Kilpatrick, born in September 1943, adapted well to life at Rossall. He became head of house and school vice-captain. 'It's odd to think back, but it didn't bother me one bit moving away from home. I just got on with it. I loved every minute. It was a tremendous environment and I got the best out of being there.' The school laid great emphasis on sport and Kilpatrick excelled. He played squash, fives and tennis. He captained the school hockey team and played for the Second XI cricket team. His main love was rugby union and he played for the first team as lock forward at a competitive level against fellow public schools such as Fettes College in Edinburgh and Sedbergh School in the Yorkshire Dales. 'We were treated like sports professionals really,' he said. 'If you consider rugby union started at public schools, it was of a very high standard. At that time *The Daily Telegraph* had a correspondent solely to cover public schools rugby. They reckoned that if you were outstanding in your university team, you were only three years away from an England cap.'

Kilpatrick passed A-levels in economics, politics and history. He entered the world of work when the financial director of Tate & Lyle, Morton Oliphant, an ex-pupil of Rossall, petitioned the school head teacher Geoffrey Sale about boys who weren't necessarily set on university. 'It wasn't like now where we have about 5,000 universities and everyone is told to get a degree. Companies liked to get you at 18 so they could train you up much earlier,' said Kilpatrick. He joined the sales department at the Tate & Lyle sugar refinery in Love Lane, Liverpool, and moved into a flat in Aigburth. 'The Beatles were having all those hits and Liverpool was a fantastic place to be. We were in the right place at the right time, in the early- to mid-1960s.' said Kilpatrick. Although he visited the Mardi Gras club and The Cavern, Kilpatrick lived a relatively sedate life. 'I'd love to say I had a wild time, but I was fairly boring. I'd have the odd pint and a few fags but I didn't do drugs. It was, shall we say, a very ordered existence.'

As a member of the sales team at Tate & Lyle, Kilpatrick had to seek out new clients and ensure orders were fulfilled. 'There were hundreds of breweries and we supplied bespoke products such as sugar-cane molasses. Jam and jelly manufacturers would want specific sucrose and glucose mixes,' he said. While living in the city, Kilpatrick watched Liverpool and Everton. 'I've stood on the Kop when it's been packed and it's true that when you got a tap on the shoulder you had to move forward a few inches so the bloke behind you could pee,' he said.

Kilpatrick did not play football at Rossall; he didn't have the time. His support of Manchester United had grown over this period, especially after the Munich air disaster in February 1958. He began attending matches at Old Trafford with two former Rossall pupils, John Jenkins, who was the son of the vicar of Stockport, and David Brew of the civil engineering family, AC Brew. Their match-day routine was exhaustive. They would meet in one of the medieval pubs in Shambles Square in the city centre before taking up their positions in the Scoreboard End at Old Trafford. After the match they visited an Indian restaurant in Rusholme – one of the first opened on a stretch of Wilmslow Road which later became known as The Curry Mile. Afterwards, they travelled to Belle Vue Stadium to watch greyhound racing. The evening often ended in the bar at the elegant Midland Hotel where they took nightcaps of gin and tonic, and smoked Black Russian cigarettes. 'It was a long day but a good day,' said Kilpatrick.

The Kilpatrick family wealth had been made in the import of granite used principally for gravestones and monuments. David's grandfather, Isaac Kilpatrick, originally from Scotland, had established the business in Littleborough. Isaac passed the business on to David's father, Frank, and it then went to David. The company's stone yard, where 20 men were employed at its busiest, was next to the family home, a Grade 2 listed hall built in the early- to mid-17th century. Staff able to work in granite were difficult to find in Rochdale, so Isaac Kilpatrick had called at Displaced Persons Camps (later known as Resettlement Camps) based in rural areas throughout the UK. He employed men principally from Eastern Europe who had fled during the Second World War. They moved into rented accommodation in the terraced houses in Rochdale, often with their families. 'It was like the League of Nations,' said Kilpatrick. 'I remember Ukrainians, Poles and Czechs all being in the yard. They were bloody good workers.' One of the men, Eliodor Leishman from Switzerland, hand-carved an eagle from marble which still stands, wings half open, set to fly, next to the communion table at St Andrew's Church in Littleborough.

David Kilpatrick's mother was Ella (Baines), the daughter of a coalminer from Leigh who had died in a pit accident, leaving behind four daughters. 'I've always felt my background has given me a balanced view because I'm from two strains of social class,' he said. In his mid-20s, Kilpatrick was unhappy working within the corporate structure at Tate & Lyle and spoke to his father about joining the family business. 'He was ticking over but there was still a decent living to be made and I much preferred the idea of being a big fish in a small pond,' he said. He had also recently met Gillian Wright, from Formby, at a house-warming party. They married and settled in Rochdale where they had three children, Joanne, Michael and Elizabeth. Kilpatrick's brother, Stuart, nine years younger, set up an undertaking company allied to the family's stonemasonry business.

The chairmanship of a football club suited Kilpatrick. 'It mirrored the values of what I came out of – team ethic, structure and discipline,' he said. 'I'm lucky, I am. I came from that wonderful regime – "Up the House", "Up the School", all that corporate structure and autocracy, which is much the same at a football club except we had seven-eighths of diddly-squat, of course. All the same, I wouldn't have missed it for the world, even if we were on the cliff edge most of the time.' Michael Kilpatrick saw his father at close quarters, in and out of football club boardrooms. 'He enjoyed the network of people he got to know as a result of his involvement with Rochdale. Even at a young age, I could tell he was very much in his element socialising on match days. Because of this, attending matches wasn't an experience I really shared with my dad and perhaps explains why I didn't develop a strong feeling of attachment to the club until many years later.'

In contrast to David Kilpatrick, Graham Morris had a typical white-collar working-class upbringing. Born in July 1941, he had lived with his parents, James and Edna (née Haldane) and brother, Brian, who was ten years older, in a 'very pleasant semi' in Blackley, north Manchester. James Morris had grown up in nearby Ancoats and was 35 when Graham was born, which made him older than most of his friends' fathers. His mother was 33. 'In my mind's eye I see dad reading the paper or doing the gardening. When he was younger, though, he was quite sporty. I still have the trophies he won for sprint races,' said Graham. James Morris had served with the RAF on the Irish border during the Second World War and later worked in pensions as a civil servant in Middleton, a few miles from Blackley. 'I didn't see my dad much when I was very young because he was away in the RAF,' said Graham. 'We were just a normal, law-abiding, rate-paying family and I have happy memories of growing up.'

James Morris regularly watched City and United; football support back then was much less partisan. 'He wanted the Manchester clubs to do well,' said Graham. 'But if he had a leaning it was more towards City.' The first game Graham attended was in April 1955 when City beat Wolverhampton Wanderers 3-0 under the floodlights at Maine Road. Three days later he went again, to see City lose against Blackpool. Both matches attracted almost 50,000 supporters. 'We took some bricks with us in a brown paper bag so that I could stand on them to make sure I could see. I was struck by the vivid colours of the shirts worn by Blackpool and Wolves, how bright and golden they looked. There was no pressure from dad for me to support City but I always felt more at home at Maine Road.'

Morris passed his eleven-plus exam and attended North Manchester Grammar School for Boys. 'I left after doing my O-levels. I felt like I would have been a drain on the family finances if I'd have gone to university,' he said. In his late teens he met his future wife, Beryl Hesketh, who had moved from Ormskirk to Alkrington, when her father took up a job for the Liverpool Victoria insurance company in Manchester. The pair are still married.

Originally unsure of a career path, his sister-in-law suggested accountancy. 'I had no real idea what this involved but called at the youth employment bureau in Deansgate [Manchester] and told them I was interested in it,' he said. Morris was taken on by the accountancy firm Binder Hamlyn, based in St Ann's Square, Manchester.

Most of the work was done laboriously, ink on paper, with very little automation. They had pull-handle comptometers which had to be replenished constantly with rolls of paper.

'It was fairly boring. I'm bloody good at maths so they threw me a cash book and said, "Add that up!"' said Morris. He was employed as an articles clerk where he was trained by the company, studied in the evenings and had to stay with the firm for at least five years. Binder Hamlyn was a long-established company and today, as BDO Global (Binder Dijker Otte), remains a multinational concern. 'I enjoyed working for them. I met a lot of people in a lot of different places,' said Morris. He would travel on the bus with his briefcase and call on companies in and around the city, helping them prepare their accounts. The Manchester Oil Refinery at Trafford Park and the petro-chemical firms at Carrington were on his regular patch.

In 1969 Morris moved with Beryl and their two daughters Helen (two) and Kathryn (new-born) to Norden, Rochdale. They later had a son, Christian. At a house party Morris met a 'rum bugger' called Roderick Wyatt. 'He pulled me to one side at this party – I'd never met him before – and started telling me how difficult it was to make any money from an accountancy practice, how it was all a waste of time. I told him if it was that bad, I'd buy him out,' said Morris. Wyatt had a staff of five based in an office in Drake Street on the outskirts of the town centre. Six months later, he phoned Morris and said he wanted to 'talk turkey'. Morris bought out his share and in January 1973 the company became Roderick Wyatt, Morris. When Wyatt moved on in 1978, Graham Morris took over the company and it later became Wyatt Morris Golland.

\* \* \*

The 1981/82 season began poorly for Rochdale. They won once in the first 12 matches and by mid-October were back in the re-election zone. The fundraising went on with potato pie suppers, quiz nights, sportsmens' dinners, appeals for match sponsors (£345 per game) and, every few weeks or so, fans tipping up the proceeds from whip-rounds they'd done at work or at the pub. One supporter, Tony Lord, called at Butterworth's sports shop and counted out, mainly in change, £125 on the counter. A local soldier on his way to fight in the Falklands War sent a cheque with a note saying it was 'to keep the club going'.

A long-running debt which had invoked several solicitors' letters was settled by David Wrigley in February 1982. He wrote to fellow directors to inform them that he (or it might have been his business) had cleared the £2,500 outstanding to a local tradesman called Suthurst, who had built a sizeable wall at the ground at a total cost of £3,200. 'This was necessary to prevent the Bailiffs taking action and I would like this to be set against my share purchase money,' he wrote.

The club was still in debt, struggling on, but the board had chosen to keep this 'in house' rather than reinforce the club's forlorn image. This policy changed drastically in the spring of 1982 when familiar headlines appeared once more in the *Rochdale Observer* and *Manchester Evening News* – 'Dale on Brink of Folding', 'Cash Crisis Strikes Dale' and 'Dale Could Fold Warns Chairman'. This new appeal was timed to coincide with the forthcoming close season when there would be no gate money coming into the club. Kilpatrick had estimated that £30,000 was needed to keep the club afloat over the summer. Savings were being made within the club. Dick Conner was made redundant from his position as assistant manager; he later became landlord of the Carters Rest pub in Spotland Road, close to the ground. The players drove themselves in their cars to away matches at Tranmere Rovers and Stockport County, to save the club hiring a coach and driver. Director Bill Dronsfield revealed that the players had also been asked to sell lottery tickets on behalf of the club.

The appeal for money was a ruse by Kilpatrick. 'There wasn't a prayer of us resigning our league position,' he said. 'There would have been no point in me going to the *Rochdale Observer* and saying, "Hello chaps, everything is terrific." We needed money and if that meant there was a bit of an element of crying wolf, it had to be.' Graham Morris was at the front line most days, placating creditors. 'We were living on a wing and a prayer,' he said. 'We owed the Inland Revenue for the PAYE. There was a chap there, in Worthing, called Mr Yeo. I was always on the phone to him. I asked him whether he'd like a Cup final ticket but he didn't go for that. He was practically on our Christmas card list.'

A friendly match was organised against Leeds United in March – top-tier clubs often made such gestures back then – and they played most of their first team on the Spotland mud. The match was staged on a Friday night and ended 3-3. Barely any funds were raised: only 1,332 fans turned up, a few hundred fewer than the league average of 1,818. Early in May, a 1-0 defeat at Hull City confirmed that Rochdale would once again finish a season in the re-election zone.

The circumstances of their appeal for re-election were markedly different from 1979/80. This time they had finished 21st, a point from safety, while Crewe Alexandra were 19 points beneath them at the bottom of the league; Crewe were clearly under the greater threat. Incidentally, Rochdale's 1-0 win against them at the end of the season had finished in high drama. Referee George Flint blew the final whistle six minutes too early. 'I lost my watch in the mud,' he said. 'And a Crewe player gave it back to me broken. I had to rely on my second watch and it was wrong. I'm sorry but according to that watch we had played 90 minutes.'

Unlike the sustained campaign mounted by Altrincham two years earlier, the non-League application for 1981/82 bordered on farcical. Runcorn were champions of the APL, and Enfield, the runners-up. Facilities at both clubs failed to meet Football League requirements, so Telford United, in third place, were put forward only two weeks before the AGM of the Football League – they had almost no time to solicit votes. David Kilpatrick had no doubt that Rochdale would be re-elected. 'Chairmen never liked voting for the demise of one of their own. It was absolutely an old pals' act. A club like Oldham, for example, would automatically vote for us. They didn't want to lose their mates from next door,' he said. In the event, Telford received 13 votes compared to Northampton Town's 53; Crewe Alexandra's 50; Scunthorpe United's 48 and Rochdale's 48.

## Chapter Fourteen

# Sleepless Nights

Fans, staff and directors assumed Andrew Hindle had quietly left town, never to be heard of again. He was, however, monitoring the situation at Spotland and eager to have his say. He wrote a letter that ran on the front page of the *Rochdale Observer*:

> I am distressed to learn of the plight of Rochdale AFC, the club of which I used to be chairman. I was prompted to write to you as I feel the sporting public of Rochdale should be totally aware of the events that have led up to the present situation.
>
> When I joined the Dale board, in October 1977, Mr Fred Ratcliffe and friends were running the club which even then was in a very parlous financial state. While the then board's outlook could be called into serious question, those gentlemen deserve unstinting praise for the way in which they put their hands in their pockets to keep the club afloat.
>
> By late 1978, the new regime, or 'Secret Six' as we were known, had taken charge, with myself

at the helm as chairman, but still the nagging demands for sporadic cash injections continued.

Ironically, at that time, I put forward a proposal to the effect that we should enter into a ground-sharing arrangement with Rochdale Hornets, thereby maximising on the use of one stadium. This was rejected as a totally unworkable idea — I need hardly remind you of subsequent happenings at Fulham, Carlisle United, Cardiff City and shortly to be at Charlton Athletic. That move would, in my opinion, have been the saviour of the club but it was not to be.

So the struggle continued and the need for money accelerated. By now, I was funding the club single-handed, until such time as it became of considerable detriment to myself and I resigned as chairman.

Around the same time, you will recall that Bob Stokoe (now flying high with Carlisle) and Jack Butterfield resigned, as did two of my co-directors, Sid Marks and Jim Valentine. The root cause of these departures was money — or the lack of it.

Surely, one cannot have a board of directors at a club like Rochdale who, to a man, are not prepared to contribute a penny-piece towards the survival of the club, and then go to public appeal, as happened in July 1980. Now, 21 months later, the public is again the target of the begging bowl.

For Mr Kilpatrick to say the club does not owe a vast amount of money is wrong. I know, because I speak by virtue of first-hand experience.

Secondly, why indeed was Martinez not sold to Bournemouth? If the club's plight is as serious as we are led to believe, surely £10,000 and a further

£10,000 pledged by contract, would have broken the back of this £30,000 shortfall to which we are asked to subscribe.

But finally, to revert to my main point. Becoming a director of a Fourth Division football club is not about advancing one's status in the locality. Nor even about having a fist full of Cup Final tickets. It is all about putting your money where your mouth is.

Possibly things have changed since I left the scene, and if so, let Mr Kilpatrick enlighten us and tell us to what extent. Then, and only then, would I as a member of the public be prepared to contribute again.

B ANDREW HINDLE
Langness,
The Promenade,
Castletown,
Isle of Man.

A few weeks later, he contributed another letter:

The central theme of my argument is that I am vehemently opposed to the public of Rochdale being called upon to finance the football club unless the present directors are putting their hands in their pockets as was not the case when I was a director of the club.

I am somewhat nonplussed as to why the question of the ground deal has cropped up — my letter certainly did not refer to it. It must be obvious to all and sundry that I have long since ceased to have anything to do with that issue. Indeed, I wonder if that topic has been introduced to divert attention from my main point.

However, I was very encouraged to read a daily newspaper report which assures us that the directors will match any money contributed to the £30,000 fund. This presumably means that the public target is reduced to £15,000 and, on that basis, is attainable. If that is the case I applaud the directors and I only hope that my remarks may have encouraged them to make this generous gesture.

Nothing would give me greater pleasure than to meet representatives of the Supporters' Club again. They are a body of tireless workers, I have the highest regard for. I would welcome a discussion on all aspects of the club's affairs during my term as chairman.

B Andrew Hindle

Graham Morris felt the letters were an unnecessary act of antagonism. 'Why was he attacking David? He didn't really know him,' he said. Kilpatrick had a more benign response. 'At the time Hindle would have felt pretty pissed off. He'd been the only person with any financial muscle,' he said. 'He was King Numero Uno when he joined the board, surrounded by sycophants. If he'd had people like David Kilpatrick and Graham Morris around him, he might have stood a chance. Remember, Graham's opening line is always, "Hang on a minute…" I'm not going to take the moral high ground and say I would have done anything differently in trying to get some of my money back.'

Andrew Hindle said he wrote the letters to 'justify himself'. 'I was getting a lot of criticism and people were

talking about me and getting arsey,' he said. 'The other
directors were not putting their hands in their pockets
and I wanted to tell fans that I had done my whack. I had
a charge on the ground as security for the bank. It was not
asset stripping. I heard people rumour-mongering but there
was no agenda to build properties on there. I felt aggrieved
being portrayed that way when I'd put in such a lot of
money. I was a useful scapegoat for some of the problems
that the club had.' Les Barlow did not believe Hindle had
set out deliberately to 'close Rochdale AFC down' or 'asset
strip' the club – two allegations that circulated the town and
later became wedged firm into folklore. 'I think all these
various directors came into the club with a good heart but
the extent of the financial problems quickly weighed them
down,' he said.

In compliance with League rules, Graham Morris wrote
to Graham Kelly, the secretary of the Football League, on
16 June 1982 and informed him that three directors had
resigned from the board of Rochdale AFC at the AGM
two days earlier: John Faulks, Trevor Butterworth and
Christopher Dunphy. Another, David Wrigley, had left on
11 May. Wrigley, Butterworth and Faulks were the last of
the 'secret six' to leave; their tenure had lasted less than four
years. The club had lost £27,132 in the financial year ending
May 1981, compared with £91,956 the year before. 'It had
come to that time again when we had to say, "Come on
fellas, who is prepared to put some cash into the pot?"' said
Kilpatrick. 'Only four of us did [himself, Morris, Dronsfield
and Walkden] so we had to say to the others that they could
not stay and vote on how you spend money that you have
not put in.' Wrigley was the only reluctant leaver. 'He did
not want to go and give up that power, but equally he did
not want to put any money in,' said Kilpatrick.

Chris Dunphy, though he got on with the other directors, had felt he was within a fiefdom run by Kilpatrick and Morris; this had also been a frequent criticism of the board under Fred Ratcliffe. Dunphy was almost ten years younger than the others – which he didn't feel was necessarily an issue – and from a different background. His father had worked as a mule spinner at Milnrow Spinning Company and his mother was a housewife. The family had lived in a semi-detached council house in St James Street, Milnrow. 'It's difficult to say why I felt a bit out of place,' he said. 'I was more practical, I suppose. I didn't know any of them when I joined the board and was from a completely different part of town. I always got on better with Trevor Butterworth. We had more in common.' Dunphy had just remarried and had moved to Hebden Bridge, West Yorkshire, with a view to starting a family. 'It seemed a good time to leave the board,' he said. Dunphy would return as a director in 1990 and become chairman in 2006.

Peter Madden wanted to make new signings through the summer and into the start of the new season, but Rochdale were continually missing out on players and clearly could not match the wages or signing-on fees being offered elsewhere. Willie Garner was a typical example. He played four games for Rochdale while on loan from Celtic, but asked for a signing-on fee of £15,000 to help cover the cost of moving his family from Scotland. The board tried to find this amount but, in the meantime, Garner was offered a job as a rep for the paint company owned by the chairman of Alloa Athletic, so he signed for them instead. Once more, Rochdale were limited to signing older players on their last club before moving into coaching or leaving the game entirely, or young, untried cast-offs from other clubs.

Graham Morris wrote to John Pierce, the borough planning and estates officer, in September 1982. The subject matter, underlined at the top of the letter, was: 'Land at Spotland occupied by Rochdale AFC Limited'. Morris wrote that he would 'be grateful to know whether, in your opinion, planning permission would be available on this land if Rochdale AFC ceased to occupy the property'. Morris, for the first time in an official document, then presented as fact what had been rumoured for nearly three years: 'We do believe that plans for a high density housing estate were drawn up by Mr Hindle some three years ago and we would like your advice as to whether this type of development would be appropriate for the area.' 'I was writing on behalf of the football club in order to get some idea of what an outside builder would be prepared to pay for the land,' said Morris. 'At that stage I did not know what the liquidator of Euroway was intending. To my mind, the only likely buyers would be speculative builders. If all had gone wrong, we would have needed to raise enough money to compete for the land purchase with these builders. Fortunately that situation did not arise, but I thought it important to find out what the chances were of planning permission being granted. Without it, the value of the land on which the ground stands would have fallen substantially.' Hindle confirmed that he had put in an enquiry to the planning department. 'It was a feasibility study for the bank. It was purely cosmetic. I had to know if it would get planning consent in case everything went tits up. I had no ulterior motive,' he said.

Six days later, Pierce wrote back to Morris and said that the council would 'be most unlikely to grant planning permission to allow the site to be redeveloped'. This was contradictory to information gleaned from the council in

December 1978 and January 1980 by chartered surveyors John Faulks and Barry Dean, working independently of one another. Both had been given the impression that planning permission for houses was a formality. Pierce pointed out that the town had a shortage of open spaces and playing pitches and that the site could still be utilised by the wider community, if no longer used by Rochdale AFC. The only caveat was that if it became derelict, 'redevelopment for residential purposes would clearly have to be considered'. While recommendations from planning officers were routinely accepted by councillors, this was not absolute. As Pierce pointed out, 'You must note that these views are my own and may not reflect the views of the Council.'

Around this time, Morris saw the same sketch, or similar, which John Faulks had seen when he visited Rochdale Council. It was a design for houses on land where Spotland stood – the pitch and the car park. 'I saw it,' he said. 'The plans and the bill for them, an architect's bill I presume, were brought to the boardroom table by Wyn Rawlinson, who was the club secretary at the time. I was shocked but I think it was Wrigley who opened his briefcase and all the paperwork disappeared rather quickly. Wrigley said, "I'll see to this." When you have no money, you don't argue if somebody offers to pay.'

It was one of the last meetings attended by Wrigley as a member of the board. He denies being part of any scheme to build houses on the ground. 'We weren't in it for the money. We always knew none of us would derive any financial benefit; I certainly did not derive any benefits,' he said. The other directors accepted that Wrigley's contribution to the football club had been generous and well-intended.

* * *

Rochdale were drawn away to Altrincham in the first round of the FA Cup. After the controversial vote two years earlier, the clubs were viewed as rivals and the media revisited the supposed enmity. Altrincham won 2-1 and four players were sent off, two from each team – this was blamed on zealous refereeing rather than a genuine feud between the clubs. In the league, Rochdale were one place above the re-election zone and familiar words had started to appear in letters written by fans to the *Rochdale Observer*: woe, bleak, appalling, angry, humiliated, frustration, negative, debacle – all these were included in a single edition. Peter Madden's after-match comments brought to mind Bob Stokoe, the man he had replaced: 'It seems there are too many players in the side that don't want to be winners and they will be told in no uncertain terms what their future at the club is. I hope the players feel it as much as the fans do.'

\* \* \*

Local visionary, Alan Ashworth of Bury Road, Rochdale, hit upon an antidote to dark, dismal Lancashire nights. Only 10 per cent of homes in the UK had a video recorder, but the 55-year-old had seen a trend developing. He paid Rochdale Council £1,500 to lease a small section in Rochdale Library from where he planned to loan video tapes. *Jesus of Nazareth*, *Rocky* and *Jaws* were among his opening stock.

The same as most libraries, Rochdale's had a selection of publications available to read on site. Missing from the racks was *Gay News*, which had proved a divisive issue when discussed at a council meeting. 'There's no need to help the permissive society to get more permissive. Libraries should enlighten people in the proper way of life,' said Councillor Clayton. Councillor Farrar went further and claimed homosexuality was 'an abnormality of nature'.

The statement from Councillor Edwards was baffling: 'Shallow-minded people jump to conclusions that it is going to corrupt, but surely television does this with all its promiscuity and gymnastics in the bedroom.' The council voted 40-16 against stocking the magazine. Meanwhile, a shopkeeper from Rochdale was fined £1,000 for offering a sleazy selection of video tapes to his customers. He had travelled to London to purchase, among others, multiple copies of *Come Softly* and *Pink Lips* at £25 each. His plan to sell them at a £15 mark-up was scuppered when an undercover police officer called at his shop and magistrates ruled that they were obscene.

\* \* \*

Peter Madden was summoned to a board meeting on Tuesday, 23 November 1982 to discuss the cup defeat against Altrincham of three days earlier. David Kilpatrick had told the press he was 'appalled' by the result and he remained in bullish mood. 'We have been totally dissatisfied with the way things have been going on the field,' he said. 'The board has agreed to a period of grace and will meet again to review the position at the end of next month.' Madden had run into the habitual mid-season misery of injuries, suspensions, loss of form and a shortage of money to bring in new players. 'I am the same man the directors offered a three-year contract to and my past record shows I can do a job. I've not become a poor manager all of a sudden,' he said. Rochdale won three of their next six games and moved up to 16th in the league table by the end of 1982.

A match was held at Spotland four days before Christmas 1982 to mark the service Fred Ratcliffe had given to the club. Rochdale played 'John McGrath's All Stars' (also listed as '4th Division All Stars & Guests') and won 4-2. Although he had not played for Rochdale, McGrath, a Mancunian living in nearby Middleton, was a regular and popular visitor to Spotland, usually on scouting missions for his various clubs. McGrath's force of personality saw him assemble a team that included well-known players such as Neville Southall, Roy McFarland, Len Cantello, Bryan Hamilton and Brian Kidd. The biggest attraction was Bobby Charlton who, at 45, could still drift past players. He scored one of the goals for the 'All Stars'. Fred Eyre, the ex-footballer and author, played in charity matches most weeks. 'I was pleased and honoured to play in a game for Fred and so was everyone else,' he said. 'I had been very complimentary about Len Hilton's pies in my book and Fred was made up because Rochdale had been mentioned.' Ratcliffe received a set of engraved goblets and a silver tray from David Kilpatrick, who announced that the newly built Willbutts Lane stand would be renamed 'The FS Ratcliffe Stand'. 'We have a good set of directors at the club. I'm proud that they're carrying on where we left off,' Ratcliffe told the press.

During most of the first week of March 1983, Mickey Bullock, the manager of Halifax Town, was taking phone calls from sick and injured players. A queue formed most mornings at the treatment table of physio Alan Sutton as he tried to push and prod hamstrings and knees and thighs back to a level of fitness which facilitated jogging, at least. By mid-week, the headcount of '100 per centers' had fallen to five and Bullock phoned League officials asking for a postponement of the forthcoming match. They refused and on the evening of Friday 4 March, a Halifax team comprising injured and sick senior professionals and youth players took the pitch at The Shay against Rochdale. The game ended goalless and for the Rochdale directors shivering in the stand, it was too much: time for a change. The team hadn't secured a win in the past seven games and had fallen to third from bottom of the division. They hadn't won away from home all season in the league and cup, and would go a full season without doing so. This was a particular ordeal for directors who, unlike supporters, were expected to attend most away matches, so would repeatedly suffer long journeys unsweetened by a win and often soured further by the patronising attitude or crowing of the other club's directors.

The board made a collective decision to sack Peter Madden. He was asked to meet David Kilpatrick at Spotland on Sunday morning; it was the first time he had dismissed a manager. 'It is awful. Anyone who says differently is lying,' he said. 'We had worked together and enjoyed success. I asked him to meet me at 10am at the club – managers know they are gone when they hear that. You have to come out with the clichés, that it's time for a parting of the ways, it's the end of the road, thank you for all your efforts and all that. They generally accept it. There is a discipline in football. They don't turn around and beg or become hostile.' Graham Morris was also sorry to end the professional relationship with Madden. 'He'd saved the club,' he said. 'When he started, the attendances were barely 800 and his enthusiasm to make it work had seen us build a strong team which was exciting to watch. He was always good company and cheerful, too.'

Madden, as managers often did, believed he was only a signing or two away from stemming the flow of poor results. He had spent several weeks piecing together a deal to bring the striker John Byrne from York City to Spotland. Madden had heard that Byrne's father was ill and the player wanted to be closer to his family in Manchester. Madden and Byrne negotiated a wage of £90 per week plus £5 appearance money, but the board said it was beyond the club's budget.

Byrne was sold two years later to Queens Park Rangers of the top flight and went on to play 23 times for the Republic of Ireland.

After leaving the club Madden stayed in the Rochdale area. He became landlord of Tophams Tavern in Smithy Bridge, Littleborough for 17 years. Almost 40 years after he had been manager, Madden met Kilpatrick by chance in the local branch of William Hill; they were both keen fans of horse racing. 'He was still raging about how we should have signed John Byrne,' said Kilpatrick. 'I kept saying "Peter, we didn't have the money," but he wouldn't let it go.'

While joining the board had been a relatively straightforward procedure for the four new directors, their positions called upon a great deal of nerve. Much as David Wrigley had warned Andrew Hindle four years earlier and similar fears had concerned Sidney Marks, they each carried a legally binding 'burden of responsibility'. Directors were obligated to trade fairly and honestly and, many times, this was not always possible to the letter at an ailing football club where often a touch of chicanery or sleight of hand was required to get by. 'I had a lot of sleepless nights,' said Graham Morris. 'Especially with my job [chartered accountant]. I had to be very careful. If the club had gone down, I'm not sure where it would have left us as directors. It was a hell of a risk. I had these visions of us being about to kick off and someone coming along with a winding-up order and stopping the game. At that point, they'd have known we'd had the cash through the turnstiles, so it would have been perfect timing on their part.' Kilpatrick was also aware of the vulnerability of their position. 'It's okay having the Corinthian attitude but it will soon founder on the harsh realities of finance. The liabilities attached to a football club and the basic requirements are exactly the same as any limited company. You're out there with the dogs of war.'

Kilpatrick and Morris continued to work well together. 'I am more impetuous than Graham but not to the point of stupidity,' said Kilpatrick. 'He is a natural worrier. Throughout all that period, he worried like hell. We were always falling out, but I love him. I call him the Morris Man. He is one of the most regular and honest people you will ever come across. He takes pleasure in the simple things. He is a Blackley lad who has done bloody well. He is rock solid and an all-round good egg.' In each other's company, Kilpatrick often talks over Morris, telling him to 'get on with it' or 'move along'. This is done in a jocular manner, often accompanied by a swear word or an air of faux exasperation. Morris speaks more quietly, sometimes adding a physical exclamation mark to a new piece of information – an upturned eyebrow or hmm-hmm cough. 'The thing with David is that he *does* listen. If I tell him to think again, he does do,' said Morris.

The appeal of directorship of a football club was easy to see in David Kilpatrick. He enjoyed the attention and the power, while understanding fully the absurdity of the small, rickety realm of Rochdale AFC. He liked being out of the house too, drinking, talking, bathing in bonhomie. He was a maverick and a reactionary and the more the little men (literally in his case, for he is 6ft 4in) told him the mission was both daft and doomed, he chipped for himself another shard of determination; granite, of course.

His son Michael said his father enjoyed the trappings and status symbols that went with running a successful business. 'But I think he values being recognised for a job well done as much as the status symbols themselves,' he said. 'He's quite comfortable holding court whether in the boardroom, at a fans' forum or the local pub, albeit much less so these days. He certainly liked to work hard and play hard over the years, but he would not want to be seen as having made a quick profit at the expense of others or trying to do things without proper foundations. He very much enjoys organising and felt duty bound to see the job through at Rochdale, despite the many challenges the club faced.'

One evening, David Kilpatrick met the author and Rochdale fan, Trevor Hoyle at a mutual friend's birthday party at a restaurant in Newhey. 'When David learnt I was a Dale fan we talked non-stop throughout the meal about the club and the players. To say he had only just met me, he was very indiscreet and revealed all kinds of dressing-room gossip,' said Hoyle. 'I could have been a hack from *The Sun* for all he knew. I mentioned that I was about to go to India for the first time and he said he went two or three times a year to buy granite. A day or two later there was a knock at the door and it was the daughter of the woman whose birthday we had attended. She gave me a handful of rupees from David, saying he thought I might need some small currency for taxis and tips on arrival. What a thoughtful gesture to someone he had met only once. That, to me, summed up the man.'

But what was in it for Graham Morris? Why stick with it? 'Well, I'd given my word, hadn't I? I'd said I'd help and sort it out.' Who had he given his word to? 'The club and the supporters, I suppose,' he said. They would not have minded him backing out, given the realisation of all the hours and sacrifice it required. The love of a football club was not without boundaries, surely. 'But I'd given my word,' he said again. The word, the promise, had been made mostly to himself, clearly. And why did it relate to this particular football club? 'I just got the bug,' he said. 'I've always been one to support the underdog. I think I must have had plenty of guts back then. I don't think I'd do it today. You're in everyone's bad books when you owe money and it was fairly big money.' His daughter Helen feels the involvement with the club enriched his and the family's life. 'There were occasions when dad was under considerable stress, notably when there was insufficient funds to pay the wages, but overall I think he has risen to the challenge and derived a great deal of satisfaction in helping to steer the ship to calmer waters. We made many friends, all with a common interest and it became a significant part of our social life.'

Christian Morris, now a partner at Wyatt Morris Golland, felt his father's personality suited the role. 'He is a real gentleman. When I say that, I don't mean in a detrimental way, like a dinosaur. In business he is polite, fair, honest, professional, but also firm. In his personal life he is not outspoken but at the same time not quiet. He certainly enjoyed the social life, a few drinks and a good laugh. He's definitely got a good sense of humour. I think he shielded us children from a lot of what was going on in the early days and it was kept between my parents. For him it was more about the work going on behind the scenes – planning the finances, budgeting, looking at players' contracts, wage bills, negotiating deals and generally keeping the club afloat. And that was all being done in addition to his day job. Saturdays were, I suppose, a release from all of that.'

The period was not without occasional upbeat moments. 'Through it all, I always found it a privilege to be a director and it was quite exciting when we won, of course,' said Morris. The board of four became close friends and had an unusual degree of purpose and union; there was none of the suspicion or jostling for power of previous incumbents. 'We actually had some fun here and there,' said Morris.

'David Walkden was great for bright ideas of how to make money. He was always scrounging competition prizes. I remember he once got some television sets but it turned out that they didn't work.' On one occasion the club was refused a safety certificate for the 'B' Stand (the Main Stand was sub-divided, A and B). 'It was something to do with weight and this was an example of where David (Kilpatrick) showed great initiative, which he often did,' said Morris. 'He brought a load of sandbags and placed them on the seats to show there was no danger of the floor going through. He got the stand re-opened again.' The 'Dronsfield Gate' was a huge, ornate metal gate supplied by Bill Dronsfield's engineering works. 'It was completely out of scale to the rest of the ground but he turned up with this great big gate and up it went,' said Morris. Another time, before a home game, it had rained heavily and pools of water had formed across the pitch. The club was desperate for attendance money to pay a slew of bills. Someone was dispatched to GNG Foam in Littleborough, to collect pieces of six-inch foam. 'You wouldn't believe how heavy foam is once it gets full of water,' said Morris. Even the referee Ken Redfern mucked in, wearing a pair of wellies. The opponents were unconvinced. 'It's a man's game. Get changed – you're playing,' Redfern told them.

Kilpatrick found respite from football through his love of flat racing. He was a regular visitor to courses up and down the country and went on to own 13 horses at different times. His most successful was Not My Choice, a chestnut gelding, pictures of which, along with other horses, adorn the walls and window sills of his home. He led an unusual work life, either dealing with relatively mundane matters on the site adjoining his house where up to ten people worked, or travelling to visit stone processing factories. He spent a great deal of time with fellow masons as a member of the Charity 3342 Lodge. On returning to Rochdale after time at boarding school and working in Liverpool, he had found himself without many friends; Freemasonry remedied this. 'I have never had an inch of benefit in terms of business from being a mason. It is a fabulously charitable organisation. For me, though, the best part is a load of lads having a night out,' he said.

In the midst of being ambushed by the ledgers and papers and folders piled high at his home and office, and also in various cubbyholes at Spotland, Morris was hoping for support from Cyril Smith. He had made frequent positive declarations about the club to the press. 'He was talking us up in the media, but behind the scenes he was saying to everyone that there was no way the club would survive. He never lifted a finger to help us,' said Morris. Much worse, Smith ramped up the pressure by reporting back on a conversation he had supposedly had on a train with Grahame Watts of Touche Ross, the liquidation company acting on behalf of Euroway. 'He passed on this message – that they were out to get us. It made my stomach turn and put the fear of God in me,' said Morris. 'I wasn't overreacting. At that point, one of about half a dozen people [creditors] could have pulled the club down and I was obviously worried who was speaking to who about the state we were in.'

After ditching the historical debt owed to former board members, the next stage for Morris and Kilpatrick was to secure once more the outright ownership of Spotland. The Allied Irish Bank had underwritten the 'purchase' of Spotland by issuing a loan to Euroway. It was not known whether Andrew Hindle had given personal guarantees to the bank, which would make him wholly liable or if the bank had been able to cash in assets such as unsold cars seized from Euroway to at least partially offset the cost of the ground purchase. Whatever the route – Allied Irish Bank to Hindle to Euroway to Rochdale AFC, most probably – the club had received payment, in stages, of about £135,000 and so, as such, had 'sold' the ground, even if the legal minefield around the issue made it difficult to say for definite who had actually bought it or, more to the point, owned it. Notwithstanding, the club was impelled to now buy back the ground at a price which would appease the bank and Touche Ross.

On a rare night off from the entanglements and woes of the football club, David Kilpatrick was with fellow Freemasons at the Masonic Hall in Richard Street. He found himself sitting next to Albert Wright, a long-established solicitor in the town and a partner of Hartley, Thomas and Wright, who had long acted on behalf of Fred Ratcliffe and Rochdale AFC. 'We were talking away and Albert asked how it was going at the football club. I started to explain how we were trying to sort out the mess of the ground sale and he stopped me in my tracks. He suddenly said, "But it's not been sold." I told him of course it had and he said, "Well how come the deeds are still in the safe at our office?"' Kilpatrick immediately left the room and headed to the public phone box in the vestibule. 'I was practically running,' he said. 'Graham [Morris] answered the phone and I said, "You're not going to believe this – Euroway never completed on the sale of the ground."'

## Chapter Fifteen

# A Most Inexplicable Affair

The realisation that the deeds had not been physically transferred produced a legal conundrum. The interested parties were now even less sure as to the status of their claim to the ground and the social club. If there was uncertainty before, it was now chaos. As the weeks went by, there was a general acceptance that the material transference of the title deeds was primarily a cosmetic procedure when measured against the moral and financial commitment. Inevitably, the actions of the solicitor who had represented the club in the 'sale' were called into question. Had it been an oversight or a deliberate piece of mismanagement, but to what gain? David Wrigley was the solicitor but he denied having anything to do with the matter. 'I do not think I got involved in the legal stage. I never prepared the contract for the ground,' he said. All other parties are adamant that he oversaw the legal issues relating to the ground sale.

On their search for funds to 'buy back' the ground, Kilpatrick and Morris called first at the Allied Irish Bank which, since the arrival of Hindle at Spotland, had become the club's de facto bank. 'It felt right that we should go there first,' said Morris. 'We met the manager and there was a solicitor there, too. I'm not sure why – it might have been to protect the bank in some way. It was ten o'clock in the morning. We'd not even sat down and the manager said in a strong Irish accent, "Come in, we're getting quietly pissed here." I was used to drinking coffee at that time of the day, but they were already at the wine. I remember thinking it was an unusual way to do business.' At several points, the solicitor expressed how angry he was with Wrigley and what he considered to be his bungling of the ground sale. 'He kept saying he was going to have Wrigley's balls in a jar,' said Kilpatrick. Despite the generally upbeat mood of the meeting, the pair learned a few days later that the loan had been declined.

Their next call was Rochdale Council – in particular John Towey, the Chief Executive and Town Clerk. Towey, six years into his role, had established himself as a supporter of community projects. Born in Leigh in 1926, he was a grammar-school boy who served as a bombardier in India during the Second World War. After the war he spent three years in the Far East before studying law at Sheffield University. He was approachable and, although not especially a football fan, understood the importance to the town of having a professional club. 'He was great, John,' said Kilpatrick. 'He had the same friendly manner with everyone he met. He was accomplished and a real gentleman. We didn't have to oversell anything, he got it straight away. He's another of the few who can be said to have saved the club.'

After several meetings Towey agreed that the council would loan the club £50,000, increased to £60,000 a few weeks later. 'We'd never have got away with offering £50,000 for the ground. We felt the minimum we could put down was £60,000,' said Morris. 'We had to stress to John that no one should hear about this, absolutely no one. If word had got out, they would have asked for a lot more.' The deal remaining confidential also suited Towey politically; it minimised the impact of any lobby from ratepayers indifferent to football, questioning such use of public funds. As part of the deal, the directors of Rochdale were asked to make personal guarantees that the money would be repaid. 'It was the usual belt-and-braces approach that the council takes when lending anyone money,' said Morris.

The social club attached to Spotland, although in a dilapidated state, was an asset which Morris realised could generate another tranche of cash. Vaux Brewery in Sunderland had a charge on the property. Although it had been closed for a year or so, the football club's debt to Vaux had grown to approximately £53,000. 'It was all boarded up,' said Morris. 'It was near-derelict. The carpets were all rotted and water was coming in through various holes in the roof.' The legal position of the social club was especially convoluted. As it sat on the club car park rather than an adopted highway, there was no right of access for vehicles. Technically, Vaux or any other supplier was not allowed to drive up to the building with supplies. This meant the social club stood a chance of being isolated, rendered impracticable, if the land on which the football club stood was sold off for any use other than a sporting venue. The social club, therefore, would only become a viable business again if Rochdale AFC took back the ground. Morris persuaded Greenall Whitley that there was a good likelihood of this happening and the brewer promised to loan Rochdale AFC £20,000 on the basis that this sum was reduced for every barrel of beer sold at the premises. This would depend, of course, on an exit deal being struck with Vaux.

A meeting was convened in Manchester specifically to resolve the various issues relating to the ground and social club. It was called for by the insurance company of the Law Society, which was due to underwrite any costs directly attributable to the failing of Wrigley & Co. It was chaired by the solicitor Maurice Watkins of James Chapman & Co. Watkins later joined the board of Manchester United and represented high-profile clients such as Eric Cantona. Representatives of the five parties – Rochdale AFC, Vaux Brewery, Euroway Car Centre, Touche Ross and the Allied Irish Bank – were deposited in different rooms. Watkins circulated each, carrying offers and counter-offers from the differing factions. 'It was like pulling teeth,' said Graham Morris. Rochdale's bargaining position was fixed. 'My absolute limit was £80,000 and not a penny more, with £20,000 of that needed for the social club.' The representative of Vaux Brewery, a solicitor called Mr Snowball – a surname which Morris and Kilpatrick had not heard before and has provided much mirth over the years – wanted to know how Wrigley had 'sold' its(Vaux's) property (the social club) when it wasn't his to sell. The representatives of Touche Ross and the Allied Irish Bank wanted to know why, if they had paid (or loaned) the money to purchase a football ground, they had not caught sight of the deeds, let alone taken possession of them.

The day, Thursday, 24 March 1983, was long. Briefcases were opened and closed. Toilet and drinks breaks were called as they peeled off for sub-meetings on the stairway or in the corridor. They each knew that procrastination was costly with legal bills growing. 'It was the most complicated and difficult negotiation I have ever been involved with,' said Morris. 'Watkins did an incredible job. I'm still not sure how he pulled it off. He must be silver-tongued.' Finally, the impasse ended and an agreement was reached, though written in near-indecipherable legalese. In simple terms, it stated that Rochdale AFC would pay £60,000 to the Allied Irish Bank and £20,000 to Vaux Brewery in return for the deeds to the ground and social club. At the same time, the bank and liquidator agreed a settlement with the Law Society's insurer to cover the shortfall of what had originally been loaned to Euroway. Everyone shook hands and left.

\* \* \*

Back at Spotland, another pressing issue was brewing. The chaps running the tea bars at the ground, known as the Fighting Fund, stood accused of despotism. On the desk of Graham Morris was an overflowing tray of correspondence from solicitors, banks, kit suppliers, plumbers et al while, in another, a letter from Allan Rabbich of Inglefield, Norden, about 'a most inexplicable affair'. It read, with original punctuation:

> Dear Mr Morris,
>
> **Re: Pearl Street Snack Bar**
>
> You have always been supportive and shown a welcome interest. I feel therefore, I should keep you in the picture regarding an unexpected and uninvited development which has left my wife Irene and myself feeling hurt and resentful.
>
> We have been told by the Chairman of the Fighting Fund Committee that our services are no longer required unless:-
>
> (a). we mix sugar in our coffee urns and not have it in separate sugar dishes on the counter.

(b). we sell coffee only and discontinue offering tea.

Experience with visiting fans has proved conclusively that tastes vary in different parts of the country. An alternative to coffee is welcomed by many, hence we have sold both for quite some time. Also, lots of customers prefer their beverages with little or no sugar.

Mr. Jack Ashworth argues it slows serving if fans have to put in their own sugar. We have not found this. It is not costing more – in fact, the reverse, as fans will and do buy more if they get what they want. Jack Ashworth has gone on record as saying that fans at their bar "get coffee with sugar in, like it or lump it".

You probably feel, as Irene and I do, that this is so trivial as to be unbelievable. All we are trying to do is provide a friendly service and improve the image of Rochdale A.F.C., which we hope visiting fans will take away with them.

We are therefore convinced there is more to this than meets the eye, and that, although denied by Jack Ashworth, it owes more to the fact that from this season, Irene and I have sold Nicholson's pies instead of Hilton's.

This decision, agreed to albeit reluctantly by the Fighting Fund Committee, followed repeated complaints by myself and Mr. Fred Kershaw, concerning the quality of Hilton's pies.

Nicholson's have supplied pies which are not brown and overbaked, and at a price considerably less than Hiltons, i.e.

Hilton's.            £2.88 per doz.
Nicholson's.         £2.58 per doz. (meat).
Nicholson's          £2.38 per doz. (meat & potato).

Purchases this season – Pearl Street bar only:-

|             | Meat (dozs) | Meat & potato (dozs) |
|-------------|-------------|----------------------|
| Crewe.      | 5           | 5                    |
| Burnley.    | 9           | 9                    |
| Northants.  | 4           | 4                    |
| Exeter.     | 2           | 2                    |
| Colchester. | 2           | 2                    |
| Watford.    | <u>15</u>   | <u>15</u>            |
|             | <u>37</u>   | <u>37</u>            |

These pies cost us:            £183.52.

If bought from Hiltons:        £213.12.

Saving to R.A.F.C., (one bar only,
6 matches):                    £29.60

What would this come to over a full season? (In addition, Mr. Fred Kershaw has ordered and sold a small number of Nicholson's pies in the Main Stand snack bar).

I think we should be astute enough to have more than one string to our bow – i.e. two bakers – this is normal commercial practice and keeps suppliers on their toes. This policy may unfortunately now go by the board with my departure.

I mention the pie situation because I strongly believe that such bizarre action by Jack Ashworth cannot possibly be put down to such a frivolous and petty reason as having sugar in sugar dishes!

In these times it is not easy to find workers willing to give their services free, and you may think it worthwhile to keep an eye on the future of the Pearl Street bar.

I take the view that you are entitled to know what is going on. At least you now have the background to what is a most inexplicable affair.

We are not asking to be reinstated. My wife is too hurt to want to come back. As for myself, I know only one football club – the one I have supported for 49 years. I shall go on supporting the club in the only way left to me – through the turnstiles, and wish R.A.F.C. every success, especially in the new image which it is bravely attempting to project.

Yours very sincerely,

ALLAN RABBICH
Shareholder , Member Supporters'
Club and Fan.

* * *

Although it had created a great deal of anxiety and a mountain of paperwork, it could be argued that Rochdale ultimately secured a good piece of business via the 'sale' to Euroway. The club had received £135,000, of which only £60,000 had been 'returned' (to the Allied Irish Bank). The involvement of Andrew Hindle with Rochdale AFC, however viewed, had indubitably led to a clear £75,000 being lodged in the club's account at a time when cash for its very survival was imperative. He had also substantially cleared outstanding debts to ex-directors. The figures appear relatively insignificant in the modern age, but were considerable at the time. Inflation from 1980 to 2019 would make the £175,000 cost of the ground £871,832, with the agreed rental charge of £35,000 becoming £174,366 per year. 'We were lucky, I suppose, in that Euroway went bust. I don't think there was any way we could have paid such a high rental charge,' said Morris. 'I know it might be tempting to raise money through the sale of your ground but I wouldn't advise any football club to do it. It's a terrible idea.'

The football club, with the binding agreement signed by the five parties, was now able to finalise its pre-negotiated deal with the council. A legal charge 'relating to land and buildings at Spotland Football Ground, Rochdale' was drawn up by Rochdale Council to Rochdale AFC. A legal charge established 'the right that an organisation that lends money has to take someone's property if that person does not pay back the money they borrowed to buy the property'. Rochdale AFC was advanced £60,000 to be repaid with interest to the council at £6,000 per year for a decade.

Finally, sole ownership of Spotland had reverted back to Rochdale AFC. The momentous nature of the announcement was reflected in the *Rochdale Observer* under the huge front-page banner headline: 'SOCCER'S SAVIOURS'. The four directors – Graham Morris, David Kilpatrick, David Walkden and Bill Dronsfield – were pictured on the Spotland turf, toasting the news, champagne in hand. Kilpatrick revealed that the council deal had been no 'matey-matey situation'. 'We had to stand up to rigorous investigation,' he said. John Towey agreed: 'We would never advance a loan to any company unless that company had a reasonable chance of prosperity,' he said. 'We are satisfied that Rochdale AFC has a sound financial structure with better than average prospects – and you can't say better than that.'

\* \* \*

The *Rochdale Observer* of Saturday, 26 March 1983, the issue containing details of the ground buy-back, provides a fascinating snapshot of the town and the times. The working men's clubs were busy. Ricky Livid, a comedian, was the star turn at the Brickcroft; Jimmy Casey, a 'hilarious' comedian, was at the Featherstall, while Walk and Windy, a 'funny duo', were the entertainment between pints of JW Lees at Kirkholt. Peter Rowan, all the way from Massachusetts, was the guest of the Kingsway Country Music Club at the Kingsway (now closed down and boarded up), a pub encircled by mills and traffic, a good few miles from the nearest hay barn. Rowan had been brought to town by folk and country aficionados Mavis and Jack Lee, who also ran a club at The Fishermen's Inn (now the Wine Press) overlooking the choppy waters of Hollingworth Lake. The Lydgate Inn (now a block of 'rural' apartments) in Littleborough had a jazz/funk night on Thursdays and, on Sundays, a 'golden oldies' night where 'the top sounds of yesteryear' were spun by Steve James. Tiffany's nightclub (now the Red and Hot World Buffet), better known as Tiff's, was holding a 'Sunday Junior Disco' while Turner's Dance School had a 'family night'. Restaurants across town were advertising their menus and prices. Rafters (now demolished) was based in Dane Street, close to Sparth Bottoms where Rochdale AFC trained, while the Lincoln Green, boasting 'golden fried fillet at £2.65', was a few yards from Wrigley & Co's office in The Butts, Rochdale. Out of town were the Manor in Norden (now Nutter's) and the Captain's Table (now the Marina Bar and Grill) in Littleborough.

Without computers, multi-channel televisions and the proliferation of video games, it was evident that people went out much more and mixed on a social basis. Scores of clubs met through the week at various church halls and community centres – among them the Dunlop Pensioners, Nalgo Retired Members Club, the National Association of Widows, the Friendly Circle, the Rochdale Stroke Club and the Inskip League of Friendship for disabled persons. In the car showrooms, the Triumph Acclaim, Austin Maestro, Hyundai Pony and Vauxhall Cavalier were heavily promoted. At the ABC Cinema, *Raiders of the Lost Ark* (PG) and *An Officer and a Gentleman* (15) were showing on the main screens. Cinema 3 at the ABC proffered *Madame Olga's Pupils* (18) three times daily and *Nympho Girls* (18) twice a day. For those preferring to stay in, the television listings included *Dynasty, Jim'll Fix It, The Dukes of Hazzard, Upstairs, Downstairs* and *Hart to Hart*.

The reunification of the football club with its ground literally and metaphorically gave it a foundation on which to build. And they did build. Almost 40 years on, Rochdale is in the midst of the most successful period in its 117-year history, about to enter a sixth season in English football's third tier. The ground, still on the same site, has three new all-seater stands and the fourth, the Sandy Lane End, has been renovated extensively.

The two old pals, Morris and Kilpatrick, attend most Rochdale home games. They are both life-presidents. Ask them about their time at the helm of the club and they don't frown; they smile. Neither of them is expansive or elaborate with words; it's not their style. 'It was good fun, most of the time,' they say. The worries and hassles and burden of responsibility do not appear to have weighed too heavily. 'Wouldn't have missed it for the world,' they say. Morris is still thin, light on his feet. Kilpatrick is more thickset, ever thus. 'Come on,' he pleads or shouts, if you don't agree with him. And you want to agree because he's so exuberant, full of it, full of personality.

Their children, now middle-aged themselves, obviously know them best. 'I think his involvement with Dale has had a very positive impact overall on his life,' says Michael Kilpatrick, a solicitor living in Madrid. 'Inevitably there have been frustrations and difficulties along the way but he is proud of the contribution he was able to make and the appreciation that is felt by people who supported the club before it saw an upturn in the 1990s. He has been able to meet and know a large number of people from all levels of the footballing world and be in privileged situations which would not have come about otherwise.' Helen Thompson, also a solicitor, says of her father, Graham Morris: 'He worked tirelessly, together with David Kilpatrick and others, to get the club into the position it is in today. I don't believe that the sacrifices and significant contributions they made over the years have been acknowledged by their successors, which is disappointing. That said, neither my dad nor David are the sort of fellows who take on something like this for accolades. Rather, it was a labour of love.'

Of the other directors, fellow overcoat men, most are still around, though subject to the various ailments commensurate with their ages. Their eyes are still lit bright, even if dust has fallen over a few memories. John Faulks lives in Norden, cheerful but fretful that he might have said too much, been too outspoken here and there. It was all a long time ago, he says. He goes to Spotland 'now and again'. Trevor Butterworth has moved back to Rochdale after many years living in Spain. He looks younger than his age (81) and, any minute now, looks as if he might ask if you fancy a kick-about or a game of table tennis, his other sporting love. I'll talk about Rochdale Football Club all day, he says. And will. He pronounces 'Rochdale' the way true Rochdalians do: 'Rochd'll'. David Wrigley lives in Newquay, Cornwall. Understandably, he's a little wary of raking over the past, but he's not unfriendly. 'I still look for Rochdale's score after United's,' he says. 'I'm pleased and proud that I was on the board at Rochdale. I tell people about it. None of us had any experience in football, you know.' He has three grown-up sons. I ask their names and he falls serious. 'Why do you want to know their names? They might not want to be in this book.' It's a fair point. In recent years he's completed a course in Teaching English to Speakers of Other Languages at Truro and Penwith College.

Andrew Hindle lives in north Yorkshire in a splendid house a few fields down from a 13th-century church. Forget-me-nots flank the dirt track leading to his door, with bluebells in the longer grass towards the trees. Rochdale in the rain in 1980 and all that gluey grimness seems a long way away. He is formal but friendly, answering every question. He smiles more than people said he would. He's magnanimous about Morris and Kilpatrick. 'Hats off to the pair of them,' he says. 'They were the keys to the revival. They did a great job.' After a couple of hours chatting, running through all that was then, why he did it, what he hoped for, how it turned out, how he is viewed, how he'd like to be remembered, he says while looking out of the window (where a deer has just passed): 'I shouldn't have got involved really. My heart was in rugby.'

Chris Dunphy played but a small role in this period of the club's history. His is another story for another book. Often, though, the same as most Rochdale fans, he ponders on the late-1970s and early-1980s. He was there, standing amid the dereliction of a falling-down Spotland. He was at the crisis meetings at Broadwater Youth Centre. He threw coins into the blanket carried by fans around the perimeter of the pitch at home games. He saw the boardroom in flux, both as a fan and as a director. He suffered the defeats. He enjoyed the occasional victories. He felt the doom and dared not trust to optimism. By staying with it, believing, he saw what happened next, the stability, the upturn, the survival. 'A lot of small decisions went our way and changed the whole history of the club for possibly the next 50 years,' he says. How true.

Across from the article in the *Rochdale Observer* of March 1983 containing the good news about Spotland returning to the club's ownership is a small item reminding readers to put forwards their clocks. Tomorrow is the first day of summer.

*Chapter Sixteen*

# Extra time and Penalties

**Saturday, 31 August 1985:** Fred Ratcliffe died in Highfield Hospital, Rochdale, aged 71. 'The footballing public of Rochdale owe him a great depth of gratitude for his efforts in keeping league football alive in the town,' said David Kilpatrick. On the day of his death Rochdale were joint top of Division Four.

**December 1985:** The Law Society made an application that David Wrigley was required to answer allegations contained in an affidavit to be put before a Solicitors' Disciplinary Tribunal.

**April 1986:** David Wrigley was struck off the Roll of Solicitors by the Law Society. The tribunal found that allegations against him were substantiated. They were: that he failed to at all times keep properly written-up such accounts as may be necessary to show all his dealings with clients' money held or paid to him and any money dealt with by him through a client; failed to carry out reconciliations between the balance of the clients' cash book and the clients' statements; drew from a client account monies not permitted to be so drawn; failed to hold a Practising Certificate; and been guilty of conduct unbefitting a solicitor. In the 'findings' section of the tribunal's report, Wrigley admitted making 'improper payments' from a bank account to reduce a deficiency in excess of £70,000.

**July 1986:** The *Rochdale Observer* carried a six-paragraph front-page story about Wrigley under the small headline, 'Lawyer Struck Off'. The information supplied by the Law Society was carried verbatim and there was no evidence of any further investigation by the paper. The piece mentioned that he had 'for a time' been joint-chairman of 'Rochdale Soccer Club'.

**February 1991:** Andrew Hindle became a director of Eventco Ltd, a sports hospitality company.

**January 1994:** Andrew Hindle resigned as a director of Eventco Ltd.

**1996:** The Main Stand was demolished and replaced.

**1998:** As part of a consortium known locally as the 'gang of four', Andrew Hindle introduced £25,000 ('Or something like that amount' – Hindle) into West Hartlepool Rugby Club. 'I lived nearby,' he said. 'I joined the board and they asked me to be chairman.' The club was promoted to the Allied Dunbar Premiership, but struggled. 'We just couldn't get the support and sustain our place at such a high level,' he said. The club sold its ground at Brierton Lane to raise funds.

**October 1997:** Nat Lofthouse opened the WMG stand (Pearl Street).

**Tuesday, 21 July 1998:** A High Court sitting in Manchester banned Andrew Hindle from acting as a company director for eight years. He had been a director of The Sporting Occasion Ltd, a corporate hospitality firm which went into liquidation with debts of £537,408. The court was told the company had traded successfully until it became involved in providing packages for the World Cup finals in France. Despite more than £200,000 worth of hospitality packages being sold to customers, less than a third of the tickets were supplied.

Allegations of unfit conduct found against Hindle included that he misappropriated more than £350,000 of company money by allowing payments to two other businesses of which he was chairman at the time. Some £210,000 was paid to another events company, known as Eventco Ltd, between 18 February and 12 May 1998, 1998. In addition, £140,025 was paid to West Hartlepool Rugby Football Club between 5 March and 8 June 1998. It was also found that Hindle had failed to ensure that full and accurate records of the payments were made, a consequence of which was that the liquidator of The Sporting Occasion Ltd was unable to establish whether any of the money could have been recovered to repay creditors. At the time, Hindle was said to be living at the Hope Island Resort, a gated community at Sanctuary Cove in the Gold Coast area of Queensland, Australia. The resort's motif is, 'Some stay for the weekend. Some stay forever.'

In an interview for this book, Hindle said the Cameroonian Football Federation or someone purporting to have connections with it had ultimately caused the collapse of The Sporting Occasion Ltd. The company had fallen foul of a 'con man' who claimed to be selling tickets for the World Cup of 1998. The tickets were said to be excess from Cameroon's allocation. This third party had 'sold' them to three or four different bulk purchasers, but failed to provide them. 'The tickets didn't come through. He did a runner, basically,' said Hindle. 'He was a con man and I'd got sucked into it.' Hindle had not moved permanently to Australia, but had spent two months there, as he usually did in the British midwinter. While there, he had attended the Australian Open tennis tournament and the Ashes cricket series. 'My lawyer told me it was okay to go away as normal and it would all be sorted out. It was bad advice because it looked as if I'd done a runner and it meant I wasn't able to defend myself at the High Court,' he said. The figures quoted in newspaper articles were inaccurate and exaggerated, he said. He had not transferred £140,025 to West Hartlepool Rugby Club – 'They would have been in clover if I had,' he said. He had not challenged press inaccuracies at the time to avoid 'raking it up all over again'.

**September 2001:** The Willbutts Lane stand was opened, containing 4,000 seats.

**February 2001:** Paul Connor became the club's record signing when he joined from Stoke City for £150,000.

**February 2000:** Andrew Hindle stood down as chairman of West Hartlepool. He said he lived in Cork, Ireland, and did not want to be an absentee chairman. Two years earlier the club had revealed debts of £600,000. Hindle told the press that he was 'very confident' that a Creditors Voluntary Arrangement (CVA) would be agreed. 'There is nothing sinister about my decision, I simply can't do it [the chairmanship] justice,' he said. On hearing this news, there was obviously a great deal of interest back in Rochdale. Rumours spread that Hindle had acted improperly. 'It's absolutely not true. How do people get hold of these things?' he said. 'I did all I could to help the club survive. There was no parallel at all in what happened at West Hartlepool and Rochdale.' He said he understood that some in the town did not view him favourably. 'It's a bit unjust,' he said. 'Rochdale is my hometown, so it means more to me than most other places. People do not have the benefit of the full facts. They'd think differently if they had. It doesn't keep me awake at night, though no one likes it when people think bad about them.'

**Thursday, 4 July 2002:** Brian Andrew Hindle was listed as a director of Hibernian Hospitality Ltd, with two shares. The company, registered in Ireland, reported a gross profit of £67,492. At the same time he was a director of Eventco Hospitality (Ireland) Ltd, registered in Cork, Ireland. The company remained dormant.

**May 2005:** David Kilpatrick left the board of Rochdale AFC. He was made life vice-president.

**January 2006:** David Walkden died, aged 78.

**May 2007:** The centenary of Rochdale AFC was celebrated with a gala dinner at the town hall attended by directors, supporters, players and fans.

**May 2008:** Rochdale appeared at Wembley for the first time. They lost 3-2 to Stockport County in the League Two play-off final.

**June 2009:** Graham Morris left the board. He was made life vice-president.

**May 2010:** Rochdale were promoted to League One after 41 seasons in the bottom division.

**September 2011:** Bill Dronsfield died after a heart attack at his holiday home in Harrogate.

**September 2011:** Andrew Hindle became chief executive of Serving Sport Ltd, a 'marketing and advertising' company.

**May 2012:** Rochdale were relegated to League Two.

**May 2014:** Rochdale were promoted back to League One.

**July 2014:** Scott Hogan was sold to Brentford for £750,000 plus sell-on clauses, the highest transfer fee ever received by Rochdale.

**November 2014**: Venue Hospitality Ltd was incorporated at Companies House with Andrew Hindle listed as 'a person with a significant role'.

**February 2018:** Rochdale played at Wembley again, losing 6-1 in an FA Cup fifth-round replay against Tottenham Hotspur. Tottenham were using Wembley as their home ground while their new stadium was being built.

**September 2018:** The three life vice-presidents who still regularly attended matches (Graham Morris, David Kilpatrick and Rod Brierley) had their season tickets revoked. They were told to request tickets on a match-to-match basis. Their season tickets and boardroom privileges were later reinstated.

**January 2019:** Serving Sport Ltd went into voluntary liquidation.

**March 2019:** Venue Hospitality Ltd went into voluntary liquidation. Andrew Hindle said he had wound up both companies because he had now retired.

**May 2019:** David Wrigley, when asked to comment about being struck off as a solicitor, responded by e-mail: 'The events to which you refer had nothing at all to do with my connection with the football club. I don't think any further comment from me is necessary.'

**May 2019:** The Crimble, now known as Crimble Hall, went into liquidation. The company owning it, Crimble Restaurant Ltd, was said to owe nearly £690,000 to 32 creditors. Twenty-nine members of staff were made redundant.

# Bibliography

Allsop, Derick, *Kicking in the Wind* (Headline, 1996)

Dennis, John, *The Oakwell Years: It Was Sometimes Like Watching Brazil* (Wharncliffe Books, 2012)

Geey, Daniel, *Done Deal* (Bloomsbury, 2019)

Giulianotti, Richard, *Sport: A Critical Sociology* (Polity Press, 2015)

Harrison, Paul, *Northern and Proud, the Biography of Bob Stokoe* (Know the Score, 2009)

Henderson Jon, *When Footballers Were Skint: A Journey in Search of the Soul of Football* (Biteback, 2019)

Hopcraft, Arthur, *The Football Man: People & Passions in Soccer* (Aurum Press, 2013)

Hoyle, Trevor, *Rule of Night* (Pomona, 2003)

Imlach, Gary, *My Father and Other Working Class Heroes* (Yellow Jersey, 2006)

Jones, Chris, *The Tale of Two Great Cities, My Footballing Journey* (Mylesiris Publishing, 2014)

Jones, Steve, *Echoes of '69* (self-published, 2003)

Jordan, Simon, *Be Careful What You Wish For* (Yellow Jersey, 2013)

Lofthouse, Nat, *Goals Galore* (Sportsmans Book Club, 1958)

Malam, Colin, *Clown Prince of Soccer?: The Len Shackleton Story* (Highdown, 2004)

Montague, James, *The Billionaires Club: The Unstoppable Rise of Football's Super-rich Owners* (Bloomsbury Sport, 2018)

Phillipps, Steven, *Rochdale AFC, the Official History, 1907–2001* (Yore Publications, 2001)

Phillipps, Steven, *The Survivors – the Story of Rochdale Association Football Club* (Sporting and Leisure Press, 1990)

Smith, Jon, *The Deal: Inside the World of a Super-Agent* (Constable, 2017)